The PERFECT SCOOP

The PERFECT SCOOP

ICE CREAMS, SORBETS, GRANITAS, and SWEET ACCOMPANIMENTS

David Lebovitz

PHOTOGRAPHY BY Lara Hata

TEN SPEED PRESS
Berkeley

Copyright © 2007 by David Lebovitz
Photography copyright © 2007 by Lara Hata

All rights reserved. Published in the United States by Ten Speed Press, an imprint
of the Crown Publishing Group, a division of Random House, Inc., New York.
www.crownpublishing.com
www.tenspeed.com

Ten Speed Press and the Ten Speed Press colophon are registered trademarks of
Random House, Inc.

Originally published in hardcover in the United States by Ten Speed Press,
Berkeley, CA, in 2007.

Library of Congress Cataloging-in-Publication Data

Lebovitz, David.
 The perfect scoop : ice creams, sorbets, granitas, and sweet accompaniments /
David Lebovitz ; photography by Lara Hata.
    p. cm.
 Includes index.
 1. Ice cream, ices, etc. I. Title.
 TX795.L45 2007
 641.8'62—dc22

                        2006037610

ISBN 978-1-58008-219-8

Printed in China

Cover and text design by Nancy Austin
Food and prop styling by George Dolese
Food stylist assistant: Elizabet der Nederlanden
Photography assistant: Ha Huynh

11 10 9 8 7 6 5 4 3 2

First Paperback Edition

CONTENTS

INTRODUCTION

I'd like to start this book with a nostalgic tale. It's one of those stories that takes place during a happier era, when I was much younger, and my sister and I spent our summer afternoons hand cranking ice cream on my grandfather's porch in the warm glow of July. Day after lazy day, we'd churn out batches of ice cream, spoons poised, barely waiting for the lid to come off the machine, before we leapt forward in a fit of happy giggles, lapping up the luscious ice cream as fast as we could.

Sometimes we'd make the most delectably creamy vanilla ice cream, using fragrant vanilla beans and churning out rich, frozen custard sweet with the taste of the farmhouse cream we'd picked up earlier that day from the neighbor's dairy farm. In late summer, we'd harvest sun-warmed peaches from the gloriously overloaded trees. Back in the kitchen we'd make a jolly mess, peeling and tossing the vibrant yellow peach slices in sugar before folding them into our ice cream.

Sometimes my grandmother would bake buttery, nut- and chocolate-loaded cookies so we could make ice cream sandwiches. Then we'd savor our homespun treats, watching the glowing sun make its early evening retreat.

That would indeed make a lovely story.

If any of it were true.

Instead, my most vivid ice cream memories are from my first and craziest, most insane summer job: scooping ice cream in a soda fountain. That ice cream shop was the most popular spot in town during the summer, and the whole town, en masse, made a beeline for us when the temperature soared. We were wildly busy from the moment the first customers practically burst through the door to closing time, when we'd have to shoo away those who invariably arrived just minutes too late.

Once we swung open that door, customers would begin swarming in, and very soon a long line would snake outside. Those of us behind the counter would spend the next few hours scooping mounds of various ice creams and piling them into crispy cones as fast as we could. We'd barely hand off one cone before the next customer would step impatiently to the counter. Luckily, we were energetic teenagers, since any normal person would have collapsed from sheer exhaustion after about five minutes of this. But we were young, and we were having the time of our lives.

I still remember the enthusiasm of each and every person who waited in line. They'd stand there forever, trying to decide which flavor to order. (Polly Ann's in San Francisco installed a wheel of flavors to aid the undecided.) Part of our allure was the quality of the ice cream we served. It was fresh and locally made, truly delicious. But another and perhaps equally important draw was that we gave unreasonably huge scoops. Absolutely enormous. Completely out of proportion to the fragile sugar cones we were constantly breaking as we tried to pack as much ice cream on as possible. Looking back, I don't know how anyone managed to eat one of those gigantic scoops, let alone two or three of them. But they did. Then they'd come back for more the next day. And the next. Come to think of it, I believe we ate almost as much of the ice cream as our customers did!

My favorite moment, though, was when I'd run out of a flavor (which was invariably mocha chip, our most popular) and have to sprint to the giant walk-in freezer out back to replace the scraped-clean bucket of ice cream. The instant I stepped into the dark, frigid chamber and closed the thick metal door, the world went away and a blissful moment would pass over me as the icy-cold blast of air hit my face. I'd stand still for a moment, inhaling the frosty vapors in the dark, gray chamber, just me and the huge cardboard canisters of ice cream packed inside, from floor to ceiling. I'd savor those few seconds of cool solitude and crisp air before heading back out to dive into the frenzy again.

Americans aren't the only ones who love ice cream. Italians line up for scoops of dense gelato at *gelaterias* like Carabé in Florence, no matter what time of the year it is. And what Parisian doesn't enjoy *un petit goûter* on the Île St. Louis? On this tiny island in the center of town, locals and tourists line up for cones of *glace* Berthillon, dainty little *boules* of ice cream with incredibly intense flavors.

In Mexico, you'll find ice creams made of everything from *guanábana* (soursop) to *aguacate* (avocado), and in most cities and villages locals gather nightly in the *zócalo*, the center square, to idle away the warm evening while chatting with friends between licks of *helado*. Across the Atlantic, audacious avant-garde Spanish chefs have obliterated the line between savory and sweet, and I've sampled ice cream combinations so curious, made with herbs, vegetables—heck, even bacon—that I wasn't sure if I was still working on dinner or had moved on to dessert.

In India, milk is concentrated and made into dense, chewy *kulfi*, often perfumed with rosewater or saffron, and while traveling through Japan I've marveled at the chewy pockets of pounded rice, called *mochi*, with a slender disk of ice cream discreetly tucked inside. These presentations are so startlingly beautiful that it seems a shame to break them open. But I do. And if you've ever visited Hawaii, you know that the islands are dotted with tiny roadside stands advertising "shave ice" on handwritten signs. I love digging into my own plastic cone heaped with sweet candied red beans or lotus seeds and a mound of crushed ice, finished with a few squirts of tropical fruit syrup and a swirl of sweetened condensed milk.

The Perfect Scoop is your guidebook to the fabulous world of ice creams, sorbets, sherbets, granitas, frozen yogurts, and gelatos. I've spent the past twenty-five years churning out all sorts of frozen desserts, at home and in restaurants, and these recipes are the result. Of course, you'll find chocolate, vanilla, and strawberry ice cream in here, but that's only the beginning. Many of the recipes are based on a cooked custard, which involves a bit of extra effort but produces ice cream of unparalleled smoothness. But there are plenty of recipes that involve no cooking at all. You'll find recipes for ice creams, frozen yogurts, and sherbets that require nothing more complicated than pressing the button on your blender.

I must confess that I love things mixed into ice cream. Big chunks of things. And lots of 'em. I want a bite—make that two bites—in every spoonful. So I've given you a whole chapter of mix-ins to choose from, offering everything from soft nuggets of Dark Chocolate Truffles (page 211) to spicy crumbled Speculoos (page 208). There are maple-glazed Wet Walnuts (page 198) and Chocolate Chip Cookie Dough (page 209) loaded with dark chocolate morsels and crispy nuts in a buttery brown sugar batter.

And when was the last time you had a freshly made ice cream sandwich? In the Vessels chapter (page 217), you'll find recipes for some favorite ways to eat ice cream. If the last ice cream sandwich you had tasted like soggy, flavorless cardboard, you're in for a real treat. Ice cream sandwiches are perfect if you've got kids, as well: Not only are they great fun to put together (even for adults), but they can be made in advance and stocked in the freezer, where they're ready at a moment's notice.

You'll discover recipes like homemade Peppermint Patties (page 206) to crumble into just-churned Chocolate Ice Cream (page 26), authentic Japanese Candied Red Beans (page 180) to spoon over exotic Green Tea Ice Cream (page 40), and Dulce de Leche (page 171), which is great on anything. Anywhere. Anytime.

Along with the basic recipes for ice creams, sorbets, and granitas, I've included lots of variations, called Perfect Pairings, which you can use to customize your scoop. You'll find simple fruit compotes to serve alongside, suggestions for making icy-cool drinks, as well as lots of ideas for creating stunning dessert compositions featuring your homemade ice cream as the centerpiece.

All of the recipes in *The Perfect Scoop* can be prepared in any home kitchen, with most of the ingredients readily available from your local supermarket. But don't neglect the ethnic markets in your community, where you'll find ingredients to make some of the more unusual ice creams, such as Vietnamese Coffee Ice Cream (page 35) and Aztec "Hot" Chocolate Ice Cream (page 29), which calls for a hint of spicy ground chiles. When making ice creams or sorbets with fresh fruit, farmer's markets are my recommended starting point; sampling means you know you're getting the most luscious hand-picked fruits available.

I've also gone out on a limb and included some flavors and ingredients that you may not be accustomed to seeing in ice cream, like cheese, herbs, and vegetables. One sip of a chilly Avocado Licuado con Leche (page 95) or a scoop of Pear-Pecorino Ice Cream (page 82), and you'll become a believer.

People have been making ice cream for hundreds of years, using all sorts of equipment. Centuries ago, it involved simply stirring fruit juice in a bucket of ice, but pastry chefs nowadays make use of high-tech machines with razor-sharp blades that'll turn anything, from bananas to bacon, into ice cream. Most home cooks will have plenty of machines from which to choose. Most of them are both incredibly simple to use and economically priced, putting homemade ice cream within the reach of anyone who wants to give it a spin. Interspersed throughout this book are tips that will help you make the most of your modern-day ice cream maker as well. To ensure success, you'll want to carefully read my instructions in Making the Perfect Ice Cream Custard (page 3), which will guide you through the steps involved in making a basic cooked custard.

The hundreds of recipes in *The Perfect Scoop* are the result of many cheerful days and nights spent churning all sorts of wonderful concoctions. I hope you have just as much fun enjoying them with your friends and family as I did creating them.

1
Basics

Whether you're a novice or a highly experienced cook, you will find it's easy to make the freshest, most unbelievably tasty ice creams, sorbets, sherbets, and granitas in your own kitchen. If you've never done it before, prepare to be wowed. Nothing beats the taste of freshly made ice cream spooned directly from the machine.

In this chapter you'll find all the information you'll need to do it. Starting with step-by-step instructions for making the perfect ice cream custard, I'll take you through the process—including some pitfalls to avoid and steps to take in case you manage to fall into one of them. The best ingredients and the right equipment are crucial to making really perfect ice creams and sorbets. I'll give you advice to help you make your choices, including information about the differences among various models of ice cream makers, if you don't have one yet.

Making the Perfect Ice Cream Custard

Many of the ice cream recipes in this book are custard-based, or French-style ice creams. Others are Philadelphia-style, which refers to ice cream made simply by mixing milk or cream with sugar and other ingredients. French-style ice creams tend to be richer and smoother, due to the emulsifying properties of egg yolks. My fruit-based ice creams tend to be Philadelphia-style, since I prefer to let the flavor of the fruits come forward without all the richness. But in some cases I offer a flavor in both styles, so you can decide which you prefer.

If you've never made a French-style stovetop ice cream custard before, follow these step-by-step instructions to ensure success (in some recipes, the procedure may vary slightly). Although I make my custards in a saucepan over moderate heat, you may wish to cook your custard in a double boiler the first few times or use a flame tamer to diffuse the heat, until you get the hang of it. It will take longer to cook, but you'll appreciate the extra time to watch and make sure it cooks to just the right consistency.

Before getting started, **prepare an ice bath** to expedite the chilling of the custard. Make one by putting some ice in a large bowl and then adding a cup or two of cold water so the ice cubes are barely floating. You can also partially fill an empty sink with ice and some water. Most custard-based ice cream recipes call for pouring the warm, just-cooked custard right into the cream, which helps stop the cooking and expedites cooling. Set the bowl of cream in the ice bath, put a strainer over the top and make sure to keep it nearby; after you've cooked the custard, you'll need to pour it into the bowl right away.

Heat the milk or the liquid called for in the recipe with the sugar in a medium-sized saucepan on the stove. Always use nonreactive cookware, such as stainless steel or anodized aluminum.

In a separate bowl, **whisk together the egg yolks.**

The next step is to temper the yolks. Here's where you need to be careful. Once the milk is hot and steamy, slowly and gradually **pour the milk into the egg yolks** (1), whisking constantly, which keeps the yolks moving and avoids the risk of cooking them into little eggy bits. I find it best to remove the saucepan from the heat and use a ladle to add the hot liquid while whisking. If you add the hot liquid too fast or don't whisk the egg yolks briskly, they'll cook and you'll end up with bits of scrambled eggs.

Scrape the warmed egg yolks back into the saucepan. Then stir the custard over moderate heat, using a heatproof utensil with a flat edge. I like to use a silicone rubber spatula, although a straight-edged wooden spatula works well too. Cook, stirring nonstop, until the mixture thickens and coats the spatula. While cooking the custard, be sure to scrape the bottom of the saucepan while stirring. Don't be timid; keep the custard mixture moving constantly while it's cooking, and *do not let the custard boil!*

You'll know your custard's done when it begins to steam and you feel it just beginning to cook as you scrape the spatula across the bottom of the pan. You can test it by running your finger across the spatula coated with custard: It's done when

your finger leaves a definite trail that doesn't flow back together (2). You can check for doneness with an instant-read thermometer too; it should read between 170°F (77°C) and 175°F (79°C) when the custard is done. Egg safety experts recommend cooking eggs to a minimum temperature of 160°F (71°C), but don't let them get above 185°F (85°C) or you'll have scrambled eggs.

It's ready! Without delay, take the custard off the heat and immediately pour the hot mixture through the strainer into the chilled bowl of cream in its ice bath, and stir (3). This will lower the temperature of the custard right away to stop the cooking (4). Stir frequently to help the custard cool down. Once it's cool, refrigerate the custard with the lid slightly ajar. It should be very cold before churning it. I recommend chilling most mixtures for at least 8 hours or overnight.

Chill the machine in advance. If you're using an ice cream maker that requires prefreezing, make sure the canister spends the required amount of time in the freezer—whatever's recommended by the manufacturer. Although it may feel frozen to the touch before the recommended time, take it from me: If you use the machine prematurely you'll end up watching the mixture go round and round without freezing—a big disappointment. Don't cheat! Most machines require 24 hours of prefreezing.

Some machines work best if you switch them on and get the dasher (the turning blade) moving before pouring in your mixture, since on some models the custard will begin freezing to the sides immediately when you pour it in, which can prevent the dasher from turning.

Although some experts say that most ice cream benefits from being allowed to "ripen" in the freezer for a few hours before serving, they can wait patiently for their rock-hard ice cream to ripen; I'm happy to enjoy the soft, freshly frozen stuff right from the machine as well. If your ice cream has been in the freezer for a long time, it will most likely benefit from being taken out 5 to 10 minutes prior to serving to allow it to soften to the best texture.

Keep It Clean and Play It Safe

Ice cream is a dairy product, so it's important to keep things as clean and hygienic as possible. Make sure all equipment is sparkling clean. Wash your hands after handling raw eggs, and clean the washable parts of your ice cream maker in very hot water (or as indicated by the manufacturer) after each use. Chill custards with eggs and dairy products promptly, and store them in the refrigerator.

All of the ice cream recipes in this book that require egg yolks are cooked as custards on the stovetop. If you have concerns about egg safety, use an instant-read thermometer to check the temperature. Most harmful bacteria don't survive at temperatures higher than 160°F (71°C). Pasteurized eggs in their shells are available in some areas and can be used if you wish.

Ingredients

ALCOHOL

Alcohol does two things in ice cream: it prevents ice creams and sorbets from freezing too hard (alcohol doesn't freeze), and it provides flavor. In some recipes you can omit it if you'll be serving kids or anyone who is avoiding alcohol. In other cases it's a vital flavor component, as in the Prune-Armagnac Ice Cream (page 78).

I frequently use kirsch, a distillation of cherries, to heighten the flavors of many fruit- or berry-based frozen desserts without interfering with the fresh fruit flavors. A few drops can transform a ho-hum fruit purée into something vibrant.

When buying liquor for cooking, my rule is to get a brand that you wouldn't mind drinking on its own, but you don't need to buy the most expensive bottle.

How Can I Make Softer Ice Cream and Sorbets?

Adding a bit of alcohol will give your ice creams and sorbets a better texture, since alcohol doesn't freeze. For fruit-based recipes, spirits like kirsch, vodka, gin, and eau-de-vie will enhance the flavor and produce a softer texture by preventing ice crystals from forming. Use caution, though: If you add too much, the mixture might not freeze at all, and you'll be left with a runny mess. In general, you can add up to 3 tablespoons (45 ml) of 40 percent (80 proof) liquor, such as rum or whiskey, to 1 quart (1 liter) of custard or sorbet mixture without any problems. I do push the limits with my boozy Eggnog Ice Cream (page 58).

BERRIES

Fresh berries are seasonal and should be used only when they're at their peak. I've never tasted a "fresh" berry that had been flown around the world that wasn't flavorless or bitter, so I never use them. I do use frozen berries, which can be quite tasty if you find a good brand, and they're generally less expensive than fresh berries. If buying frozen, choose berries that are unsweetened and individually quick frozen (IQF), rather than the sweetened ones packed like blocks of ice. When measuring frozen berries for recipes, be sure to measure them while they're frozen, since as they defrost they decrease substantially in volume.

Fresh berries should be plump and juicy when you buy them. Strawberries should be very fragrant and uniformly red, with no green "shoulders" or dark bruises. Peek under berry baskets before buying to see if there's dampness, which often indicates unseen spoilage.

I don't wash blackberries and raspberries, since they're fragile and will lose their delicacy, but fresh strawberries should always be rinsed and drained well before they're hulled and sliced to remove any grit. Fresh blueberries and cherries should be rinsed and drained as well.

BUTTER

For the recipes in this book that call for butter, use either unsalted or salted butter as noted.

CHOCOLATE

BITTERSWEET AND SEMISWEET CHOCOLATE: Unlike the old days, new brands of chocolate are being introduced all the time, and deciding which one is best to use can be a bit confusing.

Bittersweet and semisweet are interchangeable terms, and chocolates labeled as such must contain a minimum of 35 percent cocoa solids. But many premium brands nowadays have a much higher percentage so I advise you to taste as many chocolates as you can (a delicious task) to find brands you like in your price range. In a couple of recipes, I advise using chocolate with a certain percentage of cocoa solids, which you'll find listed on the packaging.

Unsweetened chocolate, often called bitter chocolate (*not* bittersweet) contains no sugar.

Buying chocolate in bulk is more economical than purchasing little bars, and dark chocolate will keep perfectly well in a cool, dark place (not the refrigerator) for several years. See Resources (page 237) for some recommended brands.

CHOCOLATE CHIPS: Most chocolate chips are formulated with less cocoa butter so they'll retain their shape when heated. I use them in baked goods like meringues and cookies (and for snacking), but not for melting. Most supermarket chocolate chips are fine to use, although I usually treat myself to premium brands.

COCOA NIBS: These crunchy bits of roasted cocoa beans are the essence of pure chocolate without any added sugar. They remain delightfully crisp even when folded into ice cream. Cocoa nibs are available at specialty shops and well-stocked supermarkets. See Resources (page 237) for online purchasing.

COCOA POWDER: All recipes that call for cocoa powder use unsweetened cocoa powder. Do *not* use cocoa drink mixes or products labeled "powdered chocolate," which contain sugar and other ingredients.

In most cases I specify Dutch-process cocoa powder, which has been acid-neutralized and is darker in color than natural cocoa powder. I find it more flavorful and prefer it for my ice creams and sorbets. If your cocoa powder has been "Dutched," it should say so somewhere on the packaging, or it will list an alkalizing agent in the ingredient list. All European brands of cocoa powder are likely to be Dutch-processed.

MILK CHOCOLATE: Milk chocolate is chocolate that's been mellowed by the addition of milk. Although ordinary brands must contain a minimum of 10 percent cocoa solids (in the U.S.), you should search out a premium brand with at least 30 percent cocoa solids and avoid using mass-marketed candy bars. They're not intended for cooking, as they contain the minimum amount of cocoa solids and are often quite sweet. Milk chocolate will keep for about one year if stored in a cool, dark place.

WHITE CHOCOLATE: Real white chocolate is made with pure cocoa butter, and that should be the only fat listed on the label. Cocoa butter is ivory colored, not truly white, so anything that is pure white is not likely to be real white chocolate. Quality is very important when selecting white chocolate, and buying a premium brand is always worth it. White chocolate will keep for about one year if stored in a cool, dark place.

Chopping Chocolate

The most effective tool for chopping chocolate is a long, serrated bread knife. You'll find a big, thick block easier to tackle if you start to chop at one corner. As you cut a wider swath, turn the block and start chopping at another corner. If a recipe calls for finely chopped chocolate, the pieces should be no larger than $1/4$ inch (1 cm). Coarsely chopped chocolate means pieces that are about $3/4$ inch (2 cm).

COCONUT AND COCONUT MILK

I prefer to use unsweetened dried coconut, rather than the sweetened flakes from the supermarket, so I can control the sweetness in the final product. Dried unsweetened coconut is available in natural and specialty food stores.

If you can't find unsweetened coconut, soak sweetened coconut in hot water. Rinse it afterward, then wring it firmly with your hands and let it dry before using.

Coconut milk is the extracted liquid from coconut meat. Very good canned brands are available in Asian and ethnic markets, as well as in well-stocked supermarkets. The best brand is from Thailand, labeled Chaokoh. (Beware of similar-sounding brand names.) Do not substitute heavily sweetened Coco López or products labeled "cream of coconut."

COFFEE

Much of the success of any coffee-based ice cream or granita depends upon the quality and strength of the coffee or espresso you use. The recipes in this book call for strong, freshly brewed coffee or espresso. If you must use instant coffee or espresso powder, be sure to use a very good brand. The substitution ratio for these recipes is 1 rounded teaspoon of top-quality instant coffee or espresso powder to $1/4$ cup (60 ml) of hot water.

CORN SYRUP

Corn syrup is an invert sugar, meaning that its chemical structure has been altered. It helps to keep ice creams and sorbets softer and more scoopable when frozen. Corn syrup also helps prevent sugar crystallization in candy recipes and is used to keep sauces from becoming grainy. I use it judiciously when I want to give extra body and thickness to sauces.

All recipes calling for corn syrup in this book use light corn syrup. Don't substitute dark corn syrup. If you live in an area where light corn syrup is unavailable, you can substitute a very mild-flavored honey, cane syrup, or golden syrup (except for the Marshmallow Sauce, page 168, and Marshmallows, page 212, where it would discolor the results). Bakers outside the United States should ideally substitute glucose, available at professional pastry supply shops.

Read the Recipe Thoroughly before Beginning

There's nothing more frustrating than getting halfway through a recipe and finding that you neglected to prepare an ingredient or component in advance. Have all the ingredients ready and all your equipment lined up and ready to go before you start.

DAIRY

HALF-AND-HALF: Half-and-half is a dairy hybrid, a mixture of milk and cream, and is between 11 and 18 percent fat. Don't use nonfat half-and-half.

HEAVY CREAM: American heavy cream is roughly 36 percent butterfat. Although there is a slight difference between products labeled "whipping cream" and those labeled "heavy cream," they are interchangeable in this book.

Look for cream that has not been ultrapasteurized (UHT). This process involves heating the cream to a very high temperature to prolong shelf life. Unfortunately, it also destroys much of the flavor. If your grocery store doesn't stock it, request that they do.

MILK: My tastes have changed over the years, and I now prefer ice creams made with whole milk in combination with heavy cream, rather than ones made with all heavy cream. But don't substitute low-fat or skim milk for the whole milk in these recipes, as the resulting ice cream will be icy and grainy.

SOUR CREAM: Sour cream has a fresh, tangy taste due to the addition of lactic acid. Buy brands with the fewest (and most natural) ingredients. Although I advise you to use regular sour cream, you can substitute low-fat sour cream if you wish in any recipe, but do not use nonfat sour cream. Crème fraîche is higher in fat than sour cream and can be used as a substitute.

YOGURT: Use only plain, whole-milk yogurt. Greek-style yogurt, which has a higher butterfat content, can be used if you wish. Or for richer results, you can substitute Strained Yogurt (page 49) in some of the frozen yogurt recipes that call for plain whole-milk yogurt, if indicated.

The Skinny on Fat

Yes, ice cream contains a rather high amount of fat. If you're concerned, try to eat French-style portions: one perfect scoop. You'll find most of the frozen desserts in this book are so full of flavor that a little goes a long way.

My ice creams often contain less cream and egg yolks than others, since I don't believe you need to overdose on fat to make food enjoyable, and too much fat can obliterate other flavors, especially fresh fruits. (Many of the fresh fruits I bring home find their way into sorbets, rather than ice creams.) So you'll find many of the recipes have milk added where cream used to be, and that instead of whisking a chicken coop's worth of egg yolks into ice cream custards, I've used a more modest amount.

DRIED FRUITS

Look for dried fruits that are plump and moist, as they'll have the best flavor. Store them in an airtight container away from the light to preserve their moisture and taste. Natural food stores are often the best places to find high-quality dried fruits. Although some people prefer unsulfured dried fruits, their darkness will affect the look of the finished ice cream.

In recipes calling for dried apricots, please use only ones from California. The imported varieties may be cheaper, but they have very little taste and you'll be disappointed in the results. Prunes, available pitted or unpitted, are sometimes labeled "dried plums." Be sure to use ones that are natural and not flavored with anything.

EGGS

All of the recipes in this book call for large eggs, and virtually all of the eggs used are cooked as a custard on the stovetop for the ice creams. If you're unsure what size your eggs are, a large egg in the shell weighs approximately 2 ounces (60 g). One yolk equals 1 tablespoon (20 g), and one white equals 2 tablespoons (30 g). Use the freshest eggs you can find and always store them in the refrigerator.

Custard-based ice cream recipes require just the yolks, not the whites. You'll find it easier to separate eggs that are very cold rather than ones at room temperature. Extra egg whites can be refrigerated or frozen or used to make Marshmallow Sauce (page 168), Meringue Nests (page 234), or Ice Cream Cones (page 228).

Egg safety means cooking eggs to at least 160°F (71°C), easily verified with an instant-read thermometer. If you have health concerns, you can find pasteurized eggs in their shell or liquid egg whites sold in some supermarkets, although if you're using them for beating into a meringue, check the package to make sure they're suitable for whipping.

EXTRACTS, FLAVORINGS, AND OILS

Good-quality extracts cost slightly more per use than inferior-quality ones and are always well worth the difference in price. To preserve their aroma, store them in a cool, dark place, as light and heat will cause their flavors to deteriorate quickly. Some manufacturers use the word "flavoring" rather than extract, so be sure to read the list of ingredients to confirm the purity of what you're buying. Avoid anything with the word "artificial" on the label.

ALMOND EXTRACT: Always purchase *pure* almond extract, not the stuff labeled "imitation." When using it, remember that a little goes a *very* long way. If a recipe calls for a few drops of extract, pour some into the cap of the bottle first, or dip a toothpick into the bottle, then dribble it carefully into the mixture.

CITRUS OILS: These oils are made by pricking citrus fruits, such as lemons and oranges, to release the intense, colorful oil found in the peel. See Resources (page 237) for online sources.

MINT EXTRACT AND OIL: Mint oil is made by steeping mint in a base of unflavored oil, whereas mint extract has a base of alcohol. Different brands vary significantly in strength, which makes calculating their use in recipes a challenge. You may want to begin by adding a smaller quantity than called for in the recipe. Taste, then add more until you're satisfied. Look for mint oil and extract at natural or specialty food stores.

VANILLA BEANS: Vanilla beans should be plump and moist. To split a bean in half and obtain the seeds, use a paring knife to cut the bean lengthwise, and then scrape out the seeds with the knife. Both the seeds and the pod have a great deal of flavor. The pods can be reused if rinsed well in water. Let the beans dry completely and then store them buried in sugar, or conserve them in a vial of bourbon, rum, or vodka.

VANILLA EXTRACT: It is imperative to use *real* vanilla extract. Shop by quality, not by price. You won't regret it once you open the bottle and take a sniff. I use vanilla extract from Mexico (the real stuff) and Bourbon vanilla from Madagascar. Tahitian vanilla has a sweet, floral aroma, and I like it with tropical fruits, although it can be harder to find.

FLOUR

Use all-purpose flour in all recipes calling for flour, such as the brownies, cookies, cones, and some mix-ins. You can use bleached or unbleached flour. Measure flour using the method listed under Measuring Cups and Spoons (page 17), or by weight.

FRESH FRUITS AND CITRUS

Choose recipes using ripe fruits only when the fruits are in season, so they're at their peak of flavor. The quality of sorbets and other fruit-based frozen desserts depends entirely on the quality of the fruit you start with. Fruit that's not going to be peeled should be rinsed and towel dried. This includes apricots, plums, and nectarines. Fruits such as mangoes, peaches, pears, and pineapples don't need to be washed, although some experts advise washing melons with soap and water before slicing, as the rind can carry microorganisms.

You may notice that in recipes calling for fresh fruits I usually specify a quantity (such as 3 large peaches) instead of a weight (1 pound peaches). Since most people shop by quantity, I've chosen to use those measurements in the ingredients list. Yet in a few instances, I do call for measuring fruit by weight, since sizes can vary rather substantially and affect the recipe outcome.

For most bush berries, like raspberries and blueberries, I've chosen to use cups (and metric weights) because baskets of berries can differ in size. If using frozen berries, be sure to measure them before thawing, since they shrink considerably as they thaw. Because strawberries are irregular in size, I find it easier to measure them by weight.

When selecting citrus, choose fruits that are heavy for their size. (I usually pick up about twenty in order to find the five or six I go home with.) To get the maximum juice from any citrus fruit, make sure the fruits are at room temperature before squeezing. Rolling them firmly on the counter will rupture the juice sacs, which will help release the juices too.

ZEST: Zest is the oil-rich, colorful part of the peel. The best tool for grating the zest from the rind is a rasp-style zester. Seek out organic or unsprayed citrus if you can, and wash and scrub all citrus well before zesting.

GELATIN

If a recipe calls for gelatin, it means unflavored powdered gelatin. If using leaf gelatin, 4 sheets equals one ¼-ounce envelope of powdered gelatin.

Whichever gelatin you use, it's necessary to soften the gelatin in cold water first. If using gelatin granules, sprinkle the granules over the cold water as indicated in the recipe and let sit for 5 minutes, until the granules are swollen and soft. Then proceed with the recipe. For leaf gelatin, soak the sheets in cold water for 5 minutes, then lift them out and warm them in a small saucepan over very low heat just until liquefied.

HONEY

Honey is a slightly acidic ingredient, and in custard-based recipes that call for a significant amount of it, you'll be directed to warm the honey separately and then add it later. Honey-based ice creams will have a smoother texture due to the high concentration of sugars.

I recommend using a good-flavored honey that is full-bodied rather than the bland supermarket varieties. Farmer's markets and specialty shops often carry good-tasting, locally produced honeys that will make any honey-based ice cream far more delectable. Look for one with a deep amber color. Honey that has crystallized can be melted gently in a saucepan or microwave oven until it returns to its liquid state.

NUTS

There's nothing like the pleasant crunch of crisp, freshly toasted nuts. And there's nothing worse than biting into an acrid, rancid nut. Since nuts have a relatively high amount of oil, you should taste a couple before using them to make sure they're still fresh. Hazelnuts, pecans, and walnuts are particularly susceptible to spoilage. Buy nuts from a store that sells in high volume and turns over its stock regularly and store them in a cool, dark place in a well-sealed container. Nuts can also be frozen in zip-top freezer bags.

Most nuts taste much better if they've been toasted, which brings out their flavors and gives them a crunchy contrast in ice cream. The only nuts I don't toast are pistachio nuts, since they'll lose their delicate green color. Buy fresh pistachios from a good source so they're crisp and vibrant green.

Toasting Nuts

1. Preheat the oven to 350°F (175°C).
2. Spread the nuts in an even layer on an ungreased baking sheet.
3. Bake the nuts in the oven for 10 to 12 minutes, stirring them once or twice while baking so they toast evenly. To see if they're done, snap one in half: it should be lightly golden brown throughout.
4. Let the nuts cool completely before using unless the recipe indicates otherwise.

PEANUT BUTTER

The recipes in this book call for commercial peanut butter. Natural-style peanut butter will release too much oil when mixed with other ingredients, so use a brand that's smooth and emulsified.

SALT

What's salt doing in an ice cream book? Salt prevents most foods from tasting flat, and that pertains to ice creams too. A little pinch will magically brighten the flavor of many ice creams and sorbets. Although you can use ordinary table salt when a pinch is required, I advise using kosher or coarse sea salt, which is especially important in recipes that ask for measuring out a specific quantity.

In a few instances, I recommend using fleur de sel, a hand-harvested sea salt from Brittany. Although you may think, "Isn't salt just salt?" fleur de sel has a delicate taste, and once you try it you're likely to start using it more and more, in spite of the price.

SPICES

Like the windshield wipers on your car, spices do not have an infinite shelf life and should be replaced when their efficacy has diminished. Most spices begin to lose their flavor and aroma after a year. Buy spices from a source that turns over its stock frequently, and replenish yours if they lose their aroma and pungency.

SUGAR

Sugar is important in ice creams and sorbets for sweetening and ensuring a nice, scoopable texture. But use too much sugar and your ice cream or sorbet won't freeze. Use too little and the ice cream or sorbet will be grainy and hard to scoop.

When a recipe calls for sugar, it means granulated white sugar. Confectioner's sugar, or powdered sugar, is simply sugar that's been pulverized to a powder with a bit of cornstarch added. Brown sugar is listed as either light brown or dark brown. Use what's indicated in the recipe, and always pack brown sugar firmly into the measuring cup to measure it accurately.

Equipment

An ice cream maker is the most important piece of equipment you'll need to use to make most of the recipes in this book. Happily, you don't need to spend a fortune, as there are many quality machines on the market that will fit within any budget. The price of a machine intended for home use can start at less than $40 but can climb upward to nearly $1,000 for a freezer of professional quality. All of the recipes in this book were tested using both an inexpensive home freezer with a canister that requires prefreezing and a moderately priced self-refrigerating machine, with virtually identical results. Although much depends on the features you want and your budget, the various types of machines also have their own advantages and drawbacks.

> ## Go By the Book
>
> No one wants to take the time to read instruction manuals. But each particular machine has specific requirements, and you should become familiar with yours prior to using it. Take a few minutes to get to know your machine by reading the instruction manual thoroughly.

ICE AND ROCK SALT MACHINES

You may find that there's nothing like the pleasure of hand-churning your own ice cream, and want the freedom to do it in the great outdoors. Or maybe you have a large brood and the smaller, 1-quart models won't churn enough at once. If so, perhaps a hand-cranked ice and rock salt freezer, or "bucket-type" freezer, may be for you.

To use an ice and rock salt machine, you fill the inner metal container (the can) with your ice cream custard or sorbet mixture, close the top, and then pack layers of ice and rock salt around the container. (The rock salt lowers the temperature so that the mixture will freeze; ice alone isn't cold enough.) Some models rotate the can with a manual hand crank, and others work with an electric motor.

PROS: These machines provide lots of old-fashioned fun, but hand-cranked models require some hard work (although it beats going to the gym). Most models can freeze larger batches at once, some up to 6 quarts (about 6 liters) at time. No electricity is needed for the hand-cranked models, nor is prefreezing the can necessary, so you can make ice cream spontaneously. Top-of-the-line brands tend to be very solid and well made.

CONS: Hand-cranked models require effort. And in addition to having a few reliable friends to help you crank, you'll also need access to a large amount of ice and rock salt. Care must be taken to be sure no grains of salt get into the ice cream when you remove the lid. Motorized models tend to be noisy and can't be opened to add mix-ins while churning. Their cost can also be high.

SELF-REFRIGERATING MACHINES

These freezers have a built-in compressor, so you just pour in your mixture, press a button, and wait. Within 30 to 45 minutes, depending on the model, you'll have freshly churned ice cream. I recommend self-refrigerating machines for people who make ice cream on a regular basis; their higher price pays off in speed, power, and efficiency. When shopping around, look for a model with a removable chilling container, which will make cleanup easier and far more hygienic. Some machines feature an automatic shutoff device, since a very powerful motor can overchurn a non-custard-based ice cream into butter if you don't keep an eye on it.

PROS: These machines are easy to use and make fast work of churning out batches of ice cream. No prefreezing of equipment is necessary, so you can make ice cream and sorbet at a moment's notice. You can freeze several batches consecutively, one right after another.

CONS: Due to their electrical components, the price is higher than other machines, although prices have dropped in recent years, and they take up more counter or cabinet space than smaller machines. You should be careful not to tip the machine, which can dislodge the liquid coolant inside. It's also possible to overfreeze certain ice creams if you're not careful.

The Pacojet: Secret of Rich and Famous Chefs

Many professionals swear by the Pacojet (see Resources, page 237) for making ice creams and sorbets. This miracle machine allows you to transform anything, from apples-and-oranges to turkey-and-mashed potatoes, into a smooth frozen treat in a flash. Any mixture, from the familiar to the funky, can simply be poured into a special metal canister and then frozen. When you're ready to serve, attach the canister to the machine and a razor-sharp blade "shaves" the mixture into a perfectly textured ice cream or sorbet in seconds. The advantage is that you can use anything you wish, such as a fruit purée without any added sugar. Or you can get inventive and freeze something savory (yes, even Thanksgiving leftovers). The disadvantage is that you need to adapt traditional recipes to use a Pacojet. And of course, there's the price. A Pacojet costs several thousand dollars, although rumors persist of a less expensive model becoming available for home cooks sometime in the future.

MACHINES REQUIRING PREFREEZING

For most people, machines that must be prefrozen are the most practical for home use, due to their low price and satisfactory performance.

These machines require that you prefreeze the canister, which is filled with a liquid coolant. You need to put the canister in the freezer 24 hours in advance. In spite of how firm or cold the canister may feel, don't try to churn anything unless the canister has been in the freezer for the amount of time recommended by the manufacturer (trust me, I've tried...). People with sufficient freezer space often store the canister in the freezer all the time.

Although it's not often mentioned in the instructions, on some models you'll find they work best if you turn the machine on and have the dasher moving before you pour in your mixture. If not, the mixture will sometimes freeze immediately to the sides of the prefrozen canister, causing the dasher to stall.

PROS: The low cost of these machines makes them accessible to everyone. Many units cost around $50. They produce good ice cream and don't take up too much cabinet space when not in use, and there's a large variety of models and brands to choose from. Most have a large opening, which allows mix-ins to be added while churning.

CONS: The canister must be prefrozen, which requires freezer space and advance planning. It needs to be completely refrozen between batches. The canister shouldn't be run through the dishwasher.

Why Does My Ice Cream Freeze Harder Than What I Buy in the Store?

Commercial ice creams are made in high-speed machines, which are able to whip extra air (called overrun) into the ice cream. This, of course, is done both for reasons of economy (more air equals more profit) and to improve the texture. Sometimes a long list of unpronounceable ingredients are added too, which can make the texture more scoopable.

The majority of home ice cream machines don't churn as fast and aren't as powerful as commercial machines, so the ice cream you make at home will have less air and is invariably denser (but tastier) than what you buy in the store. In addition, most home freezers are very cold and are not intended for keeping ice cream at the ideal serving temperature. For this reason, it's best to remove homemade ice creams, sorbets, and sherbets from the freezer 5 to 10 minutes prior to serving.

OTHER MACHINES

Making homemade ice cream has become so popular that a myriad of other options have become available for freezing ice cream. KitchenAid offers a snap-on canister for its powerful standing electric mixers. Once the canister is prefrozen, you pour the mixture inside and churn away with the mixer set on low speed.

There's also the Donvier freezer, which requires the canister to be prefrozen before the mixture is added. You must hand crank the machine every so often during the freezing time, meaning that little air is incorporated into the ice cream. No electricity is needed for churning.

Which Ice Cream Machine Should I Buy?

If you're going to make ice cream infrequently, say once or twice a month, a unit with a canister that you prefreeze is probably your best bet. If you're tempted by the idea of churning ice cream in the great outdoors, a hand-cranked ice and rock salt model that requires no electricity and has sufficient capacity to feed a hungry crowd may be what you're looking for.

If you're serious about making ice cream and you have the space, a freezer with self-contained coolant is the way to go. These machines require no advance preparation, and you can freeze one batch right after the other. Of course, they're more expensive, but if you're a big ice cream aficionado, you'll find it a solid investment.

OTHER EQUIPMENT

Fortunately, making ice creams, sorbets, and granitas requires very little in the way of specialty equipment, aside from an ice cream maker. The following list describes a few other items you may need or simply want to have on hand.

BAKING DISH: You'll need a shallow dish of some sort to make granitas. It should be made of a nonreactive material: stainless steel, porcelain, earthenware, and plastic are all suitable. The exact size isn't important, but it should be between 8 and 12 inches (20 and 30 cm) across and should have sides that are at least 2 inches (5 cm) high to contain the icy crystals as you stir the granita up.

BLENDER, FOOD MILL, OR FOOD PROCESSOR: Aside from your ice cream maker, a blender will be your second most important piece of equipment and your best pal for making smooth purées. Stick or wand blenders do an effective job and can be used to purée anything directly in a saucepan or mixing bowl.

You can also use a food processor with a sharp blade or a low-tech food mill for puréeing. Some cooks like to chop nuts in their food processor, although I find the results uneven and prefer to use a chef's knife.

CHERRY PITTER: A handheld, spring-loaded metal cherry pitter is a small tool that you'll find handy when cherry season comes around. The best and sturdiest of the bunch are made in Germany.

ESPRESSO MAKER: Several of the recipes call for espresso. I use an Italian stovetop espresso maker—an inexpensive metal pot that makes good, strong coffee. If you don't have an espresso maker, see the suggested substitution on page 7, although I encourage you to use true espresso for the best results.

ICE CREAM CONE MAKER: While a cone maker is definitely a niche item, I can't think of anything more fun than rolling up your own cones and filling them with a scoop of home-churned ice cream. Most machines have nonstick coating to make life easier and are relatively inexpensive. They come with a cone-rolling mold, and wire stands are available to hold the cones as they cool and for serving.

Machines called pizzelle irons will make smaller cones that, when rolled up, will hold one tiny scoop.

KNIVES: A good, sharp knife is invaluable for slicing fruit and chopping nuts. A paring knife with a 3- to 4-inch (8- to 10-cm) blade and an 8-inch (20-cm) chef's knife will perform most tasks required for the recipes in this book.

MEASURING CUPS AND SPOONS: For measuring liquids, use cups made of clear plastic or glass, so you can get an accurate measurement. Graduated measuring cups, the metal or plastic kind with handles that nest within each other ($1/4$ cup, $1/3$ cup, etc.), are best for measuring dry ingredients. Flour should always be measured in a graduated measuring cup: Spoon the flour into the cup, then level it off with the sweep of a flat-edged utensil. I like to have several sets of each kind of measuring cup on hand.

MIXING BOWLS: Any kind of bowl will do for ice cream making, although if you can find them, heavy plastic or stainless steel bowls with a rubber bottom make stirring mixtures and tempering eggs easier, since pouring one ingredient into another while simultaneously whisking can be challenging. The rubber foot keeps the bowl from wobbling around.

When a recipe calls for a small bowl, I mean one that holds 1 quart (1 liter). A medium bowl holds about 2 to 3 quarts (2 to 3 liters), and a large bowl is anything bigger. When in doubt, use a large bowl to avoid surprises.

Tempering Tantrums

If you're all by yourself in the kitchen and you're trying to pour warm liquid into egg yolks while simultaneously whisking, chances are the bowl of egg yolks is going to want to move around a bit. This can be frustrating for the solitary cook. Here are a few strategies for stabilizing the mischievous bowl:

- Soak a kitchen towel with water. Hold one corner and spin the towel into a long twist (like a gym towel intended for a locker-room snap). Form it into a closed circle on the countertop and nestle your bowl in the center.
- Buy mixing bowls with rubber bottoms. You'll find them available at stores specializing in cookware and at online shops. I own several and love them.
- Set a pair of rubber dishwashing gloves on the countertop, side by side, and then set your bowl on the gloves. The gloves will stabilize the bowl.
- Find a friend to help in the kitchen. Make sure you reward him or her with ice cream!

SAUCEPANS AND SKILLETS: Use heavy-duty pots and pans, which dissipate heat and will help ensure even heating when cooking on the stovetop.

For fruit-based mixtures like granitas and sorbets, or anything with an acidic ingredient like wine, always use nonreactive cookware. These include saucepans made of anodized aluminum, heatproof glass, or anything lined with stainless steel. The acid in the fruit can react with other metals and leave a nasty aftertaste.

A small saucepan means one that holds 1 to 3 quarts (1 to 3 liters), a medium saucepan holds around 4 quarts (4 liters), and a large saucepan refers to anything larger than 4 quarts (4 liters).

SCALE: A scale is necessary to weigh out the correct amount of some of the ingredients called for in the recipes, such as chocolate. For dry ingredients, measurements are given in both cup measurements and metric weights so that you can measure them by weight if you prefer.

SCOOPS: There are basically two types of ice cream scoops. **Solid scoops** are one-piece tools, often filled with antifreeze, that boast the ability to scoop through even the firmest ice cream. They shouldn't be run through the dishwasher, which can damage the finish and reduce the effectiveness of the antifreeze inside. Some single-piece scoops are coated with nonstick material to help the ice cream release. These kinds of scoops have no moving parts to break.

Spring-loaded scoops, sometimes called trigger scoops, usually require a bit more effort when scooping but have the advantage of a thin arc of metal that helps release the ice cream into a neat, perfectly rounded scoop. Cheaper models are flimsy and tend to slip gears and break easily, so I advise purchasing only professional-quality spring-loaded scoops.

SPATULAS: Spatulas made of heatproof material are the invention of the decade for home cooks and professionals. The flexible heads are made of silicone and can withstand temperatures well over 400°F (200°C) without melting. I keep lots of them on hand when cooking.

Some ice cream makers come with specially designed plastic spatulas that fit nicely into the freezing canister for removing just-churned ice cream. Don't use them for any other purpose, since you want them to last as long as possible and they may be hard to replace.

STORAGE CONTAINERS: My preferred containers for storage are ones that are square, plastic, and heavy-duty, with tight-sealing lids. Square containers, rather than round ones, fit more neatly in the freezer if space is at a premium, and heavy-duty plastic ensures that they won't crack in the freezer. Restaurant supply shops often carry a great selection of sturdy plastic food-safe containers.

STRAINERS: Strainers with medium-sized mesh screens are useful for removing seeds from berry purées and for straining just-cooked custards to remove any bits of cooked egg. Buy strainers with stainless steel screens that feel sturdy and solid. You'll find that these can take a lot of firm pressure when straining purées.

THERMOMETER: I recommend having an instant-read thermometer on hand when making custard-based ice creams if you're a beginner. For the uninitiated, it takes much of the guesswork out of the process of making custard. You may find that digital instant-read thermometers take faster readings than the dial type. When checking the temperature, be sure the end of the probe is submerged in the liquid but is not touching the bottom of the pan, which is hotter than the liquid itself.

VEGETABLE PEELER: Vegetable peelers made of nonreactive stainless steel are preferable for peeling fruit and shaving off wide strips of citrus zest. I make sure mine is sharp. Some now come with replaceable blades.

WHISKS: As with flexible spatulas, I like to keep several whisks on hand when cooking. Like other kitchen tools that take a beating, well-made whisks will last far longer than flimsy ones.

ZESTERS AND GRATERS: If you don't have a rasp-style grater, I suggest you make one your next purchase. They scrape off the most delicate, flavorful part of the peel and leave any bitter white pith behind. See page 11 for zesting tips.

2

Ice Creams

For some of us, the perfect scoop is a simple dish of creamy Vanilla Ice Cream flecked with lots of aromatic vanilla seeds (pages 24 and 25). Others get their frosty fix from a cone of Chocolate Ice Cream (pages 26 and 28). But in between chocolate and vanilla, there's a whole world of flavors to explore, and you'll find them all in this chapter, from rosy-pink Strawberry-Sour Cream Ice Cream (page 90) made from sweet, juicy strawberries to silky Lavender-Honey Ice Cream (page 64) to the liveliest lemon ice cream (page 85) you've ever eaten. While youngsters will certainly go wild for Peanut Butter and Jelly Ice Cream (page 50), few adults can resist an eye-opening scoop of Coffee Ice Cream (page 34), richly infused with a jolt of dark-roasted coffee beans. And if there's anyone who can resist a scoop of Tin Roof Ice Cream (page 54), chock-full of chocolate-dipped peanuts and gooey ripples of fudge, I'd like to meet them.

In this chapter you'll find all the classic ice creams as well as a myriad of modern flavors that are sure to please. There are also a handful of frozen yogurts and a gelato or two. Many of these recipes are simple enough to whiz up in a blender before freezing them in an ice cream maker, while others involve custards gently cooked in a saucepan until rich and satiny smooth. If you've never made a stovetop custard before, it's quite simple, and I've offered step-by-step instructions (page 3), with pictures and lots of pointers and tips to ensure success.

There's no reason why you can't create your own flavor combinations by adding mix-ins to your scoop—perhaps a swirl of Fudge Ripple (page 210), chewy nuggets of truffles (pages 211 and 212), chopped bits of candied nuts, or chunks of buttery-soft Chocolate Chip Cookie Dough (page 209). You'll find all these and more in chapter 6, Mix-Ins. Your imagination is the only limit.

Vanilla Ice Cream

Everyone needs a terrific vanilla ice cream recipe in their repertoire, and here it is. Keeping a tub of homemade vanilla ice cream in my freezer is standard policy, since I can't think of any dessert that isn't made better with a soft scoop of vanilla ice cream melting alongside.

1 cup (250 ml) whole milk

¾ cup (150 g) sugar

2 cups (500 ml) heavy cream

Pinch of salt

1 vanilla bean, split in half lengthwise

6 large egg yolks

¾ teaspoon vanilla extract

Warm the milk, sugar, 1 cup (250 ml) of the cream, and salt in a medium saucepan. Scrape the seeds from the vanilla bean into the warm milk and add the bean as well. Cover, remove from the heat, and let steep at room temperature for 30 minutes.

Pour the remaining 1 cup (250 ml) cream into a large bowl and set a mesh strainer on top. In a separate medium bowl, whisk together the egg yolks. Slowly pour the warm mixture into the egg yolks, whisking constantly, then scrape the warmed egg yolks back into the saucepan.

Stir the mixture constantly over medium heat with a heatproof spatula, scraping the bottom as you stir, until the mixture thickens and coats the spatula. Pour the custard through the strainer and stir it into the cream. Put the vanilla bean into the custard, add the vanilla extract, and stir until cool over an ice bath.

Chill the mixture thoroughly in the refrigerator. When ready to churn, remove the vanilla bean, rinsing and reserving it for another use, and then freeze the mixture in your ice cream maker according to the manufacturer's instructions.

PERFECT PAIRINGS: Make Chocolate Chip Ice Cream by drizzling in one recipe of dark chocolate Stracciatella (page 210).

I may not fit the profile of a bourbon drinker, but I do like (and sometimes need) a good shot of whisky every now and then...even in my ice cream! To make Bourbon and Spiced Pecan Ice Cream, stir 3 tablespoons (45 ml) bourbon (I like Jack Daniels) into the custard just before freezing, then mix in one recipe coarsely chopped Spiced Pecans (page 197) just after churning the ice cream.

Vanilla Ice Cream, Philadelphia-Style

MAKES ABOUT 1 QUART (1 LITER)

Philadelphia-style ice cream is made with no eggs, so it can be mixed together in a New York minute. It gets it name because at one time there was a proliferation of dairy farms around Philadelphia. I've made this vanilla ice cream successfully with all heavy cream as well as with a mixture of cream and milk, and I like it both ways.

> 3 cups (750 ml) heavy cream, or 2 cups (500 ml) heavy cream and 1 cup (250 ml) whole milk
>
> ¾ cup (150 g) sugar
>
> Pinch of salt
>
> 1 vanilla bean, split in half lengthwise
>
> ¾ teaspoon vanilla extract

Pour 1 cup (250 ml) of the cream into a medium saucepan and add the sugar and salt. Scrape the seeds from the vanilla bean into the saucepan and add the pod to the pot. Warm over medium heat, stirring, until the sugar is dissolved.

Remove from the heat and add the remaining 2 cups (500 ml) cream (or the remaining 1 cup, 250 ml, cream and the milk) and the vanilla extract.

Chill the mixture thoroughly in the refrigerator. When ready to churn, remove the vanilla bean, rinsing and reserving it for another use, and then freeze the mixture in your ice cream maker according to the manufacturer's instructions.

PERFECT PAIRING: To make Caramel-Chocolate Ripple Ice Cream, layer 1 cup each Fudge Ripple (page 210) and Salted Butter Caramel Sauce (page 174) into the just-churned custard.

French vs. American

There are two basic styles of ice cream: French-style, which is a cooked custard made with egg yolks, and Philadelphia-style, made with cream or a combination of cream and milk, but without eggs.

French-style ice creams tend to be smoother and silkier, due to the emulsifying power of the egg yolks, which get cooked on the stovetop, requiring a bit of cooking prowess. Philadelphia-style ice creams can simply be mixed or puréed together, chilled thoroughly, and then frozen. Philadelphia-style ice creams have no egg yolks, so they tend to be a bit firmer, freeze harder, and have a somewhat chewier texture. The advantage is that they're a little lighter tasting and are easier to make.

Chocolate Ice Cream

My search for the ultimate chocolate ice cream ended the day I opened my ice cream maker and took a taste of this version. And before I knew it, I'd licked the dasher as clean as the day I bought it! Intense cocoa powder blended with unctuous dark chocolate results in a perfect chocolate ice cream that's so irresistible you won't be able to wait to dig in either. I don't know why, but homemade ice cream always tastes best scraped (or, if no one's watching, licked) directly from the machine.

> 2 cups (500 ml) heavy cream
>
> 3 tablespoons (21 g) unsweetened Dutch-process cocoa powder
>
> 5 ounces (140 g) bittersweet or semisweet chocolate, chopped
>
> 1 cup (250 ml) whole milk
>
> ¾ cup (150 g) sugar
>
> Pinch of salt
>
> 5 large egg yolks
>
> ½ teaspoon vanilla extract

Warm 1 cup (250 ml) of the cream with the cocoa powder in a medium saucepan, whisking to thoroughly blend the cocoa. Bring to a boil, then reduce the heat and simmer at a very low boil for 30 seconds, whisking constantly. Remove from the heat and add the chopped chocolate, stirring until smooth. Then stir in the remaining 1 cup (250 ml) cream. Pour the mixture into a large bowl, scraping the saucepan as thoroughly as possible, and set a mesh strainer on top of the bowl.

Warm the milk, sugar, and salt in the same saucepan. In a separate medium bowl, whisk together the egg yolks. Slowly pour the warm milk into the egg yolks, whisking constantly, then scrape the warmed egg yolks back into the saucepan.

Stir the mixture constantly over medium heat with a heatproof spatula, scraping the bottom as you stir, until the mixture thickens and coats the spatula. Pour the custard through the strainer and stir it into the chocolate mixture until smooth, then stir in the vanilla. Stir until cool over an ice bath.

Chill the mixture thoroughly in the refrigerator, then freeze it in your ice cream maker according to the manufacturer's instructions. (If the cold mixture is too thick to pour into your machine, whisk it vigorously to thin it out.)

PERFECT PAIRINGS: To make Chocolate-Mint Ice Cream, stir ⅛ teaspoon mint oil or extract into the custard before freezing, then fold in one recipe of homemade Peppermint Patties (page 206) or 2 cups crumbled store-bought peppermint patties.

To make Rocky Road Ice Cream, fold in 1½ cups (90 g) homemade (or miniature store-bought) Marshmallows (page 212) and 1 cup (150 g) roasted peanuts or toasted, coarsely chopped almonds (see page 13).

Chocolate Ice Cream, Philadelphia-Style

MAKES ABOUT 1 QUART (1 LITER)

Unsweetened chocolate provides the maximum chocolate flavor in this non-custard-based chocolate ice cream. But bitter chocolate can be stubborn to melt, so whiz the mixture in a blender until it's silky smooth.

2¼ cups (560 ml) heavy cream

6 tablespoons (50 g) unsweetened Dutch-process cocoa powder

1 cup (200 g) sugar

Pinch of salt

6 ounces (170 g) unsweetened chocolate, chopped

1 cup (250 ml) whole milk

1 teaspoon vanilla extract

Whisk together the cream, cocoa powder, sugar, and salt in a large saucepan. Heat the mixture, whisking frequently, until it comes to a full, rolling boil (it will start to foam up). Remove from the heat and whisk in the chocolate until it's completely melted, then whisk in the milk and vanilla. Pour the mixture into a blender and blend for 30 seconds, until very smooth.

Chill the mixture thoroughly in the refrigerator, then freeze it in your ice cream maker according to the manufacturer's instructions.

PERFECT PAIRINGS: Make Double Chocolate Ice Cream by folding in one recipe of Dark Chocolate Truffles (page 211) or White Chocolate Truffles (page 212).

For Chocolate-Peanut Butter Patty Ice Cream, fold in one recipe of Peanut Butter Patties (page 204) instead.

What's That "About"?

In my recipes for ice cream and sorbets, I use the word "about" when indicating the quantity the recipe will make. In general, a custard or other mixture frozen in an ice cream machine designed for home use will increase in volume by around 25 percent once churned. The air incorporated into ice cream during churning, by the way, is called the overrun, and commercial ice cream can have up to 120 percent overrun!

Most of the recipes in this book will make 1 quart (1 liter) of frozen ice cream or sorbet. I tested the recipes using two of the most commonly used types of machines—one with a canister that you prefreeze and the other a powerful, self-refrigerated model. I found that the ice cream increased in volume in proportion to the power and speed of the machine. Hence, the recipes may yield slightly more or slightly less for you.

Aztec "Hot" Chocolate Ice Cream

The Aztecs were such trendsetters. Although it's become fashionably chic, from Soho to South Beach, to spice up chocolate with a bit of chile pepper, in fact it's a custom that goes back more than a thousand years. And I wonder if, even back then, there were paparazzi stalking luminaries in Central America, hoping to catch them in spicy situations. When your guests taste this decadent, zippy chocolate ice cream, you'll understand what all the fuss is about—and perhaps develop a few over-zealous followers yourself.

2¼ cups (560 ml) heavy cream

6 tablespoons (50 g) unsweetened Dutch-process cocoa powder

¾ cup (150 g) sugar

3 ounces (85 g) semisweet or bittersweet chocolate, chopped

1¼ cups (310 ml) whole milk

1 teaspoon vanilla extract

Pinch of salt

1¼ teaspoons ground cinnamon

2 to 3 teaspoons chile powder (see Note)

2 tablespoons brandy

Whisk together the cream, cocoa powder, and sugar in a large saucepan. Heat the mixture, whisking frequently, until it comes to a full, rolling boil (it will start to foam up). Remove from the heat and add the chocolate, then whisk until it is completely melted. Stir in the milk, vanilla, salt, cinnamon, chile powder, and brandy. Pour the mixture into a blender and blend for 30 seconds, until very smooth.

Chill the mixture thoroughly in the refrigerator, then freeze it in your ice cream maker according to the manufacturer's instructions.

NOTE: I like the taste of smoky ancho or chipotle chile powder, available in Mexican markets. They can vary in intensity, so if you're unsure of the strength of your chile powder, add the smaller amount and let it sit for a while, then see if you like it before adding more. The subtle warmth can heat up as it stands.

PERFECT PAIRING: For Mexican Chocolate and Cajeta Ice Cream, layer in one recipe of Cajeta (page 173). Include some Spiced Pecans (page 197) if you'd like.

Chocolate-Peanut Butter Ice Cream

MAKES ABOUT 1 QUART (1 LITER)

Two great tastes—smooth, creamy peanut butter and pure unadulterated cocoa—merge together to make one terrific ice cream.

> 2 cups (500 ml) half-and-half
>
> 1/4 cup (25 g) unsweetened Dutch-process cocoa powder
>
> 1/2 cup (100 g) sugar
>
> Pinch of salt
>
> 1/2 cup (130 g) smooth peanut butter

Whisk together the half-and-half, cocoa powder, sugar, and salt in a large saucepan. Heat the mixture, whisking frequently, until it comes to a full, rolling boil (it will start to foam up). Remove from the heat and whisk in the peanut butter, stirring until thoroughly blended.

Chill the mixture thoroughly, then freeze it in your ice cream maker according to the manufacturer's instructions.

PERFECT PAIRING: For Chocolate Fudge Swirl Peanut Butter Ice Cream, layer in one recipe of Fudge Ripple (page 210) and mix in Peanut Butter Patties (page 204).

Chocolate-Raspberry Ice Cream

MAKES ABOUT 3 CUPS (750 ML)

If you're one of those people who finds the combination of raspberries with dark chocolate the ultimate luxury, you'll adore this ice cream. It's the perfect indulgence: rich, dark chocolate with the bright flavor of tangy raspberries.

> 1 1/2 cups (375 ml) heavy cream
>
> 5 tablespoons (40 g) unsweetened Dutch-process cocoa powder
>
> 2/3 cup (130 g) sugar
>
> 2 cups (240 g) raspberries, fresh or frozen

Whisk together the cream, cocoa powder, and sugar in a large saucepan. Heat the mixture, whisking frequently, until it comes to a full, rolling boil (it will start to foam up). Remove from the heat and add the raspberries. Cover and let stand for 10 minutes.

Purée the mixture in a food processor or blender. If you wish, press the mixture through a mesh strainer to remove the seeds.

Chill the mixture thoroughly, then freeze it in your ice cream maker according to the manufacturer's instructions.

Milk Chocolate Ice Cream

MAKES ABOUT 1 QUART (1 LITER)

I finally understand the allure of milk chocolate. While writing a book exploring the world of chocolate, I became determined to get over my skepticism, and I taste-tested as many milk chocolates as I could. Yes, it was tough work, but I felt compelled to do it. I became a convert after sampling premium milk chocolates made with a high percentage of cocoa solids, and a whole new world opened up to me.

Mixing in cocoa nibs adds a crunchy counterpoint to this milky-smooth ice cream. I like biting into the little bits of pure, unadulterated chocolate, but I've made them optional, since you may not have them readily available (you can substitute chocolate chips). But once you taste a few, you'll find yourself adding them to chocolate desserts all the time, like I do. (See Resources, page 237, for online sources.)

> 8 ounces (230 g) milk chocolate with at least 30 percent cocoa solids, finely chopped
>
> 1½ cups (375 ml) heavy cream
>
> 1½ cups (375 ml) whole milk
>
> ¾ cup (150 g) sugar
>
> Big pinch of salt
>
> 4 large egg yolks
>
> 2 teaspoons Cognac
>
> ¾ cup (120 g) cocoa nibs or semisweet or bittersweet chocolate chips (optional)

Combine the milk chocolate and cream in a large, heatproof bowl set over a saucepan of simmering water. Stir until the chocolate is melted, then remove the bowl from the saucepan. Set it aside with a mesh strainer over the top.

Warm the milk, sugar, and salt in a medium saucepan. In a separate medium bowl, whisk together the egg yolks. Slowly pour the warm milk mixture into the egg yolks, whisking constantly, then scrape the warmed egg yolks back into the saucepan.

Stir the mixture constantly over medium heat with a heatproof spatula, scraping the bottom as you stir, until the mixture thickens and coats the spatula. Pour the custard through the strainer into the milk chocolate mixture, add the Cognac, and mix together. Stir until cool over an ice bath.

Chill the mixture thoroughly in the refrigerator, then freeze it in your ice cream maker according to the manufacturer's instructions. During the last few minutes of churning, add the cocoa nibs, if using.

PERFECT PAIRINGS: Make Milk Chocolate and Brownie Ice Cream by folding 2 cups of crumbled Chewy-Dense Brownies (page 221) into the just-churned ice cream.

For Milk Chocolate and Chocolate-Covered Peanut Ice Cream, fold in one recipe of Chocolate-Covered Peanuts (page 199).

Guinness–Milk Chocolate Ice Cream

MAKES ABOUT 1 QUART (1 LITER)

If you like the hearty taste of Guinness Stout, this is the ice cream for you. I was curious as to whether the beer flavor was too strong, so I asked my friend Heather, a knockout whose microscopic waistline belies the fact that the girl really knows her beer, to come by and taste. She gave this one a big thumbs up, so I sent her home with the whole container. The next day the phone rang. It was Heather, telling me that she offered some to her good-looking new neighbor, whom she'd been looking for an excuse to approach, and he was smitten enough to ask her out on a date between spoonfuls. While I can't promise that sharing this ice cream will wind up being an icebreaker for you, I don't see any reason not to give it a try.

> 7 ounces (205 g) milk chocolate, finely chopped
>
> 1 cup (250 ml) whole milk
>
> 1/2 cup (100 g) sugar
>
> Pinch of salt
>
> 4 large egg yolks
>
> 1 cup (250 ml) heavy cream
>
> 3/4 cup (180 ml) Guinness Stout
>
> 1 teaspoon vanilla extract

Put the chocolate pieces in a large bowl and set a mesh strainer over the top.

Warm the milk, sugar, and salt in a medium saucepan. In a separate medium bowl, whisk together the egg yolks. Slowly pour the warm mixture into the egg yolks, whisking constantly, then scrape the warmed egg yolks back into the saucepan.

Stir the mixture constantly over medium heat with a heatproof spatula, scraping the bottom as you stir, until the mixture thickens and coats the spatula. Pour the custard through the strainer over the milk chocolate, then stir until the chocolate is melted. Once the mixture is smooth, whisk in the cream, then the Guinness and vanilla. Stir until cool over an ice bath.

Chill the mixture thoroughly in the refrigerator, then freeze it in your ice cream maker according to the manufacturer's instructions.

PERFECT PAIRING: Make Guinness, Milk Chocolate, and Oatmeal Ice Cream by folding one recipe of Oatmeal Praline (page 205) into the just-churned ice cream.

White Chocolate Ice Cream

MAKES ABOUT 1 QUART (1 LITER)

Sometimes I'm afraid to admit that I love white chocolate. Purists argue, "It's not real chocolate." Although that may technically be true, who cares? (French fries aren't "real chocolate" either…yet they're pretty darn good.) So I don't compare it to dark chocolate, since it's a whole other ballgame.

White chocolate's creamy-smooth, delicate cocoa butter flavor is perfect when melted and stirred into ice cream, and the result makes a truly outstanding dessert when topped with Sour Cherries in Syrup (page 185). And I've yet to come across any chocolate cake that couldn't be improved by a scoop of white chocolate ice cream melting seductively alongside.

> 8 ounces (230 g) white chocolate, finely chopped
>
> 1 cup (250 ml) whole milk
>
> 2/3 cup (130 g) sugar
>
> Pinch of salt
>
> 5 large egg yolks
>
> 2 cups (500 ml) heavy cream

Put the chocolate pieces in a large bowl and set a mesh strainer over the top.

Warm the milk, sugar, and salt in a medium saucepan. In a separate medium bowl, whisk together the egg yolks. Slowly pour the warm milk into the egg yolks, whisking constantly, then scrape the warmed egg yolks back into the saucepan.

Stir the mixture constantly over medium heat with a heatproof spatula, scraping the bottom as you stir, until the mixture thickens and coats the spatula. Pour the custard through the strainer over the white chocolate. Stir until the white chocolate is completely melted and the mixture is smooth, then stir in the cream. Stir until cool over an ice bath.

Chill the mixture thoroughly in the refrigerator, then freeze it in your ice cream maker according to the manufacturer's instructions.

PERFECT PAIRINGS: Make White Chocolate–Cherry Ice Cream by folding very well-drained and coarsely chopped Sour Cherries in Syrup (page 185) or Candied Cherries (page 215) into the just-churned ice cream.

For Black and White Chocolate Ice Cream, layer one recipe of Fudge Ripple (page 210), Dark Chocolate Truffles (page 211), or Stracciatella (page 210) into the just-churned ice cream.

Coffee Ice Cream

When I was a kid growing up in puritanical New England, dessert was a seldom-seen treat. When temptation raised its devilish head, a few scoops of unadulterated ice cream were allowed and served forth without much fanfare. Our reward was often coffee ice cream, curiously one of the few "adult" flavors that kids seem to like as much as grown-ups. And in case you're feeling sorry for my dessert-deprived childhood, not to worry; I'm definitely making up for lost time nowadays.

> 1½ cups (375 ml) whole milk
>
> ¾ cup (150 g) sugar
>
> 1½ cups (125 g) whole coffee beans
>
> Pinch of salt
>
> 1½ cups (375 ml) heavy cream
>
> 5 large egg yolks
>
> ¼ teaspoon vanilla extract
>
> ¼ teaspoon finely ground coffee

Warm the milk, sugar, whole coffee beans, salt, and ½ cup (125 ml) of the cream in a medium saucepan. Once the mixture is warm, cover, remove from the heat, and let steep at room temperature for 1 hour.

Rewarm the coffee-infused milk mixture. Pour the remaining 1 cup (250 ml) cream into a large bowl and set a mesh strainer on top. In a separate medium bowl, whisk together the egg yolks. Slowly pour the warm coffee mixture into the egg yolks, whisking constantly, then scrape the warmed egg yolks back into the saucepan.

Stir the mixture constantly over medium heat with a heatproof spatula, scraping the bottom as you stir, until the mixture thickens and coats the spatula. Pour the custard through the strainer and stir it into the cream. Press on the coffee beans in the strainer to extract as much of the coffee flavor as possible, then discard the beans. Mix in the vanilla and the finely ground coffee and stir until cool over an ice bath.

Chill the mixture thoroughly in the refrigerator, then freeze it in your ice cream maker according to the manufacturer's instructions.

PERFECT PAIRING: Make Coffee Ice Cream Brownie Sundaes by topping Brownies (pages 220 and 221) with scoops of Coffee Ice Cream, then spooning Mocha Sauce (page 166) over the top, and finishing with a final flourish of French Almonds (page 189).

Coffee Frozen Yogurt

MAKES ABOUT 1 QUART (1 LITER)

When my father was in the army, he and his bunkmates would eagerly anticipate the care packages that would arrive from home, filled with cookies and cakes. But in lieu of homemade goodies, their Brazilian bunkmate would get sacks of aromatic coffee beans. He'd carefully prepare single, tiny cups of coffee by crushing a few of the highly prized beans between two metal spoons and then drizzling boiling water over them, creating perhaps the most labor-intensive cup of coffee ever. But I'm sure the effort was well worth it. Make sure the espresso you use for this recipe is excellent; your effort will be appreciated as well.

    1 cup (240 g) plain whole-milk yogurt

    3/4 cup (150 g) sugar

    Pinch of salt

    3/4 cup (180 ml) heavy cream

    1 cup (250 ml) brewed espresso, cooled to room temperature

    1/4 teaspoon finely ground dark roast coffee

Whisk together the yogurt, sugar, salt, cream, espresso, and ground coffee. Chill for 2 hours. Freeze the mixture in your ice cream maker according to the manufacturer's instructions.

Vietnamese Coffee Ice Cream

MAKES ABOUT 1 QUART (1 LITER)

Vietnamese food is perhaps my favorite of all the cuisines in the world, and I would eat it every single night if I could. At the start of every Vietnamese meal, I order a Vietnamese coffee. A glass with a sweet dose of condensed milk is brought to the table with a well-worn stainless-steel filter balanced on top, dripping steaming hot coffee into the thick, sweet milk. Once brewed, it all gets stirred up and ice is added. I thought the flavors would make an excellent ice cream, and I was right.

    1 1/2 cups (600 g) sweetened condensed milk

    1 1/2 cups (375 ml) brewed espresso (or very strongly brewed coffee)

    1/2 cup (125 ml) half-and-half

    Big pinch of finely ground dark roast coffee

Whisk together the condensed milk, espresso, half-and-half, and ground coffee. Chill the mixture thoroughly, then freeze it in your ice cream maker according to the manufacturer's instructions.

Anise Ice Cream

If you've never tasted anise and chocolate together, prepare yourself for an unexpected treat. I don't even like anise, but for some improbable reason this is one of my favorite ice creams, especially when nestled alongside a slice of dense chocolate cake or used to fill profiteroles doused in warm chocolate sauce (see the Perfect Pairings at the end of the recipe).

> 2 teaspoons anise seeds
>
> 2 cups (500 ml) heavy cream
>
> 1 cup (250 ml) whole milk
>
> $^2/_3$ cup (130 g) sugar
>
> $1^1/_2$ tablespoons good-flavored honey
>
> Pinch of salt
>
> 5 large egg yolks

Toast the anise seeds in a medium saucepan over moderate heat for about 3 minutes, until they smell fragrant. Pour in 1 cup (250 ml) of the cream, then add the milk, sugar, honey, and salt. Heat until warm, then cover, remove from the heat, and let steep at room temperature for 1 hour.

Rewarm the anise-infused milk mixture. Pour the remaining 1 cup (250 ml) cream into a large bowl and set a mesh strainer over the top. In a separate medium bowl, whisk together the egg yolks. Slowly pour the warm anise-infused mixture into the egg yolks, whisking constantly, then scrape the warmed egg yolks back into the saucepan.

Stir the mixture constantly over medium heat with a heatproof spatula, scraping the bottom as you stir, until the mixture thickens and coats the spatula. Pour the custard through the strainer and stir it into the cream. Discard the anise seeds and stir until cool over an ice bath.

Chill the mixture thoroughly in the refrigerator, then freeze it in your ice cream maker according to the manufacturer's instructions.

VARIATION: To make Biscotti Ice Cream, warm $^1/_2$ cup (80 g) mixed dark and light raisins with $^1/_4$ cup (60 ml) Marsala, simmering until the wine is absorbed. Let cool. Coarsely chop $^1/_2$ cup (65 g) toasted almonds (see page 13). During the last few minutes of churning, add the soaked raisins and almonds to the ice cream.

> PERFECT PAIRINGS: Make Anise Ice Cream Puffs (pictured opposite) by tucking scoops of Anise Ice Cream into airy Profiteroles (page 232), then surround them with Lean Chocolate Sauce (page 165). Or finely chop Candied Citrus Peel (page 178) made with orange peel and stir it in during the last few minutes of churning to make Orange-Anise Ice Cream.

Cinnamon Ice Cream

MAKES ABOUT 1 QUART (1 LITER)

Spicy cinnamon sticks give this ice cream a stronger, far more complex flavor than ground cinnamon does. Around the winter holidays, skip the bowl of whipped cream to accompany pumpkin pie or apple crisp and treat your lucky guests to cinnamon ice cream instead. It is also very good alongside any favorite chocolate dessert, such as devil's food cake or perched atop a homemade Brownie (pages 220 and 221).

1 cup (250 ml) whole milk

¾ cup (150 g) sugar

Pinch of salt

Ten 3-inch (8-cm) cinnamon sticks, broken up

2 cups (500 ml) heavy cream

5 large egg yolks

Warm the milk, sugar, salt, cinnamon sticks and 1 cup (250 ml) of the cream in a medium saucepan. Once warm, cover, remove from the heat, and let steep at room temperature for 1 hour

Rewarm the cinnamon-infused milk mixture Remove the cinnamon sticks with a slotted spoon and discard them. Pour the remaining 1 cup (250 ml) cream into a large bowl and set a mesh strainer on top.

In a separate medium bowl, whisk together the egg yolks. Slowly pour the warm mixture into the egg yolks, whisking constantly, then scrape the warmed egg yolks back into the saucepan.

Stir the mixture constantly over medium heat with a heatproof spatula, scraping the bottom as you stir, until the mixture thickens and coats the spatula. Pour the custard through the strainer and into the cream. Stir until cool over an ice bath.

Chill the mixture thoroughly in the refrigerator, then freeze it in your ice cream maker according to the manufacturer's instructions.

PERFECT PAIRING: Marble this ice cream with Aztec "Hot" Chocolate Ice Cream (page 29) to make Aztec Cinnamon-Chocolate Ice Cream.

Black Currant Tea Ice Cream

There's something about the slightly smoky, potent, and fruity flavor of black currant tea that makes it the perfect complement to chocolate (see Perfect Pairings, below). But if black currants aren't your cup of tea, substitute another aromatic infusion, such as Earl Grey, scented with bergamot, or smoky oolong instead.

> 1 cup (250 ml) whole milk
>
> 2 cups (500 ml) heavy cream
>
> ¾ cup (150 g) sugar
>
> ¼ cup (15 g) loose black currant tea leaves
>
> 5 large egg yolks

Warm the milk, 1 cup (250 ml) of the cream, sugar, and tea leaves in a medium saucepan. Cover, remove from the heat, and let steep at room temperature for 1 hour.

Rewarm the tea-infused milk. Pour the remaining 1 cup (250 ml) cream into a large bowl and set a mesh strainer on top. In a separate medium bowl, whisk together the egg yolks. Slowly pour the warm mixture into the egg yolks, whisking constantly, then scrape the warmed egg yolks back into the saucepan.

Stir the mixture constantly over medium heat with a heatproof spatula, scraping the bottom as you stir, until the mixture thickens and coats the spatula. Pour the custard through the strainer into the cream, pressing gently on the tea leaves to extract the maximum flavor from them, then discard the leaves. Stir until cool over an ice bath.

Chill the mixture thoroughly in the refrigerator, then freeze it in your ice cream maker according to the manufacturer's instructions.

PERFECT PAIRINGS: Make Black Currant Tea and Chocolate Truffle Ice Cream by adding Dark Chocolate Truffles (page 211), or swirl this ice cream with Fudge Ripple (page 210) to make Black Currant Tea and Fudge Ripple Ice Cream.

Green Tea Ice Cream

Green tea powder, called *matcha*, is found in tea shops and stores that sell Japanese products, which I'm always looking for an excuse to visit since they're great places for poking around. *Matcha* has a slightly pungent yet powerful taste, but its color is the real showstopper. Frothing the tea turns the custard a vivid green color.

1 cup (250 ml) whole milk

¾ cup (150 g) sugar

Pinch of salt

2 cups (500 ml) heavy cream

4 teaspoons matcha (green tea powder)

6 large egg yolks

Warm the milk, sugar, and salt in a medium saucepan. Pour the cream into a large bowl and whisk in the green tea powder. Set a mesh strainer on top.

In a separate medium bowl, whisk together the egg yolks. Slowly pour the warm mixture into the egg yolks, whisking constantly, then scrape the warmed egg yolks back into the saucepan.

Stir the mixture constantly over medium heat with a heatproof spatula, scraping the bottom as you stir, until the mixture thickens and coats the spatula. Pour the custard through the strainer and stir it into the cream, then whisk it vigorously until the custard is frothy to dissolve the green tea powder. Stir until cool over an ice bath.

Chill the mixture thoroughly in the refrigerator, then freeze it in your ice cream maker according to the manufacturer's instructions.

PERFECT PAIRINGS: Make Green Tea and Red Bean Ice Cream by folding one recipe of drained Candied Red Beans (page 183) into the just-churned ice cream. Or prefreeze scoops of Green Tea Ice Cream and sprinkle them with kinako powder (roasted soybean powder, available in stores selling Japanese groceries) before serving (pictured opposite).

Kinako Ice Cream

A few years back, I visited Tokyo for the first time, and while there I detected a curious flavor in one of the desserts I tasted. None of the pastry-chef students I was there to teach was able to tell me exactly what it was. But later, when a couple of the students and I were poking around at the 100-yen shop (the fabulously fun Japanese equivalent of a 99¢ store), I randomly picked up a packet of beige powder with a colorful riot of Japanese lettering. My easily enthused guides got even more enthused, letting me know that I'd found exactly what I was looking for. When I got home, I discovered kinako in my local Japanese food shop and learned that it was roasted soybean powder. It has a taste similar to roasted nuts but more elusive and certainly more exotic.

> 1 cup (250 ml) whole milk
>
> 3/4 cup (150 g) sugar
>
> 6 tablespoons (55 g) kinako powder
>
> Pinch of salt
>
> 2 cups (500 ml) heavy cream
>
> 6 large egg yolks

Whisk together the milk, sugar, kinako, and salt in a medium saucepan. Pour the cream into a large bowl and set a mesh strainer on top.

Warm the kinako-flavored mixture. In a separate medium bowl, whisk together the egg yolks. Slowly pour the warm mixture into the egg yolks, whisking constantly, then scrape the warmed egg yolks back into the saucepan.

Stir the mixture constantly over medium heat with a heatproof spatula, scraping the bottom as you stir, until the mixture thickens and coats the spatula. Pour the custard through the strainer and stir it into the cream. Pour the mixture into a blender and purée for 30 seconds.

Chill the mixture thoroughly in the refrigerator, then freeze it in your ice cream maker according to the manufacturer's instructions.

VARIATION: To make a nondairy version of this ice cream, warm 2 1/2 cups (625 ml) plain soy milk with 3/4 cup (150 g) sugar and whisk in 3 1/2 tablespoons (35 g) kinako powder. Once warm, remove the mixture from the heat and chill thoroughly. Whiz it in the blender, and then freeze it in your ice cream maker.

PERFECT PAIRING: Make Kinako Chocolate Ice Cream Sandwiches, using the Chocolate Ice Cream Sandwich Cookies (page 223) and rolling the edges of the sandwiches in finely chopped Salt-Roasted Peanuts (page 188).

Fresh Ginger Ice Cream

The cleansing zing of fresh ginger is always welcome after dinner. Its not-so-subtle spiciness is a pleasing juxtaposition to the cool creaminess of ice cream. Ginger is also reputed to aid digestion, and adding nuggets of soft Dark Chocolate Truffles (page 211) or layering the ice cream with Stracciatella (page 210) would certainly make this "medicine" go down quite easily.

> 3 ounces (85 g) unpeeled fresh ginger
>
> 1 cup (250 ml) whole milk
>
> 2 cups (500 ml) heavy cream
>
> $^3/_4$ cup (150 g) sugar
>
> Pinch of salt
>
> 5 large egg yolks

Cut the ginger in half lengthwise (making it more stable for slicing), and then cut it into thin slices. Place the ginger in a medium, nonreactive saucepan. Add enough water to cover the ginger by about $^1/_2$ inch (2 cm), and bring to a boil. Boil for 2 minutes, then drain, discarding the liquid.

Return the blanched ginger slices to the saucepan, then add the milk, 1 cup (250 ml) of the cream, sugar, and salt. Warm the mixture, cover, and remove from the heat. Let steep at room temperature for 1 hour.

Rewarm the mixture. Remove the ginger slices with a slotted spoon and discard. Pour the remaining 1 cup (250 ml) heavy cream into a large bowl and set a mesh strainer on top.

In a separate medium bowl, whisk together the egg yolks. Slowly pour the warm mixture into the egg yolks, whisking constantly, then scrape the warmed egg yolks back into the saucepan.

Stir the mixture constantly over medium heat with a heatproof spatula, scraping the bottom as you stir, until the mixture thickens and coats the spatula. Pour the custard through the strainer and stir it into the cream. Stir until cool over an ice bath.

Chill the mixture thoroughly in the refrigerator, then freeze it in your ice cream maker according to the manufacturer's instructions.

VARIATION: To make Lemon–Fresh Ginger Ice Cream, grind the zest of 2 lemons with the sugar in a blender or food processor and warm it with the milk.

PERFECT PAIRINGS: Make Ginger and Candied Lemon Ice Cream by draining a handful of Candied Lemon Slices (page 214), coarsely chopping them, and folding them into the just-churned ice cream.

For Ginger-Gingersnap Ice Cream, mix in one recipe of Speculoos (page 208).

Butterscotch Pecan Ice Cream

MAKES ABOUT 1¼ QUARTS (1¼ LITERS)

There seems to be no agreement as to the origin of the word "butterscotch." Some culinary scholars argue that its name is taken from "butter-scorched," a theory worthy of consideration, since the process does indeed require cooking butter. Yet others academically assert that the term is derived from the word "butter scoring," as in "cutting." Not as in, "Dude, I scored some awesome Butterscotch Pecan Ice Cream from David!"

So I'd like to offer my own theory, one that's a bit simpler: It's because buttery butterscotch always tastes better with a shot of scotch in it.

5 tablespoons (70 g) butter, salted or unsalted

¾ cup (170 g) packed dark brown sugar

½ teaspoon coarse salt

2 cups (500 ml) heavy cream

¾ cup (180 ml) whole milk

6 large egg yolks

½ teaspoon vanilla extract

1 tablespoon scotch whisky

Buttered Pecans (page 195)

Melt the butter in a medium saucepan, then stir in the brown sugar and salt until well moistened. Whisk in 1 cup (250 ml) of the cream and the milk.

Warm the brown sugar and cream mixture. Pour the remaining 1 cup (250 ml) cream into a large bowl and set a mesh strainer on top.

In a separate medium bowl, whisk together the egg yolks. Slowly pour the warm brown sugar mixture into the egg yolks, whisking constantly, then scrape the warmed egg yolks back into the saucepan.

Stir the mixture constantly over medium heat with a heatproof spatula, scraping the bottom as you stir, until the mixture thickens and coats the spatula. Pour the custard through the strainer and stir it into the cream. Add the vanilla and scotch, then stir until cool over an ice bath.

Chill the mixture thoroughly in the refrigerator, then freeze it in your ice cream maker according to the manufacturer's instructions. During the last few minutes of churning, add the Buttered Pecans.

PERFECT PAIRING: Go all out and make Blondie Sundaes, serving Butterscotch Pecan Ice Cream atop Blondies (page 222), drizzling with Lean Chocolate Sauce (page 165) or Classic Hot Fudge (page 164).

Date, Rum, and Pecan Ice Cream

This is the perfect date ice cream. Ha ha...er, sorry about that.

Ahem. Anyway, sweet dates and rum make a good duo, but having lived in San Francisco for many years, where it's often whispered that there's no better way to liven up a pairing than by adding a third element, I offer you this ménage à trois of flavors in one sybaritic ice cream.

Be careful when heating the rum and dates: The rum can flame up, so keep an eye on the action before it gets too hot to handle.

DATES

> 12 dates (4 ounces, 115 g), pitted
>
> ¼ cup (60 ml) dark rum

ICE CREAM

> 1 cup (250 ml) whole milk
>
> ⅔ cup (130 g) sugar
>
> Big pinch of salt
>
> 1¼ cups (310 ml) heavy cream
>
> 6 large egg yolks
>
> ½ teaspoon vanilla extract
>
> 2 tablespoons dark rum
>
> 1 cup (100 g) pecans, toasted (see page 13) and coarsely chopped (see Note)

To prepare the dates, chop them into ½-inch (2-cm) pieces. Combine the date pieces with the rum in a small saucepan and bring to a boil. Remove from the heat and stir. Cover and let macerate at room temperature for at least 4 hours (this can be done up to 1 day ahead).

To make the ice cream, warm the milk, sugar, and salt in a medium saucepan. Pour the cream into a large bowl and set a mesh strainer on top.

In a separate medium bowl, whisk together the egg yolks. Slowly pour the warm mixture into the egg yolks, whisking constantly, then scrape the warmed egg yolks back into the saucepan.

Stir the mixture constantly over medium heat with a heatproof spatula, scraping the bottom as you stir, until the mixture thickens and coats the spatula. Pour the custard through the strainer and stir it into the cream. Mix in the vanilla and rum, then stir until cool over an ice bath.

Chill the mixture thoroughly in the refrigerator, then freeze it in your ice cream maker according to the manufacturer's instructions. During the last few minutes of churning, add the nuts and date pieces.

NOTE: Feel free to substitute 1 cup Wet Pecans (page 198) or 1 cup Spiced Pecans (page 197) for the toasted pecans.

Gianduja Gelato

On my first visit to Torino, I arrived in rabid pursuit of *gianduja*, a confection made from local hazelnuts ground with milk chocolate that is a specialty of the Piedmont region. I'd also never had *gianduja* gelato at the source. I did not leave disappointed. I watched with anticipation as the gelato maker at Caffè San Carlo smeared dense gelato from his gleaming freezer into a cone. It was hazelnut heaven. Use top-quality milk chocolate with at least 30 percent cocoa solids.

1½ cups (185 g) hazelnuts, toasted (see page 13)

1 cup (250 ml) whole milk

2 cups (500 ml) heavy cream

¾ cup (150 g) sugar

¼ teaspoon coarse salt

4 ounces (115 g) milk chocolate, finely chopped

5 large egg yolks

⅛ teaspoon vanilla extract

Rub the hazelnuts in a kitchen towel to remove as much of the papery skins as possible, then finely chop them in a food processor or blender.

Warm the milk with 1 cup (250 ml) of the cream, sugar, and salt in a saucepan. Once warm, remove from the heat and add the chopped hazelnuts. Cover and let steep at room temperature for 1 hour.

Put the milk chocolate pieces in a large bowl. Heat the remaining 1 cup (250 ml) cream in a medium saucepan until it just begins to boil. Pour it over the milk chocolate pieces and stir until the chocolate is completely melted and smooth. Set a mesh strainer over the top.

Pour the hazelnut-infused milk through a strainer into a medium saucepan, squeezing the nuts firmly with your hands to extract as much of the flavorful liquid as possible. Discard the hazelnuts.

Rewarm the hazelnut-infused mixture. In a separate medium bowl, whisk together the egg yolks. Slowly pour the warm hazelnut mixture into the egg yolks, whisking constantly, then scrape the warmed egg yolks back into the saucepan.

Stir the mixture constantly over medium heat with a heatproof spatula, scraping the bottom as you stir, until the mixture thickens and coats the spatula. Pour the custard through the strainer and stir it into the milk chocolate mixture. Add the vanilla and stir until cool over an ice bath.

Chill the mixture thoroughly in the refrigerator, then freeze it in your ice cream maker according to the manufacturer's instructions.

PERFECT PAIRING: Make Gianduja-Stracciatella Gelato (pictured opposite) by adding Stracciatella (page 210) to the gelato. Scoop it into Ice Cream Cones (page 228) to serve.

Maple Walnut Ice Cream with Wet Walnuts

I once visited a sugar shack in Canada, a magical place where sticky maple sap gets boiled down into glistening maple syrup. I watched the process until I could stand it no more, and then my wildest dreams came true: We sat down to a lunch where everything came to the table drenched with pure, precious maple syrup. And in case there wasn't enough, a big pitcher of warm maple syrup also sat within reach so we could help ourselves to as much as we wanted. If my shoulder bag had been syrup-proof, I would have been very tempted to take some of the obvious overflow off their hands. Maple syrup is usually graded dark amber or light amber. The darker the syrup, the deeper the flavor, so I always use the darker type, since there's no such thing as too much maple syrup flavor. Adding Wet Walnuts (page 198) drenched in maple syrup ensures a delivery of delicious maple flavor with each bite.

> 1^{1}/$_{2}$ cups (375 ml) whole milk
>
> 2 tablespoons sugar
>
> 1^{1}/$_{2}$ cups (375 ml) heavy cream
>
> 5 large egg yolks
>
> ^{3}/$_{4}$ cup (180 ml) dark amber maple syrup
>
> ^{1}/$_{8}$ teaspoon coarse salt
>
> ^{1}/$_{4}$ teaspoon vanilla extract
>
> Wet Walnuts (page 198)

Warm the milk and sugar in a medium saucepan. Pour the cream into a large bowl and set a mesh strainer on top.

In a separate medium bowl, whisk together the egg yolks. Slowly pour the warm mixture into the egg yolks, whisking constantly, then scrape the warmed egg yolks back into the saucepan.

Stir the mixture constantly over medium heat with a heatproof spatula, scraping the bottom as you stir, until the mixture thickens and coats the spatula. Pour the custard through the strainer and stir it into the cream to cool. Add the maple syrup, salt, and vanilla, and stir until cool over an ice bath.

Chill the mixture thoroughly in the refrigerator, then freeze it in your ice cream maker according to the manufacturer's instructions. During the last few minutes of churning, add the Wet Walnuts.

PERFECT PAIRING: Use Salted Butter Caramel Sauce (page 174) to make Maple Walnut Ice Cream Sundaes, resting the ice cream on a Chewy-Dense Brownie (page 221) and topping it off with a Candied Cherry (page 215).

Vanilla Frozen Yogurt

I really like frozen yogurt, but only if it's homemade. So don't expect this to taste like the frozen yogurt that squirts out of the machine at the mall. That kind is loaded with so much other stuff that any similarity to real yogurt is purely coincidental. Homemade frozen yogurt has a delightful tanginess and is a bit lighter than traditional ice cream. I choose to keep mine pure, relying on good whole-milk yogurt to provide much of the flavor. If you do want to make a dense, richer frozen yogurt, see the variation below.

> 3 cups (720 g) plain whole-milk yogurt
>
> 1 cup (200 g) sugar
>
> 1 teaspoon vanilla extract

Mix together the yogurt, sugar, and vanilla. Stir until the sugar is completely dissolved. Refrigerate for 1 hour.

Freeze in your ice cream maker according to the manufacturer's instructions.

VARIATION: To make Rich Vanilla Frozen Yogurt, substitute 3 cups (720 g) of strained yogurt (see below) or Greek-style yogurt for the plain whole-milk yogurt and reduce the amount of sugar to ³⁄₄ cup (150 g).

> PERFECT PAIRING: Yes, you can have yogurt and granola for dessert. Just top a scoop of Vanilla Frozen Yogurt with Honey-Crunch Granola (page 186).

Strained Yogurt

Draining yogurt allows the whey to run off, leaving you with very thick yogurt with a higher concentration of butterfat, which makes a smoother, creamier frozen yogurt that's naturally more tangy. I like both, and my choice on any given day depends on my mood and what I'm serving alongside.

So when a little extra richness is called for, use these instructions to make strained yogurt, which you can substitute cup for cup for the yogurt called for in any of the frozen yogurt recipes in this book. (I do give two different recipes for vanilla frozen yogurt, one using strained yogurt and one using unstrained yogurt.)

To make 1 cup (240 g) of strained yogurt, line a mesh strainer with a few layers of cheesecloth. Then scrape 16 ounces or 2 cups (480 g) of plain whole-milk yogurt into the cheesecloth. Gather the ends and fold them over the yogurt, then refrigerate for at least 6 hours.

You can also use Greek-style yogurt, which is much higher in fat than plain yogurt, in place of strained yogurt in all of the frozen yogurt recipes.

Peanut Butter Ice Cream

Kids, naturally, love this ice cream. And it's easy enough that kids can put it together themselves with a minimum of help from Mom or Dad. To make it even more fun, layer in a swirl of their favorite jam.

> $^3/_4$ cup (180 g) smooth peanut butter
>
> $^3/_4$ cup plus 2 tablespoons (180 g) sugar
>
> $2^2/_3$ cups (660 ml) half-and-half
>
> Pinch of salt
>
> $^1/_8$ teaspoon vanilla extract

Purée the peanut butter, sugar, half-and-half, salt, and vanilla in a blender or food processor until smooth.

Chill the mixture thoroughly in the refrigerator, then freeze it in your ice cream maker according to the manufacturer's instructions.

VARIATION: To make Peanut Butter and Jelly Ice Cream, as you remove the ice cream from the machine, layer it with $^3/_4$ cup (240 g) of your favorite jam or jelly.

Orange Popsicle Ice Cream

This ice cream is for those who are nostalgic for those orange-and-cream-flavored popsicles. If you miss that taste, you'll discover it again here.

> $^2/_3$ cup (130 g) sugar
>
> Grated zest of 3 oranges, preferably unsprayed
>
> $1^1/_4$ cups (310 ml) freshly squeezed orange juice (from 4 or 5 large oranges)
>
> 1 cup (240 g) sour cream
>
> $^1/_2$ cup (125 ml) half-and-half
>
> 2 teaspoons Grand Marnier or another orange liqueur

In a blender, pulverize the sugar and orange zest until the zest is very fine. Add the orange juice, sour cream, half-and-half, and Grand Marnier and blend until the sugar is completely dissolved.

Chill the mixture thoroughly in the refrigerator, then freeze it in your ice cream maker according to the manufacturer's instructions.

PERFECT PAIRING: If you like oranges and cream, dip small scoops of Orange Popsicle Ice Cream in melted white chocolate, using the directions for Tartufi (page 230).

Malted Milk Ice Cream

I froze lots and lots and lots of ice cream when writing this book. It was a treat having freshly made ice cream every day, but space in my freezer soon became an issue, and more than once a frozen brick of ice cream slipped out, nearly crashing down on my foot. I eventually realized that it was impossible (and a little dangerous) to coexist with too many flavors all at once. Consequently, I passed off lots of ice cream to friends, neighbors, local shopkeepers, and occasionally a startled delivery man. All were more than happy to take a quart off my hands. But I guarded this Malted Milk Ice Cream, saving it all for myself.

The recipe calls for malt powder, which is usually found in the ice cream aisle of your supermarket. Sometimes, however, it's stocked alongside chocolate drink mixes like Ovaltine, which isn't the same thing and shouldn't be used here. The most common brands of malt powder are Carnation and Horlicks. (See Resources, page 237, for online sources.)

> 1 cup (250 ml) half-and-half
>
> ¾ cup (150 g) sugar
>
> Pinch of salt
>
> 2 cups (500 ml) heavy cream
>
> ¼ teaspoon vanilla extract
>
> ⅔ cup (90 g) malt powder
>
> 6 large egg yolks
>
> 2 cups (350 g) malted milk balls, coarsely chopped

Warm the half-and-half, sugar, and salt in a medium saucepan. In a large bowl, whisk together the heavy cream, vanilla, and malt powder and set a mesh strainer on top.

In a separate medium bowl, whisk together the egg yolks. Slowly pour the warm mixture into the egg yolks, whisking constantly, then scrape the warmed egg yolks back into the saucepan.

Stir the mixture constantly over medium heat with a heatproof spatula, scraping the bottom as you stir, until the mixture thickens and coats the spatula. Pour the custard through the strainer and whisk it into the malted milk mixture. Stir until cool over an ice bath.

Chill the mixture thoroughly in the refrigerator, then freeze it in your ice cream maker according to the manufacturer's instructions. As you remove the ice cream from the machine, fold in the chopped malted milk balls.

PERFECT PAIRING: Add crumbled Chewy-Dense Brownies (page 221) or Dark Chocolate Truffles (page 211) for Chocolate–Malted Milk Ice Cream.

Oatmeal-Raisin Ice Cream

This ice cream tastes just like a big, moist, chewy oatmeal cookie, thanks to the winning combination of plump raisins and crunchy oatmeal praline folded into a custard made with just the right touch of brown sugar.

RAISINS

> 1/4 cup (60 ml) water
>
> 2 tablespoons sugar
>
> 1/2 cup (80 g) raisins
>
> 2 teaspoons whiskey

ICE CREAM

> 1 cup (250 ml) whole milk
>
> 1/2 cup (100 g) granulated sugar
>
> Pinch of salt
>
> 2 cups (500 ml) heavy cream
>
> 1/3 cup (70 g) packed light brown sugar
>
> 1/4 teaspoon ground cinnamon
>
> 5 large egg yolks
>
> 1/2 teaspoon vanilla extract
>
> Oatmeal Praline (page 205)

To prepare the raisins, heat the water and sugar in a small saucepan. Add the raisins and cook over low heat, stirring frequently, until all but about 2 tablespoons of the syrup has been absorbed, about 5 minutes. Remove from the heat and add the whiskey.

To make the ice cream, warm the milk, granulated sugar, and salt in a medium saucepan. Whisk the cream, brown sugar, and cinnamon together into a large bowl and set a mesh strainer on top.

In a separate medium bowl, whisk together the egg yolks. Slowly pour the warm milk mixture into the egg yolks, whisking constantly, then scrape the warmed egg yolks back into the saucepan.

Stir the mixture constantly over medium heat with a heatproof spatula, scraping the bottom as you stir, until the mixture thickens and coats the spatula. Pour the custard through the strainer and stir it into the cream. Mix in the vanilla and stir until cool over an ice bath.

Chill the mixture thoroughly in the refrigerator, then freeze it in your ice cream maker according to the manufacturer's instructions. During the last few minutes of churning, add the raisins and Oatmeal Praline.

PERFECT PAIRING: For Oatmeal-Raisin Tartufi, follow the instructions on page 230.

Rum Raisin Ice Cream

The first time I discovered "gourmet" ice cream, the flavor was rum raisin, made by one of those premium brands with lots of vowels in its name. Aside from all those vowels, it also had lots and lots of raisins plumped in real, honest-to-goodness rum, and I had never had store-bought ice cream that was so smooth and so creamy. Coincidentally, at about the same time I discovered those little round pints of premium ice cream, I learned a new way to eat ice cream: right from the little round pint container. Which, by strange coincidence (or shrewd marketing, more likely), fit just perfectly in my hand.

^{2}/$_3$ cup (100 g) mixed dark and light raisins

^{1}/$_2$ cup (125 ml) dark rum

1-inch (3-cm) strip of orange or lemon zest

^{3}/$_4$ cup (180 ml) whole milk

^{2}/$_3$ cup (130 g) sugar

1^1/$_2$ cups (375 ml) heavy cream

Pinch of salt

4 large egg yolks

Heat the raisins, rum, and orange zest in a small saucepan. Let simmer for 2 minutes, then remove from the heat. Cover and let stand for a few hours. (The raisins can be macerated 1 day in advance.)

Warm the milk, sugar, ^{1}/$_2$ cup (125 ml) of the heavy cream, and salt in a medium saucepan. Pour the remaining 1 cup (250 ml) cream into a large bowl and set a mesh strainer on top.

In a separate medium bowl, whisk together the egg yolks. Slowly pour the warmed milk into the egg yolks, whisking constantly, then scrape the warmed egg yolks back into the saucepan.

Stir the mixture constantly over medium heat with a heatproof spatula, scraping the bottom as you stir, until the mixture thickens and coats the spatula. Pour the custard through the strainer and into the cream. Stir until cool over an ice bath, then chill the mixture thoroughly in the refrigerator.

When ready to freeze the ice cream, drain the raisins over a bowl and reserve the rum. Discard the orange zest. Measure the drained rum and add more, if necessary, so that you have a total of 3 tablespoons (45 ml). Stir the rum into the custard.

Freeze the mixture in your ice cream maker according to the manufacturer's instructions. During the last few minutes of churning, add the rum-soaked raisins.

PERFECT PAIRING: Make Rum Raisin Vacherins, filling Meringue Nests (page 234) with Rum Raisin Ice Cream topped with Whipped Cream (page 170) and thin strips of Candied Citrus Peel (page 178) made with orange zest.

Tin Roof Ice Cream

MAKES ABOUT 1¼ QUARTS (1¼ LITERS)

Do you know how tin roof ice cream got its name? Neither do I. Nor does anyone, it seems. I've tried to find out but have always come up empty-handed. I do know that it's one of my favorite ice cream combinations, and I guess I need to be content with that. Tin roof sundaes are traditionally made of vanilla ice cream topped with chocolate sauce and a scattering of red-skinned Spanish peanuts. I couldn't resist using chocolate-covered peanuts instead and folding them into the ice cream, where they become embedded between layers of fudge ripple.

> ¾ cup (180 ml) whole milk
>
> ¾ cup (150 g) sugar
>
> Pinch of salt
>
> 1½ cups (375 ml) heavy cream
>
> ½ vanilla bean, split lengthwise
>
> 4 large egg yolks
>
> ¼ teaspoon vanilla extract
>
> ¾ cup Chocolate-Covered Peanuts (page 199)
>
> Fudge Ripple (page 210)

Warm the milk, sugar, salt and ½ cup (125 ml) of the cream in a medium saucepan. With a sharp paring knife, scrape the flavorful seeds from the vanilla bean and add them, along with the pod, to the hot milk mixture. Cover, remove from the heat, and let steep at room temperature for 30 minutes.

Rewarm the vanilla-infused mixture. Pour the remaining 1 cup (250 ml) cream into a large bowl and set a mesh strainer on top. In a separate medium bowl, whisk together the egg yolks. Slowly pour the warm mixture into the egg yolks, whisking constantly, then scrape the warmed egg yolks back into the saucepan.

Stir the mixture constantly over medium heat with a heatproof spatula, scraping the bottom as you stir, until the mixture thickens and coats the spatula. Pour the custard through the strainer and stir it into the cream to cool. Remove the vanilla bean, wipe it clean of any egg bits, and add it back to the custard. Stir in the vanilla and stir until cool over an ice bath. Chill thoroughly in the refrigerator.

When ready to churn the ice cream, remove the vanilla bean (it can be rinsed and reused). Freeze the ice cream in your ice cream maker according to the manufacturer's instructions. While the ice cream is freezing, chop the peanuts into bite-sized pieces.

Fold the peanut pieces into the frozen ice cream as you remove it from the machine, and layer it with Fudge Ripple.

PERFECT PAIRING: To make Tin Roof Sundaes, serve this ice cream with plenty of Marshmallow–Hot Fudge Sauce (page 166) and Salt-Roasted Peanuts (page 188), topped off with a Candied Cherry (page 215).

Zabaglione Gelato

True zabaglione—a foamy custard of egg yolks, wine, and sugar—is often made to order in Italian restaurants. Moments after the waiter takes your order, you'll hear the frenetic "clang-clack-clang" of the whisk hitting the copper bowl in the kitchen. Once it's reached a billowy peak, it's heaped into a glass quickly but not necessarily neatly (speed trumps presentation with zabaglione) and served straight up and warm. In season, you'll often find sliced strawberries buried underneath all that delicious froth. Zabaglione Gelato captures the taste of a true zabaglione in a cool scoop of ice cream without the last-minute flurry of activity, and it's just as good served with lots of juicy strawberries.

> 1 cup (250 ml) whole milk
>
> $^2/_3$ cup (130 g) sugar
>
> Big pinch of salt
>
> 1 lemon, preferably unsprayed
>
> $1^1/_2$ cups (375 ml) heavy cream
>
> 6 large egg yolks
>
> $^1/_2$ cup (125 ml) dry Marsala wine

Warm the milk, sugar, and salt in a medium saucepan. Zest half of the lemon directly into the warm milk. Pour the cream into a large bowl and set a mesh strainer on top.

In a separate medium bowl, whisk together the egg yolks. Slowly pour the warm lemon-infused milk into the egg yolks, whisking constantly, then scrape the warmed egg yolks back into the saucepan.

Stir the mixture constantly over medium heat with a heatproof spatula, scraping the bottom as you stir, until the mixture thickens and coats the spatula. Pour the custard through the strainer and stir it into the cream. Add the Marsala and stir until cool over an ice bath.

Chill the mixture thoroughly in the refrigerator, then freeze it in your ice cream maker according to the manufacturer's instructions.

PERFECT PAIRING: Pair Zabaglione Gelato with Mixed Berry Coulis (page 181), or spoon lots of sugared strawberries into a wine goblet and top with a scoop of the ice cream.

Chartreuse Ice Cream

MAKES ABOUT 1 QUART (1 LITER)

Maybe I'm not the sharpest knife in the drawer. When I visited the Chartreuse distill-ery in the French Alps, our guide told us that the exact recipe for the famed herbal liqueur was a closely guarded secret, known only by three brothers who worked at the monastery.

Astounded, I spoke up. "Wow, that's incredible. What is the likelihood of three brothers going into the same business together, as well as becoming monks at the same monastery?" The other guests on the tour simply stopped and looked at me with their mouths slightly agape. Then our guide enlightened me and we moved on, but not before I overheard a few hushed conversations evaluating my intellect.

This is a very light ice cream, and it's so simple that anyone, regardless of their intelligence level, can easily put it together.

> $2^2/_3$ cups (660 ml) whole milk
>
> $1^1/_3$ cups (320 g) sour cream
>
> $^3/_4$ cup (150 g) sugar
>
> 3 tablespoons (45 ml) green Chartreuse liqueur

Purée the milk, sour cream, sugar, and Chartreuse in a blender or food proces-sor until smooth.

Chill the mixture thoroughly in the refrigerator, then freeze it in your ice cream maker according to the manufacturer's instructions.

VARIATION: Substitute another liquor or liqueur for the Chartreuse, such as dark rum, Cognac, or Grand Marnier.

PERFECT PAIRING: Fill Profiteroles (page 232) with Chartreuse Ice Cream, then ladle warm Lean Chocolate Sauce (page 165) over them, topping them with a shower of crisp French Almonds (page 189).

Brrrr...

Store your ice creams and sorbets in a freezer set at 0°F (-18°C), which you can verify with the use of a freezer thermometer, available in any supermarket or hardware store. Once your ice cream or sorbet mix is churned, quickly scrape it into a chilled container and press plastic wrap on top to prevent ice crystals from forming on the surface. Then pop it right into the freezer.

Alas, although the freezer is the best (and only) place for storing ice creams and sor-bets, the low temperature does not make for easy scooping and serving. So you'll want to remove your ice cream or sorbet from the freezer at least 5 minutes before serving to allow it to come to a temperature and consistency that is easy to scoop, and even easier to enjoy.

Eggnog Ice Cream

If you need to liven things up around your holiday table, this tipsy ice cream will do the trick. Warm apple crisp, cranberry upside-down cake, or the ever-popular pumpkin pie—all are improved with a sidecar of this frozen version of eggnog. This will definitely make those obligatory family get-togethers a bit less traumatic...which I offer on very good authority.

The simplest way to measure freshly grated nutmeg, which is the only kind you should use, is to fold a sheet of paper in half, reopen it, and grate the nutmeg over the paper. Then fold the paper again to direct the nutmeg into the measuring spoon.

> 1 cup (250 ml) whole milk
>
> 2/3 cup (130 g) sugar
>
> Pinch of salt
>
> 2 cups (500 ml) heavy cream
>
> 6 large egg yolks
>
> 1 teaspoon freshly grated nutmeg, or more to taste
>
> 2 tablespoons brandy
>
> 2 tablespoons dark rum
>
> 2 teaspoons vanilla extract

Warm the milk, sugar, and salt in a medium saucepan. Pour the cream into a large bowl and set a mesh strainer on top.

In a separate medium bowl, whisk together the egg yolks. Slowly pour the warm mixture into the egg yolks, whisking constantly, then scrape the warmed egg yolks back into the saucepan.

Stir the mixture constantly over medium heat with a heatproof spatula, scraping the bottom as you stir, until the mixture thickens and coats the spatula. Pour the custard through the strainer and stir it into the cream to cool. Mix in the nutmeg, brandy, rum, and vanilla and stir until cool over an ice bath.

Chill the mixture thoroughly in the refrigerator. Once the mixture is cold, taste it, and grate in more fresh nutmeg if you wish. Freeze in your ice cream maker according to the manufacturer's instructions.

PERFECT PAIRING: Make Eggnog Ice Cream Cups by serving scoops of Eggnog Ice Cream in punch cups, drizzled with Whiskey Caramel Sauce (page 175) and dusted with freshly grated nutmeg.

Crème Fraîche Ice Cream

Crème fraîche is the cultured French cousin to American sour cream, although it's far richer and more unctuous, with a distinct nutty-tangy-sweet flavor.

This ice cream is made in a slightly different manner than other recipes, since mixing the crème fraîche with the other ingredients too far in advance can cause the whole batch to turn into a whole lot of crème fraîche, perhaps more than you bargained for.

> 1 cup (250 ml) whole milk
>
> ³⁄₄ cup (150 g) sugar
>
> Big pinch of salt
>
> 5 large egg yolks
>
> 2 cups (480 g) crème fraîche (see Note)

Prepare a medium-sized bowl with a mesh strainer over the top and set it in an ice bath.

Warm the milk, sugar, and salt in a medium saucepan. In a separate medium bowl, whisk together the egg yolks. Slowly pour the warm milk into the egg yolks, whisking constantly, then scrape the warmed egg yolks back into the saucepan.

Stir the mixture constantly over medium heat with a heatproof plastic spatula, scraping the bottom as you stir, until the mixture thickens and coats the spatula. Pour the custard through the strainer and stir until cool over an ice bath. Chill thoroughly in the refrigerator.

Once cool, whisk in the crème fraîche, then freeze the mixture in your ice cream maker according to the manufacturer's instructions.

NOTE: Crème fraîche is available at cheese shops and well-stocked supermarkets. You can make your own version by stirring together 2 cups (500 ml) heavy cream and ¹⁄₄ cup (60 ml) buttermilk. Let stand at room temperature for 24 hours, until thick. Refrigerate until ready to use.

VARIATION: If crème fraîche is your refined cousin from France, mascarpone is the rugged Italian uncle from New Jersey that no one in the family likes to talk about. To make Mascarpone Ice Cream, substitute 2 cups (480 g) mascarpone for the crème fraîche. Mascarpone ice cream makes a terrific *affogato*: douse a couple of scoops with a shot of warm espresso.

PERFECT PAIRING: Make Cherries Jubilee by warming Candied Cherries (page 215) with 2 tablespoons kirsch or curaçao (or another liqueur) and then spooning the warm cherries over scoops of Crème Fraîche Ice Cream.

Toasted Almond and
Candied Cherry Ice Cream

MAKES ABOUT 1½ QUARTS (1½ LITERS)

Crack open a cherry or apricot pit and you'll discover a soft kernel inside with the pronounced scent of bitter almonds. I took a cue from whatever higher power designed these two flavors together and paired cherries with almonds in one heavenly ice cream. Adding anything chocolate makes this ice cream amazingly good.

Be sure to drain the cherries in a strainer very well before folding them into the ice cream. They should be dry and sticky before you chop them up and mix them in.

> 1 cup (250 ml) whole milk
>
> ¾ cup (150 g) sugar
>
> Pinch of salt
>
> 2 cups (500 ml) heavy cream
>
> 2 cups (270 g) whole almonds, toasted (see page 13) and coarsely chopped
>
> 5 large egg yolks
>
> ¼ teaspoon almond extract
>
> 1 cup (200 g) well-drained Sour Cherries in Syrup (page 185) or Candied Cherries (page 215), coarsely chopped

Warm the milk, sugar, salt, and 1 cup (250 ml) of the cream in a medium saucepan. Finely chop 1 cup (135 g) of the almonds and add them to the warm milk. Cover, remove from the heat, and let steep at room temperature for 1 hour.

Strain the almond-infused milk into a separate medium saucepan. Press with a spatula or squeeze with your hands to extract as much flavor from the almonds as possible. Discard the almonds.

Rewarm the almond-infused milk. Pour the remaining 1 cup (250 ml) cream into a large bowl and set a mesh strainer on top. In a separate medium bowl, whisk together the egg yolks. Slowly pour the warm mixture into the egg yolks, whisking constantly, then scrape the warmed egg yolks back into the saucepan.

Stir the mixture constantly over medium heat with a heatproof spatula, scraping the bottom as you stir, until the mixture thickens and coats the spatula. Pour the custard through the strainer and stir it into the cream. Stir in the almond extract and stir until cool over an ice bath.

Chill the mixture thoroughly in the refrigerator, then freeze it in your ice cream maker according to the manufacturer's instructions. During the last few minutes of churning, add the remaining 1 cup (135 g) chopped almonds. When you remove the ice cream from the machine, fold in the chopped cherries.

PERFECT PAIRINGS: Try layering this ice cream with Fudge Ripple (page 210) for Almond, Cherry, and Chocolate Ice Cream (pictured opposite), or add Dark Chocolate Truffles (page 211) or Stracciatella (page 210) instead.

Goat Cheese Ice Cream

MAKES ABOUT 3 CUPS (750 ML)

The first time I ever saw fresh goat cheese was when we started serving it on salads at Chez Panisse. This being Berkeley, most of the customers thought it was tofu. Nowadays goat cheese has become far more familiar. Especially in Berkeley.

Adding goat cheese to ice cream gives it the surprising taste of a blue-ribbon cheesecake. Use a moist, fresh goat cheese for best results.

> $1^1/_2$ cups (375 ml) whole milk
>
> $^2/_3$ cup (130 g) sugar
>
> 8 ounces (230 g) fresh goat cheese
>
> 6 large egg yolks

Warm the milk and sugar in a medium saucepan. While the milk is warming, crumble the goat cheese into a large bowl and set a mesh strainer on top.

In a separate medium bowl, whisk together the egg yolks. Slowly pour the warm mixture into the egg yolks, whisking constantly, then scrape the warmed egg yolks back into the saucepan.

Stir the mixture constantly over medium heat with a heatproof spatula, scraping the bottom as you stir, until the mixture thickens and coats the spatula. Pour the custard through the strainer and stir it into the goat cheese. Keep stirring until the cheese is melted, then stir until cool over an ice bath.

Chill the mixture thoroughly in the refrigerator, then freeze it in your ice cream maker according to the manufacturer's instructions.

PERFECT PAIRING: Mix the cheese course and dessert by serving Goat Cheese Ice Cream with Honey and Walnuts. Toast some very delicious walnut halves (see page 13) and let cool. To serve, drizzle a scoop of Goat Cheese Ice Cream with strongly flavored honey (I like chestnut or lavender honey). Scatter the toasted walnut halves over the top.

Cheesecake Ice Cream

MAKES ABOUT 3 CUPS (750 ML)

When I first started to travel to France regularly, the French, when they found out I was American, would rhapsodize *"J'adore le Philadelphia!"*

It took me a while to realize they were enthralled with our cream cheese, which is indeed worthy of international acclaim. They've adopted cheesecake too, calling it *le gâteau fromage* or simply *le cheesecake.*

8 ounces (230 g) cream cheese

1 lemon, preferably unsprayed

1 cup (240 g) sour cream

$^1/_2$ cup (125 ml) half-and-half

$^2/_3$ cup (130 g) sugar

Pinch of salt

Cut the cream cheese into small pieces. Zest the lemon directly into a blender or food processor, then add the cream cheese, sour cream, half-and-half, sugar, and salt, and purée until smooth.

Chill the mixture thoroughly in the refrigerator, then freeze it in your ice cream maker according to the manufacturer's instructions.

PERFECT PAIRING: For Blueberry Cheesecake Ice Cream, layer Cheesecake Ice Cream with Blueberry Sauce (page 182).

Tiramisù Ice Cream

MAKES ABOUT 1$^1/_4$ QUARTS (1$^1/_4$ LITERS)

I live above a *huilerie* in Paris, a shop that sells top-quality oils from all over the world. I decided that Colette, the owner, would be my primary ice cream taste tester. Not only did she have an excellent palate and love to taste things, but I knew that, being French, she'd have absolutely no problem expressing her opinions, good or bad. This was her favorite of all the ice creams I made. Her eyes rolled back in her head when she slipped the first spoonful in her mouth. "Oh lá lá," she exclaimed.

2 cups (450 g) mascarpone

1 cup (250 ml) half-and-half

$^2/_3$ cup (130 g) sugar

Pinch of salt

$^1/_4$ cup (60 ml) coffee-flavored liqueur, such as Kahlúa

3 tablespoons (45 ml) brandy or dark rum

Mocha Ripple (page 211)

Purée the mascarpone, half-and-half, sugar, salt, liqueur, and brandy together in a blender or food processor until smooth and the sugar is dissolved. Chill thoroughly in the refrigerator.

Freeze in your ice cream maker according to the manufacturer's instructions. As you remove it from the machine, alternate layers of Mocha Ripple with the frozen ice cream in the storage container.

PERFECT PAIRING: Make a classic *affogato*, which means "drowned" in Italian, by pouring warm espresso over Tiramisù Ice Cream served in a small bowl.

Lavender-Honey Ice Cream

The Marché d'Aligre is the liveliest market in Paris. In the center, there's a marvelous *épicerie*, with bins brimming with things familiar and unusual: various grains and spices, plump dried fruits, organic honey, bars of chocolate, and artisan candies from all over France. It's my one-stop shop for anything *délicieux!*

When I stopped by to get some lavender flowers, José Ferré, the proprietor, shooed me away from the basket in his window and stepped into the back room. A minute later he returned dragging an enormous sack of dark purple lavender flowers that had just arrived from Provence. He gestured toward the bag, so I stuck my head in and inhaled deeply. The perfumed bouquet of the freshly harvested lavender flowers was ethereal. Of course, those lavender flowers made amazing ice cream.

Try to find the most fragrant lavender flowers you can, wherever you live, and be sure to use lavender flowers that are intended for consumption.

1/2 cup (125 ml) good-flavored honey

1/4 cup (8 g) dried or fresh lavender flowers

1 1/2 cups (375 ml) whole milk

1/4 cup (50 g) sugar

Pinch of salt

1 1/2 cups (375 ml) heavy cream

5 large egg yolks

Heat the honey and 2 tablespoons of the lavender in a small saucepan. Once warm, remove from the heat and set aside to steep at room temperature for 1 hour.

Warm the milk, sugar, and salt in a medium saucepan. Pour the cream into a large bowl and set a mesh strainer on top. Pour the lavender-infused honey into the cream through the strainer, pressing on the lavender flowers to extract as much flavor as possible, then discard the lavender and set the strainer back over the cream.

In a separate medium bowl, whisk together the egg yolks. Slowly pour the warm mixture into the egg yolks, whisking constantly, then scrape the warmed egg yolks back into the saucepan.

Stir the mixture constantly over medium heat with a heatproof spatula, scraping the bottom as you stir, until the mixture thickens and coats the spatula. Pour the custard through the strainer and stir it into the cream. Add the remaining 2 tablespoons lavender flowers and stir until cool over an ice bath.

Chill the mixture overnight in the refrigerator. The next day, before churning, strain the mixture, again pressing on the lavender flowers to extract their flavor. Discard the flowers, then freeze the mixture in your ice cream maker according to the manufacturer's instructions.

VARIATION: To make Honey-Sesame Ice Cream, follow the recipe but omit the steps that call for infusing lavender flowers in the honey and the custard. Prepare one recipe of Honey-Sesame Brittle (page 204) and crumble it into the ice cream during the last few minutes of churning.

PERFECT PAIRING: To make Figs Roasted in Pernod, for 4 to 6 servings, slice 10 fresh figs in half and place them in a baking dish. Drizzle with 3 tablespoons (45 ml) of good honey (such as lavender honey) and 2 tablespoons Pernod. Cover with aluminum foil and bake in a preheated 375°F (190°C) oven for 20 minutes, until tender. Serve the figs warm or at room temperature, along with some of the sauce and a scoop of Lavender-Honey Ice Cream. Top with a few strips of Candied Citrus Peel (page 178) if you like.

Roquefort-Honey Ice Cream

MAKES 3 CUPS (750 ML)

This curious combination of flavors will surprise you, as it did the unsuspecting friends I invited over to taste test it. One was so enamored of it that she kept digging her spoon in until the container was scraped clean! I like to serve this with warm oven-baked pears. Not only do they taste very good together, but the combination does double duty as the cheese course *and* the dessert.

A few helpful tips: You can replace the Roquefort with a favorite blue cheese, with excellent results. Also, if your honey is very strong, you may wish to use the smaller amount indicated. And be a bit careful when making the custard; because it has no sugar, it will cook quickly.

6 to 8 tablespoons (90 to 125 ml) good-flavored honey

4 ounces (115 g) Roquefort or blue cheese

1 cup (250 ml) whole milk

4 large egg yolks

1 cup (250 ml) heavy cream

Warm the honey in a small saucepan, then set aside. Crumble the cheese into a large bowl and set a mesh strainer over the top.

Warm the milk in a medium saucepan. In a separate medium bowl, whisk together the egg yolks. Slowly pour the warm milk into the egg yolks, whisking constantly, then scrape the warmed egg yolks back into the saucepan.

Stir the mixture constantly over medium heat with a heatproof spatula, scraping the bottom as you stir, until the mixture thickens and coats the spatula. Pour the custard through the strainer and stir it into the cheese. Stir until most of the cheese is melted (some small bits are fine and are rather nice in the finished ice cream, I think). Stir in the cream and honey, then stir until cool over an ice bath.

Chill the mixture thoroughly in the refrigerator, then freeze it in your ice cream maker according to the manufacturer's instructions.

PERFECT PAIRING: Roquefort-Honey Ice Cream is lovely drizzled with warm honey and served with toasted pecans or walnuts scattered over the top.

Turrón Ice Cream

While navigating my way through the Barcelona train station, I was suddenly surrounded by a squadron of Spanish police, guns drawn, barking orders at me in Spanish. Aimed and ready, they gestured to me to open up the suspiciously overstuffed valise I was dragging.

I carefully unzipped my bulky suitcase, revealing rows and rows of peculiar brown paper-wrapped bundles, all packed neatly in rows. An officer demanded that I unwrap one of the packages. I slowly tore the paper off the first one and held it high for all to see. The policemen let down their guns and had a good laugh. My crime? Smuggling home blocks of crispy Spanish *turrón*.

This ice cream duplicates the taste of *turrón* with crispy almonds, honey, and a touch of candied orange, and it can be made, without raising any suspicions, in your ice cream maker at home.

> 1½ cups (375 ml) half-and-half
>
> ½ cup (100 g) sugar
>
> ¼ cup (60 ml) good-flavored honey
>
> Pinch of salt
>
> 1 orange, preferably unsprayed
>
> 1½ cups (375 ml) heavy cream
>
> 5 large egg yolks
>
> 1 teaspoon orange-flower water
>
> 2 tablespoons chopped candied orange peel (see Note)
>
> ⅔ cup (75 g) almonds, toasted (page 13) and very coarsely chopped
>
> ¼ cup (30 g) shelled unsalted pistachio nuts, very coarsely chopped

Warm the half-and-half, sugar, honey, and salt in a medium saucepan. Zest the orange directly into the mixture. Pour the cream into a large bowl and set a mesh strainer on top.

In a separate medium bowl, whisk together the egg yolks. Slowly pour the warm half-and-half into the egg yolks, whisking constantly, then scrape the warmed egg yolks back into the saucepan.

Stir the mixture constantly over medium heat with a heatproof spatula, scraping the bottom as you stir, until the mixture thickens and coats the spatula. Pour the custard through the strainer and stir it into the cream to cool. Add the orange-flower water and stir until cool over an ice bath.

Chill the mixture thoroughly in the refrigerator, then freeze it in your ice cream maker according to the manufacturer's instructions. As you remove it from the machine, fold in the candied orange peel, almonds, and pistachio nuts.

NOTE: To order candied orange peel, see Resources (page 237). You can also make Candied Citrus Peel (page 178) using orange zest.

Sweet Potato Ice Cream with Maple-Glazed Pecans

MAKES ABOUT 1 QUART (1 LITER)

I've spent many a summer night enjoying an ice cream cone, flanked by Mexican and Filipino families, at Mitchell's Ice Cream in San Francisco's Mission District. This ice cream is inspired by *ube,* the sweet potato ice cream they serve up in addition to all the other exotic flavors they offer. Mitchell's is so popular that the place is just as packed when the inevitable summer fog rolls in and chills things down as it is when the sun is shining. There's always a line. But don't think for a minute that the flavor of this ice cream is too adventurous. Imagine a nice slab of spiced pumpkin pie; this ice cream delivers that classic flavor in one neat scoop of ice cream.

The best sweet potatoes to use are a vivid, electric orange. I try to find the brightest orange ones when shopping. Don't tell, but sometimes I scrape a bit of the skin off one, just to check.

1 pound (450 g) sweet potatoes, peeled

1 cup plus 2 tablespoons (280 ml) whole milk

$^2/_3$ cup (140 g) packed light brown sugar

$^1/_4$ teaspoon ground cinnamon

$^1/_2$ teaspoon vanilla extract

Pinch of salt

A few drops freshly squeezed lemon juice

Wet Pecans (page 198)

Cut the sweet potatoes into 1-inch (3-cm) cubes. Place the cubed potatoes in a medium saucepan and cover with water. Bring to a boil, reduce the heat to a simmer, and cook for 20 minutes, or until tender when poked with a sharp knife. Drain the sweet potatoes and let cool to room temperature.

Pour the milk into a blender and add the brown sugar, sweet potato pieces, cinnamon, vanilla, and salt. Purée until very smooth, at least 30 seconds. Add lemon juice to taste. Press the mixture through a mesh strainer, using a flexible rubber spatula.

Chill the mixture thoroughly in the refrigerator, then freeze it in your ice cream maker according to the manufacturer's instructions. During the last few minutes of churning, add the pecans and their syrup.

PERFECT PAIRINGS: Top with Whiskey Caramel Sauce (page 175) or Pecan-Praline Sauce (page 176).

Panforte Ice Cream

Fortunately, I once worked with pastry chef Mary Canales. Unfortunately, our time together lasted merely a few hours. I was ending my tenure at Chez Panisse, and she was just beginning hers. But I liked her instantly, and we kept in touch. Years later, she decided to open an ice cream shop, Ici, in Berkeley, and I was thrilled when her ice creams became legendary in the Bay Area. Here's the most popular flavor from her vast repertoire. *Panforte* is a Italian cake, a Tuscan specialty that's so dense and delicious that it's practically a confection. And like the best *panforte,* Mary's ice cream has the perfect balance of spices, toasted almonds, and candied orange peel.

1 cup (250 ml) half-and-half

2/3 cup (130 g) sugar

1 cinnamon stick, broken in half

1/4 teaspoon ground cloves

1/4 teaspoon freshly grated nutmeg

2 cups (500 ml) heavy cream

4 large egg yolks

3 tablespoons (45 ml) full-flavored honey

1/4 cup (30 g) mixed candied citrus peel (see Note)

1/2 cup (65 g) almonds, toasted (see page 13) and coarsely chopped

Warm the half-and-half, sugar, and spices in a medium saucepan. Cover, remove from the heat, and let steep at room temperature for 30 minutes.

Rewarm the spice-infused mixture. Pour the cream into a large bowl and set a mesh strainer on top. In a separate medium bowl, whisk together the egg yolks. Slowly pour the warm mixture into the egg yolks, whisking constantly, then scrape the warmed egg yolks back into the saucepan.

Stir the mixture constantly over medium heat with a heatproof spatula, scraping the bottom as you stir, until the mixture thickens and coats the spatula. Pour the custard through the strainer and mix it into the cream. Discard the cinnamon stick. Stir the custard until cool over an ice bath. While it's cooling, warm the honey in a small saucepan, then stir it into the custard.

Chill the mixture thoroughly in the refrigerator, then freeze it in your ice cream maker according to the manufacturer's instructions. During the last few minutes of churning, add the candied citrus peel and almonds.

NOTE: You can find good-quality candied peel in well-stocked markets (but no icky green things, please!) or by mail order (see Resources, page 237). Or you can use the recipe for Candied Citrus Peel on page 178.

PERFECT PAIRING: Pair Panforte Ice Cream with a scoop of Black Pepper Ice Cream (page 102).

Rice Gelato

Many apartment buildings in Paris, including mine, have a *gardienne*. Although their official duties are accepting deliveries and overseeing maintenance, they're equally famous for being a steady (and remarkably reliable) source of gossip about your neighbors.

My *gardienne* is Madame André, who has young children, so she was always quite happy to accept ice cream while I churned out recipes for this book. Of all the ice creams I gave her, this was her absolute favorite, and she went into Gallic raptures whenever she saw me for days and days afterward. I should probably recommend her for a job as my publicist too, since shortly thereafter I got a reputation in the building as being *L'Américain qui fait des glaces, toujours!* (the American who makes ice cream, all the time!). If you're a rice pudding lover, this is the ice cream for you. And be sure to spread the word.

½ cup (100 g) Italian Arborio rice

3 cups (750 ml) whole milk

¾ cup (150 g) sugar

Pinch of salt

1 vanilla bean, split in half lengthwise

Two 1-inch-wide (3-cm) strips of orange zest

5 large egg yolks

1 cup (250 ml) half-and-half or cream

Pinch of freshly grated nutmeg

To cook the rice, preheat the oven to 350°F (175°C). In a 2-quart (2-liter) baking dish, stir together the rice, milk, ¼ cup (50 g) of the sugar, and the salt. Add the vanilla bean and strips of orange zest. Cover the dish snugly with aluminum foil and bake for 1 hour.

Remove the rice from the oven and remove the foil. Stir in the remaining ½ cup (100 g) sugar, then continue to bake the rice, uncovered, for another 30 minutes, until it is tender. There should be about ½ inch (2 cm) of milk covering the rice.

Remove the rice from oven, remove the vanilla bean (it can be rinsed and saved for another use), and briskly whisk in the egg yolks all at once. Then whisk in the half-and-half or cream and nutmeg.

Purée half of the rice mixture in a blender or food processor until chopped quite fine, then stir it back into the cooked rice.

Chill the mixture thoroughly in the refrigerator, then freeze it in your ice cream maker according to the manufacturer's instructions.

NOTE: It's best to serve this ice cream the same day you churn it, or remove it from the freezer at least 5 to 10 minutes before you plan to scoop it, so the grains are chewy-soft.

PERFECT PAIRING: Sour Cherries in Grand Marnier are perfect over Rice Gelato. For about 6 servings, combine ¾ cup (90 g) dried sour cherries, 6 tablespoons (90 ml) Grand Marnier, 2 tablespoons water, and 3 tablespoons (45 g) sugar in a small, nonreactive saucepan. Heat until the liquid comes to a full boil. Remove from the heat, cover, and let stand until cool. Spoon the cherries over the Rice Gelato.

What's Gelato?

In my quest to learn more about gelato, I talked with Italian food expert Maureen Fant, who lives in Rome. She explained that *gelato* is simply the Italian name for ice cream. More generally, *gelato* means "frozen" and can refer to any frozen dessert churned with milk or cream.

Italian gelato is usually less sweet than traditional ice cream, and it is very thick and somewhat sticky. One reason for its distinctively dense texture is that very little air is whipped into it. If you peer into the special machines used in Italy for churning gelato, you'll find a slowly spinning drum with a paddle that systematically moves up and down, scraping the gelato off the sides as it turns and freezes, rather than the rapidly spinning dasher used for American ice cream production. The freezers used to hold gelato in Italy are also kept at a slightly higher temperature—around 10°F (-12°C)—to keep it soft, whereas regular ice cream is stored at 0°F (-18°C).

Although some gelatos do have egg yolks, they are often thickened with a starch instead. The result is a chewy gelato that tastes less rich than a custard-based one made with eggs. Faith Willinger, who writes about Italian cuisine in Florence, told me that thickening gelato with a starch is a Sicilian trait, and it is done because egg yolks are less digestible than starch, important during their hot summers.

In most Italian cities, *gelaterias* are everywhere you look. Some are great, and some are ordinary. Always look for a place crammed full of Italians, since they're very passionate about their gelato and don't tolerate anything but the best. One thing almost all Italians agree on is that gelato is best eaten from a cone while walking. But as in everything Italian, there's lots of lively debate on this point, and at Il Gelato di San Crispino, one of the top *gelaterias* in Rome, the Alongi brothers, who make the gelato, believe cones to be unhygienic and insist on serving their gelato in stiff paper cups.

Roasted Banana Ice Cream

Bill Fujimoto, the produce expert at Monterey Market in Berkeley, grew up in Japan. He once told me about the produce market where his father worked, which featured a wall covered with tarantulas, each individually nailed in place. In days past, native islanders would hoist bunches of bananas onto ships heading landward, and the bananas would sometimes include a little something extra from the jungle lurking beneath the stem. Sometimes people would bring home bananas only to discover an unwelcome houseguest the next day, enjoying a morning stroll across the kitchen counter.

In spite of their risky reputation, bananas have become the most popular, and least intimidating, fruit in America. I've eaten more than my fair share and have yet to see any hazardous signs of life. (But that doesn't mean I don't take a peek every now and then.)

Roasting bananas in butter and brown sugar gives them a deep, rich butterscotch flavor, which enhances their abundant natural sweetness.

> 3 medium-sized ripe bananas, peeled
>
> $1/3$ cup (70 g) packed light brown sugar
>
> I tablespoon butter, salted or unsalted, cut into small pieces
>
> $1^1/2$ cups (375 ml) whole milk
>
> 2 tablespoons granulated sugar
>
> $1/2$ teaspoon vanilla extract
>
> $1^1/2$ teaspoons freshly squeezed lemon juice
>
> $1/4$ teaspoon coarse salt

Preheat the oven to 400°F (200°C).

Slice the bananas into $1/2$-inch (2-cm) pieces and toss them with the brown sugar and butter in a 2-quart (2-liter) baking dish. Bake for 40 minutes, stirring just once during baking, until the bananas are browned and cooked through.

Scrape the bananas and the thick syrup in the baking dish into a blender or food processor. Add the milk, granulated sugar, vanilla, lemon juice, and salt, and purée until smooth.

Chill the mixture thoroughly in the refrigerator, then freeze it in your ice cream maker according to the manufacturer's instructions. If the chilled mixture is too thick to pour into your machine, whisking will thin it out.

PERFECT PAIRING: Roasted Banana Ice Cream makes a terrific foundation for an updated banana split. Drench the ice cream in warm Classic Hot Fudge (page 164), and add ripe banana slices and Whipped Cream (page 170) or Marshmallow Sauce (page 168). Top it off with a Candied Cherry (page 215), of course!

Sour Cherry Frozen Yogurt

What do you say when a nice Jewish boy gives up a promising career as a lawyer to become a self-appointed "amateur gourmet"? ("Oy!" his mom probably said.)

When the audacious amateur himself, Adam Roberts, used my recipe for Strawberry Frozen Yogurt (page 91) as inspiration for churning up a batch of Sour Cherry Frozen Yogurt, he posted the results on his web site, www.amateurgourmet.com. It was an idea too delicious not to include in this book. However, when pressed for minor details like, say, a recipe or exact quantities, Adam played the amateur card and feigned ignorance, forcing a certain professional to do his duty.

This recipe calls for sour cherries, which are different from their sweeter counterparts and sometimes require a bit of foraging to find (Adam found his at Manhattan's Greenmarket). Their tiny little pits can easily be slipped out by squeezing the cherries with your fingers or with the help of a cherry pitter.

> 1 pound (450 g) fresh sour cherries (about 3 cups, measured unpitted)
>
> ¾ cup (150 g) sugar
>
> 1 cup (240 g) plain whole-milk yogurt (see Note)
>
> 2 drops almond extract

Stem and pit the cherries. Put them in a medium, nonreactive saucepan with the sugar. Cover, bring to a boil, then lower the heat and simmer for 5 minutes, stirring frequently to encourage the juices to flow, until the cherries are tender and cooked through. Remove from the heat and let cool to room temperature.

Purée the cooked sour cherries and any liquid in a blender or food processor with the yogurt and almond extract until smooth.

Chill for 2 hours, then freeze in your ice cream maker according to the manufacturer's instructions.

NOTE: I don't recommend using Strained Yogurt (page 49) for making this, as I find the flavor too tart when combined with the sour cherries. If you'd like to make it richer, use Greek-style yogurt instead.

PERFECT PAIRING: Make Sour Cherry Profiteroles by filling Profiteroles (page 232) with Sour Cherry Frozen Yogurt and topping them off with a few Sour Cherries in Syrup (page 185) and a scribble of Lean Chocolate Sauce (page 165).

Dried Apricot-Pistachio Ice Cream

I love, love, *love* dried apricots. They're one of my favorite foods on earth, as long as they're the ones from California. People are often tempted by Turkish and Chinese dried apricots, since they're usually more colorful and far more plump (and cheaper), but I find them terribly sweet, and ice cream made with them lacks the delicious flavor and intensity of dried apricots.

The combination of pistachio nuts and apricots is particularly good. Don't toast the pistachio nuts or they'll lose their lovely green hue. Make sure the pistachio nuts you're using are fresh and crisp.

> 5 ounces (140 g) dried California apricots, quartered
>
> $^3/_4$ cup (180 ml) white wine, dry or sweet
>
> $^1/_2$ cup (70 g) shelled unsalted pistachio nuts
>
> $^2/_3$ cup (130 g) sugar
>
> 2 cups (500 ml) half-and-half
>
> A few drops freshly squeezed lemon juice

In a small saucepan, warm the apricot pieces in the wine. Simmer for 5 minutes, cover, remove from the heat, and let stand for 1 hour. Coarsely chop the pistachio nuts.

Purée the apricots with the wine in a blender with the sugar, half-and-half, and lemon juice until smooth.

Chill the mixture thoroughly in the refrigerator, then freeze it in your ice cream maker according to the manufacturer's instructions. During the last few minutes of churning, add the chopped pistachio nuts.

PERFECT PAIRING: You can make Apricot-Pistachio Crêpes (pictured opposite) by warming Crêpes (page 233) and serving them, folded, on plates, topped with scoops of Dried Apricot-Pistachio Ice Cream, a drizzling of acacia honey, and a scattering of chopped pistachios.

Fresh Apricot Ice Cream

MAKES ABOUT 1 QUART (1 LITER)

If you're lucky enough to live in an area where fresh apricots are bountiful in the summer, be sure to take advantage of their brief season by churning up a batch of this ice cream. Don't be put off by apricots that are übersoft, as plump and fragile as an overfilled water balloon, seemingly ready to burst at the slightest touch. Those are invariably the best-tasting fruits.

1 pound (450 g) squishy-ripe fresh apricots (10 to 16, depending on size)

1/2 cup (125 ml) water

1/2 cup (100 g) sugar

1 cup (250 ml) heavy cream

3 drops almond extract

A few drops freshly squeezed lemon juice

Slice open the apricots and remove the pits, then cut each apricot into sixths. Cook the apricot pieces with the water in a covered medium, nonreactive saucepan over medium heat until tender, about 8 minutes, and stirring occasionally. Remove from the heat and stir in the sugar until disolved. Let cool to room temperature.

Once cool, purée the apricots and any liquid in a blender or food processor until smooth. Taste a big spoonful; if there are any small fibers, press the mixture through a mesh strainer to remove them. Stir in the cream, almond extract, and lemon juice.

Chill the mixture thoroughly in the refrigerator, then freeze it in your ice cream maker according to the manufacturer's instructions.

PERFECT PAIRING: It's easy to assemble Apricot Vacherins with Sour Cherries in Syrup. Fill Almond Meringue Nests (page 235) with Fresh Apricot Ice Cream and top with Sour Cherries in Syrup (page 185). You might want to add some Whipped Cream (page 170) and candied French Almonds (page 189).

Plum Ice Cream

MAKES ABOUT 1 QUART (1 LITER)

For many years, I was delighted to work with Lindsey Shere, the founding pastry chef at Chez Panisse. She was constantly surprising us with amazing fruits and berries from neighbors' backyards and nearby farms. Without fail, Lindsey would come in one weekend each summer carrying a big plastic Tupperware container, which, due to its distinctive rounded shape, left no question that it was precisely designed to hold a canned ham. But instead of a ham, inside would be a jumble of tiny, tender, smushed wild plums picked by her mother. Eaten raw, they were puckery-tart, but once stewed, they made an incredibly flavorful plum ice cream. Each year I would wait patiently for that one late-summer weekend when Lindsey would walk though the door lugging her now-infamous canned ham container. Although wild plums may be hard to come by, you can use whatever plums are available with equal success.

> 1 pound (450 g) plums (about 8)
>
> 1/3 cup (80 ml) water
>
> 3/4 cup plus 2 tablespoons (180 g) sugar
>
> 1 cup (250 ml) heavy cream
>
> 1/2 teaspoon kirsch

Slice the plums in half and remove the pits. Cut the plums into eighths and put them in a medium, nonreactive saucepan with the water. Cover and cook over medium heat, stirring occasionally, until tender, about 8 minutes. Remove from the heat, and stir in the sugar until dissolved. Let cool to room temperature.

Once cool, purée in a blender or food processor with the cream and kirsch until smooth.

Chill the mixture thoroughly, then freeze it in your ice cream maker according to the manufacturer's instructions.

PERFECT PAIRING: To make Plum–Raspberry Swirl Ice Cream, layer the just-churned plum ice cream with Raspberry Swirl Ice Cream (page 92), or make Plum–Blackberry Swirl Ice Cream by substituting blackberries for the raspberries.

Prune-Armagnac Ice Cream

MAKES ABOUT 1 QUART (1 LITER)

One winter I visited my friend Kate Hill, who lives in Gascony, a region famous for its tasty prunes, *les pruneaux d'Agen.* As a means of prying me away from the cozy kitchen hearth, where I could happily eat cassoulet and drink Armagnac all day by the fire, we decided to do something cultural and visit the local prune museum. It was all rather exciting: an entire museum full of educational displays on the history of prunes, including informative dioramas showing the various phases of prune production. We ended our visit with a thrilling film explaining prune cultivation and harvesting, which was a real nail-biter.

On our way out, near the prune-filled gift shop (there was a comic book about a prune-fueled superhero...I'm not kidding), was a shrine with a jar holding what they claimed was the world's oldest prune, dating back to the mid-1800s.

For this recipe, you should use prunes that are wrinkled but not necessarily that old, and be alert that it's become *au courant* to call them dried plums in America.

PRUNES

> 20 large prunes (about 10 ounces, 280 g), also known as dried plums
>
> $^1/_2$ cup (125 ml) Armagnac
>
> 2 tablespoons sugar

ICE CREAM

> 1 cup (240 g) sour cream
>
> 1 cup (250 ml) whole milk
>
> $^1/_2$ cup (100 g) sugar
>
> 1 teaspoon freshly squeezed lemon juice
>
> $^1/_2$ teaspoon vanilla extract

To prepare the prunes, remove the pits and cut the prunes into quarters. Put the prune pieces in a small saucepan with the Armagnac and the 2 tablespoons sugar. Heat until the Armagnac starts bubbling. Stir the prunes, then cover and let stand for at least 2 hours. (The prunes can be macerated a few days in advance.)

To make the ice cream, purée the prunes and any liquid in a food processor or blender along with the sour cream, milk, sugar, lemon juice, and vanilla. Pulse the mixture until it's almost smooth, with a few bits of prune remaining.

Chill the mixture thoroughly in the refrigerator, then freeze it in your ice cream maker according to the manufacturer's instructions.

PERFECT PAIRING: If you've never had prunes and chocolate together, try studding this ice cream with Dark Chocolate Truffles (page 211).

Pear-Caramel Ice Cream

MAKES ABOUT 1 QUART (1 LITER)

This ice cream combines the best of two worlds: deeply caramelized sugar and sweet, juicy pears. Use the ripest, most flavorful pears you can find, since you want the flavor of the pears to stand up to the slightly burnt taste of the caramel. I recommend Comice or Bartlett pears, which have a heady, roselike aroma when ripe. Don't be alarmed if the sugar hardens and crackles when you add the pears. Keep cooking, and the pears will dissolve the caramelized sugar nicely.

> 3 medium-sized ripe pears, peeled and cored
>
> $3/4$ cup plus 2 tablespoons (180 g) sugar
>
> 2 cups (500 ml) heavy cream
>
> $1/8$ teaspoon coarse salt
>
> A few drops freshly squeezed lemon juice

Dice the pears into $1/4$-inch (1-cm) pieces.

Spread the sugar in a large, nonreactive, heavy-bottomed saucepan. Cook the sugar over medium heat, watching it carefully. When it begins to liquefy and darken at the edges, use a heatproof spatula to very gently stir the sugar, encouraging the heat of the liquefied sugar around the edges to moisten and melt the sugar crystals in the center.

Once the sugar becomes deep amber, stir in the pear pieces. Some of the caramel will seize and harden, but as you cook the pears, use a heatproof utensil to stir them and melt any bits of hard caramel. Continue to cook the pears for 10 minutes, until the pieces are cooked through.

Remove from the heat and stir in $1/2$ cup (125 ml) of the cream, then mix in the remaining cream, along with the salt and a few drops of lemon juice.

Let cool to room temperature, then purée in a blender or food processor until smooth. Press the mixture through a mesh strainer with a flexible rubber spatula to remove any tough pear fibers.

Chill the mixture thoroughly in the refrigerator, then freeze it in your ice cream maker according to the manufacturer's instructions.

VARIATION: For Pear, Caramel, and Ginger Ice Cream, add $1/3$ cup (35 g) very finely chopped candied ginger to the ice cream during the last few minutes of churning.

PERFECT PAIRING: Make Pear-Caramel Cream Puffs with Salted Butter Caramel and Chocolate Sauces and Buttercrunch Toffee Bits. Fill Profiteroles (page 232) with Pear-Caramel Ice Cream, and set them on a pool of Salted Butter Caramel Sauce (page 174). Scribble Lean Chocolate Sauce (page 165) over the cream puffs, then top with bits of well-crumbled Buttercrunch Toffee (page 200).

Fresh Fig Ice Cream

Surprisingly, a lot of people have never seen a fresh fig. When they do, they invariably ask, "What is *that?*" Indeed, a majority of the fig harvest gets dried and made into the familiar bar cookies. But fresh figs have a sweet succulence that is unmatched by their dried counterparts. A fig is ripe when the sides crack and split and a dewy drop of juice starts to ooze from the tiny hole in the bottom. Once picked, figs don't ripen any more, so buy only figs that are dead-ripe. For best results, use Black Mission figs, which will give the ice cream a lovely deep-violet color.

> 2 pounds (1 kg) fresh figs (about 20)
>
> $1/2$ cup (125 ml) water
>
> 1 lemon, preferably unsprayed
>
> $3/4$ cup (150 g) sugar
>
> 1 cup (250 ml) heavy cream
>
> $1/2$ teaspoon freshly squeezed lemon juice, or more to taste

Remove the hard stem ends from the figs, then cut each fig into 8 pieces. Put the figs in a medium, nonreactive saucepan with the water, and zest the lemon directly into the saucepan. Cover and cook over medium heat, stirring occasionally, until the figs are tender, 8 to 10 minutes.

Remove the lid, add the sugar, and continue to cook, stirring frequently, until the figs are a jamlike consistency. Remove from the heat and let cool to room temperature. Once cool, purée the fig paste in a blender or food processor with the cream and lemon juice. Taste, then add more lemon juice if desired.

Chill the mixture thoroughly, then freeze it in your ice cream maker according to the manufacturer's instructions.

Pear-Pecorino Ice Cream

MAKES ABOUT 1 QUART (1 LITER)

When friends found out I was writing a book on ice cream, many felt compelled to "help out" by passing along really odd flavor combinations they'd either seen or heard of. But somehow, I just couldn't seem to get enthusiastic about combinations like Clam-Raisin or Duck Fat Swirl. However, when Judy Witts raved about this combination, which she'd enjoyed at her local *gelateria* in Florence, it piqued my interest.

After a bit of trial and error, I discovered that the key to preserving the character of pecorino is to very finely dice the cheese rather than grating it. The little bites of salty cheese are the perfect counterpoint to the fruity, pear-flavored custard.

3 ripe pears, such as Bartlett or Comice, peeled and cored

$^1/_3$ cup (80 ml) water

4 ounces (115 g) pecorino cheese

$^1/_2$ cup (120 g) sour cream

1 cup (250 ml) half-and-half

$^2/_3$ cup (130 g) sugar

3 large egg yolks

$^1/_4$ teaspoon freshly squeezed lemon juice

Cut the pears into $^1/_2$-inch (2-cm) pieces. Cook them with the water in a medium, nonreactive saucepan, covered, over medium heat, stirring occasionally, until the pears are cooked through, about 10 minutes. Purée in a food processor or blender until smooth. You should have about $1^1/_2$ cups (375 ml) purée.

Use a chef's knife to cut the pecorino into very thin slices, then chop the slices into small pieces about the size of grains of rice. Put them in a large bowl, add the sour cream, and set a mesh strainer over the top.

Warm the half-and-half and sugar in a medium saucepan. In a separate medium bowl, whisk together the egg yolks. Slowly pour the warm half-and-half into the egg yolks, whisking constantly, then scrape the warmed egg yolks back into the saucepan.

Stir the mixture constantly over medium heat with a heatproof spatula, scraping the bottom as you stir, until the mixture thickens and coats the spatula. Pour the custard through the strainer and stir it into the pecorino and sour cream. Mix in the lemon juice and pear purée, then stir until cool over an ice bath.

Chill the mixture thoroughly in the refrigerator, then freeze it in your ice cream maker according to the manufacturer's instructions.

PERFECT PAIRING: Serve with Marsala-Roasted Pears. For 6 servings, lop a small piece off the bottom of 6 Bosc pears. Set them upright in a baking dish just big enough to fit them all snugly and pour $^3/_4$ cup (180 ml) Marsala wine over the pears. Sprinkle with $^1/_3$ cup (65 g) sugar, then bake in a preheated 375°F (190°C) oven for 40 minutes, basting the pears with the juices occasionally. Serve warm or at room temperature, with a scoop of Pear-Pecorino Ice Cream and a spoonful of the Marsala syrup.

Olive Oil Ice Cream

My well-meaning hostess, knowing that I had come to Italy to sample chocolate and gelato, planned a special dinner in my honor. As we drove up the mountain to the restaurant, she turned to me and said, "We've arranged a special dinner just for you. Each and every course is going to have chocolate in it!" Gulp.

Dinner was, um, interesting, and chocolate was indeed incorporated into each and every course—except for dessert! However, the chef presented us with a selection of ice creams, including one flavored with a fruity, locally pressed olive oil.

Olive oil ice cream pairs remarkably well with summer fruits such as strawberries and apricots, and if you use a fruity Spanish Arbequina olive oil, you'll find this ice cream is sublime drizzled with Lean Chocolate Sauce (page 165) too. Be sure to try it flecked with a few grains of coarse sea salt over the top.

> 1$\frac{1}{3}$ cups (330 ml) whole milk
>
> $\frac{1}{2}$ cup (100 g) sugar
>
> Pinch of salt
>
> 1 cup (250 ml) heavy cream
>
> 6 large egg yolks
>
> $\frac{1}{2}$ cup (125 ml) fruity olive oil

Warm the milk, sugar, and salt in a medium saucepan. Pour the cream into a large bowl and set a mesh strainer on top.

In a separate medium bowl, whisk together the egg yolks. Slowly pour the warm mixture into the egg yolks, whisking constantly, then scrape the warmed egg yolks back into the saucepan.

Stir the mixture constantly over medium heat with a heatproof spatula, scraping the bottom as you stir, until the mixture thickens and coats the spatula. Pour the custard through the strainer and stir it into the cream. Whisk the olive oil into the custard vigorously until it's well blended, then stir until cool over an ice bath. Chill the mixture thoroughly in the refrigerator, then freeze it in your ice cream maker according to the manufacturer's instructions.

VARIATION: For Lemon-Olive Oil Ice Cream, very, very finely grate the zest of 1 lemon, preferably unsprayed, into the olive oil and warm it gently. Remove from the heat and let it infuse while you make the custard. Whisk the oil along with the zest into the ice cream custard.

PERFECT PAIRING: To make Honey-Roasted Apricots to serve along with Olive Oil Ice Cream, for 6 servings, split 12 fresh apricots in half and remove the pits. Arrange them cut side down in a baking dish and drizzle with 3 tablespoons (45 ml) honey, 6 tablespoons (90 ml) white wine, and $\frac{1}{2}$ vanilla bean, split lengthwise. Bake, uncovered, for 20 minutes, or until the apricots are tender, basting them with their juices midway during baking. Serve the apricots warm or at room temperature with a scoop of Olive Oil Ice Cream and some French Almonds (page 189).

Orange-Szechwan Pepper Ice Cream

MAKES ABOUT 1 QUART (1 LITER)

After a big meal, when I feel like I can't eat another bite, I like a dessert that's been infused with an intriguing flavor, like Szechwan pepper, to coax my taste buds back to life. This ice cream starts off comfortably, with the familiar flavor of orange, and then comes alive with a kick from the Szechwan peppercorns.

  3 tablespoons (10 g) Szechwan peppercorns

  1 1/2 cups (375 ml) whole milk

  1 1/2 cups (375 ml) heavy cream

  1 cup (200 g) sugar

  4 oranges, preferably unsprayed

  6 large egg yolks

Coarsely grind the Szechwan peppercorns in a mortar and pestle, or place them in a heavy-duty freezer bag and crack them with a rolling pin or hammer.

Heat the milk, 1/2 cup (125 ml) of the cream, and sugar with the crushed Szechwan peppercorns in a medium saucepan. Zest the oranges directly into the saucepan. Once warm, cover, remove from the heat, and let steep at room temperature for 1 hour.

Rewarm the Szechwan pepper-infused mixture. Pour the remaining 1 cup (250 ml) heavy cream into a large bowl and set a mesh strainer on top. In a separate medium bowl, whisk together the egg yolks. Slowly pour the warm mixture into the egg yolks, whisking constantly, then scrape the warmed egg yolks back into the saucepan.

Stir the mixture constantly over medium heat with a heatproof spatula, scraping the bottom as you stir, until the mixture thickens and coats the spatula. Pour the custard through the strainer and stir it into the cream. Stir until cool over an ice bath.

Chill the mixture thoroughly in the refrigerator, then freeze it in your ice cream maker according to the manufacturer's instructions.

VARIATIONS: For Orange-Cardamom Ice Cream, substitute 2 teaspoons cardamom seeds, crushed, for the Szechwan pepper.

For Orange-Clove Ice Cream, substitute 10 to 15 crushed whole cloves (depending on how clovey you want your ice cream) for the Szechwan pepper.

PERFECT PAIRING: Serve with Red Wine-Poached Rhubarb Compote (page 129).

Super Lemon Ice Cream

This recipe comes from Barbara Tropp, the woman who introduced many Americans to the wonders of Chinese cooking. But she was also one of those people who was just absolutely lovely to be around in every respect. She was deservedly popular in the food community and left many great recipes behind as her legacy, including this famous lemon ice cream. It was passed on to me by Susan Loomis, a dear friend we both had in common. I made it, ate one spoonful, and immediately found another reason to love, and miss, Barbara. It's superbly lemony and clean...and as zesty as Barbara was herself.

> 2 lemons, preferably unsprayed
>
> $1/2$ cup (100 g) sugar
>
> $1/2$ cup (125 ml) freshly squeezed lemon juice (from about 3 lemons)
>
> 2 cups (500 ml) half-and-half
>
> Pinch of salt

Zest the lemons directly into a food processor or blender. Add the sugar and blend until the lemon zest is very fine. Add the lemon juice and blend until the sugar is completely dissolved. Blend in the half-and-half and salt until smooth.

Chill for 1 hour, then freeze the mixture in your ice cream maker according to the manufacturer's instructions.

PERFECT PAIRING: **Make Mock Lemon Meringue Pie by folding Marshmallows (page 212) into the just-churned ice cream or by topping it off with fluffy Marshmallow Sauce (page 168).**

Marbling

You can marble together several flavors of ice cream and sorbet. First, pick any two (or more) flavors that sound complementary. Chocolate, vanilla, and strawberry ice creams combined will make Neapolitan ice cream, for example. Toasted Coconut Ice Cream (page 96) and Mango Sorbet (page 108), when marbled together, become a tropical combination that's as great tasting as it looks (see photograph page 97). Get the idea?

Make and freeze the ice creams or sorbets you plan to marble. Once they're frozen, and while they're still relatively soft, take a separate container and alternate large scoopfuls of the ice creams or sorbets, one after the other, rapping the container on the counter to release any air pockets as you go. When you're done, cover the container and freeze until solid.

If your ice cream maker requires 24 hours in the freezer between batches, remove the previously frozen ice cream from the freezer to soften a bit before marbling it with the second batch.

Lemon-Speculoos Ice Cream

MAKES ABOUT 1½ QUARTS (1½ LITERS)

The Belgians have their own version of gingersnaps, called *speculoos* (SPEC-ou-looze). They're meant to be nibbled alongside the copious amounts of beer that Belgians drink, which was one of the many lessons I learned when I went to chocolate school there, at Callebaut College. The Belgians like their beer so much that the outdoor beer gardens are busy all year long, even during the freezing cold winters. You have to brush the snow off your table to put down your glass! The good news is that you don't have to worry about your beer getting warm.

Back home, I found that *speculoos* go equally well when crumbled and folded into lemon ice cream, which can be consumed any time of the year.

3 large lemons, preferably unsprayed

¾ cup (150 g) sugar

1 cup (250 ml) whole milk

2 cups (500 ml) heavy cream

Pinch of salt

5 egg yolks

Speculoos (page 208), crumbled

Zest the lemons directly into a food processor or blender. Add the sugar and blend until the lemon zest is very fine.

Warm the milk with the lemon-scented sugar, ½ cup (125 ml) of the heavy cream, and salt in a medium saucepan. Cover, remove from the heat, and let infuse for 1 hour.

Rewarm the lemon-infused mixture. Pour the remaining 1½ cups (375 ml) cream into a large bowl and set a mesh strainer on top.

In a separate medium bowl, whisk together the egg yolks. Slowly pour warm lemon-infused milk into the egg yolks, whisking constantly, then scrape the warmed egg yolks back into the saucepan.

Stir the mixture constantly over medium heat with a heatproof spatula, scraping the bottom as you stir, until the mixture thickens and coats the spatula. Pour the custard through the strainer and stir it into the cream. Discard the lemon zest and stir until cool over an ice bath.

Chill the mixture thoroughly in the refrigerator, then freeze it in your ice cream maker according to the manufacturer's instructions. As you remove it from the machine, fold in the crumbled *speculoos*.

PERFECT PAIRING: Since *speculoos* are meant to be enjoyed with beer, try pairing this ice cream with a fruity Belgian beer for dessert. I recommend the sour cherry-flavored *kriek* (the best brand is Lindemans), which you can find in well-stocked supermarkets and liquor stores.

Blueberry Frozen Yogurt

MAKES ABOUT 1 QUART (1 LITER)

When I wrote my first book on desserts, I told the story of the blueberry bush my father planted when I was growing up, which was an early lesson in disappointment (there were many more to come, but that was the first). As soon as the berries would ripen, the wily and evil blackbirds would come and snag any and all berries before I got to taste even one.

When I returned home about a year ago, my sister had just sold the house and was moving away, and I noticed that the lonely berry bush was still there. And still devoid of berries. Although I gave up hope a long time ago, I considered warning the family moving in not to get their hopes up for any ripe blueberries. But I decided to let them find out on their own. They'll learn the same lesson I did, and end up buying blueberries at the store, where the blackbirds can't get them. Hopefully they'll spare themselves the disappointment of a life as unfulfilled as mine, devoid of home-grown blueberries.

> 1½ cups (360 g) plain whole-milk yogurt
>
> ¾ cup (150 g) sugar
>
> 3 cups (340 g) blueberries, fresh or frozen
>
> 1 teaspoon kirsch
>
> 2 teaspoons freshly squeezed lemon juice

In a blender or food processor, blend together the yogurt, sugar, and blueberries. Press the mixture through a strainer to remove the seeds. Stir in the kirsch and lemon juice. Chill for 1 hour.

Freeze in your ice cream maker according to the manufacturer's instructions.

VARIATIONS: To make a richer version, substitute 1½ cups (360 g) of Greek-style yogurt or Strained Yogurt (page 49) for the plain yogurt.

To make Raspberry Frozen Yogurt, purée 2 cups (480 g) plain whole-milk yogurt, ¾ cup (150 g) sugar and 2 cups (240 g) fresh or frozen raspberries with 1 teaspoon freshly squeezed lemon juice. Press the mixture through a strainer to remove the seeds. Chill for 1 hour, then freeze in your ice cream maker.

PERFECT PAIRING: Serve scoops of Blueberry Frozen Yogurt in Honey-Cornmeal Ice Cream Cones (page 230).

Peach Ice Cream

This is the first ice cream that springs to mind when people recall hand-cranked, old-fashioned fruit ice creams from their past. More than any other homemade ice cream, this is perhaps the most beloved of all flavors and is indeed best when spooned right out of the machine, just moments after it's been churned.

An easy way to peel peaches is to cut an X at the bottom and then lower them in a pot of boiling water for about 20 seconds. Using a slotted spoon, transfer the peaches to a colander and shock them with cold water, then let them cool. Afterward, you'll find their fuzzy peels just slip right off.

> 1⅓ pounds (600 g) ripe peaches (about 4 large peaches)
>
> ½ cup (125 ml) water
>
> ¾ cup (150 g) sugar
>
> ½ cup (120 g) sour cream
>
> 1 cup (250 ml) heavy cream
>
> ¼ teaspoon vanilla extract
>
> A few drops freshly squeezed lemon juice

Peel the peaches, slice them in half, and remove the pits. Cut the peaches into chunks and cook them with the water in a medium, nonreactive saucepan over medium heat, covered, stirring once or twice, until soft and cooked through, about 10 minutes.

Remove from the heat, stir in the sugar, then cool to room temperature.

Purée the cooked peaches and any liquid in a blender or food processor with the sour cream, heavy cream, vanilla, and lemon juice until almost smooth but slightly chunky.

Chill the mixture thoroughly in the refrigerator, then freeze it in your ice cream maker according to the manufacturer's instructions.

VARIATION: To make Nectarine Ice Cream, simply substitute nectarines for the peaches. There's no need to peel the nectarines, since their tender skins soften during cooking.

> PERFECT PAIRING: Make a Peaches and Cream Compote by serving Peach Ice Cream with Crème Fraîche Ice Cream (page 59). Peel and slice several peaches (allow 2 peaches for 4 people), then toss the slices with a sprinkle of sugar and let stand for about 30 minutes, until juicy. Put a scoop of each of the two ice creams in a bowl and pile peach slices around them.

Peach Frozen Yogurt

MAKES ABOUT 3 CUPS (750 ML)

Unlike some of the other frozen yogurts in this book, I only make this with plain, unstrained yogurt. Since the peach purée is so velvety thick, this frozen yogurt has a lovely consistency when frozen.

$1^{1}/_{2}$ pounds (675 g) ripe peaches (about 5 large peaches)

$^{1}/_{2}$ cup (125 ml) water

$^{3}/_{4}$ cup (150 g) sugar

I cup (240 g) plain whole-milk yogurt

A few drops freshly squeezed lemon juice

Peel the peaches, slice them in half, and remove the pits. Cut the peaches into chunks and cook them with the water in a medium, nonreactive saucepan over medium heat, covered, stirring occasionally, until soft and cooked through, about 10 minutes. Remove from the heat, stir in the sugar, then chill in the refrigerator.

When the peaches are cool, purée them in a food processor or blender with the yogurt until almost smooth but slightly chunky. Mix in a few drops of lemon juice.

Freeze the mixture in your ice cream maker according to the manufacturer's instructions.

PERFECT PAIRING: Serve Peach Frozen Yogurt with a summertime Mixed Fruit Coulis (page 181).

Strawberry-Sour Cream Ice Cream

MAKES ABOUT $1^{1}/_{4}$ QUARTS ($1^{1}/_{4}$ LITERS)

Brilliant pink fresh strawberry ice cream is a classic flavor and, along with chocolate and vanilla, is an American favorite. I'm a big fan of any kind of berries served with tangy sour cream, but I think strawberries are the most delicious, especially when frozen into a soft, rosy red scoop of ice cream. Macerating the strawberries beforehand magically transforms even so-so berries into fruits that are brilliantly red. Try to eat this ice cream soon after it's been churned.

I pound (450 g) fresh strawberries, rinsed and hulled

$^{3}/_{4}$ cup (150 g) sugar

I tablespoon vodka or kirsch

I cup (240 g) sour cream

I cup (250 ml) heavy cream

$^{1}/_{2}$ teaspoon freshly squeezed lemon juice

Slice the strawberries and toss them in a bowl with the sugar and vodka or kirsch, stirring until the sugar begins to dissolve. Cover and let stand at room temperature for 1 hour, stirring every so often.

Pulse the strawberries and their liquid with the sour cream, heavy cream, and lemon juice in a blender or food processor until almost smooth but still slightly chunky.

Refrigerate for 1 hour, then freeze in your ice cream maker according to the manufacturer's instructions.

Strawberry Frozen Yogurt

MAKES ABOUT 1 QUART (1 LITER)

This frozen yogurt is a snap to put together, especially welcome in the summer which is when you may want to limit your time in a warm kitchen. But don't let its ease of preparation fool you; this vibrantly colored frozen yogurt provides the biggest blast of strawberry flavor imaginable.

> 1 pound (450 g) fresh strawberries, rinsed and hulled
>
> $2/3$ cup (130 g) sugar
>
> 2 teaspoons vodka or kirsch (optional)
>
> 1 cup (240 g) plain whole-milk yogurt
>
> 1 teaspoon freshly squeezed lemon juice

Slice the strawberries into small pieces. Toss in a bowl with the sugar and vodka or kirsch, if using, stirring until the sugar begins to dissolve. Cover and let stand at room temperature for 1 hour, stirring every so often.

Purée the strawberries and their liquid with the yogurt and lemon juice in a blender or food processor until smooth. If you wish, press the mixture through a mesh strainer to remove any seeds.

Refrigerate for 1 hour, then freeze in your ice cream maker according to the manufacturer's instructions.

PERFECT PAIRING: For Strawberry Frozen Yogurt Meringues (pictured on page 235), fill Meringue Nests (page 234) with Strawberry Frozen Yogurt. Add a dollop of Whipped Cream (page 170), and surround the frozen yogurt and meringue shell with lots of sliced sweetened strawberries, adding a few raspberries or mango slices if you like.

Raspberry Swirl Ice Cream

I'm a firm believer in being very nice to the people who feed me, which comes from working in restaurants and seeing what can happen to people who aren't. I have a particular soft spot for the young folks at my local fish market, who wake early each morning to unpack, bone, and clean icy cold fish all day long. Since their freezer has a much larger capacity than mine, and their capacity for eating ice cream follows suit, I got into the habit of bringing them lots of ice creams and sorbets. Each time I'd bring them another flavor, they'd drop whatever work they were doing, rip off the lid, and dig right in. They liked this Raspberry Swirl Ice Cream the most, and it earned me VIP status instantly.

Since that day, I've gotten the quickest and most helpful service of anyone who shops at that fish store. This perplexes the other shoppers, who have no idea of the power of homemade ice cream. For best results, layer the just-churned ice cream with the raspberry swirl and avoid stirring it to preserve the colorful contrast between the frozen vanilla custard and the gorgeous swirl of raspberries.

ICE CREAM

> 1 cup (250 ml) whole milk
>
> ⅔ cup (130 g) sugar
>
> Pinch of salt
>
> 1½ cups (375 ml) heavy cream
>
> 5 large egg yolks
>
> ½ teaspoon vanilla extract

RASPBERRY SWIRL

> 1½ cups (160 g) raspberries, fresh or frozen
>
> 3 tablespoons (45 g) sugar
>
> 1 tablespoon vodka

To make the ice cream, warm the milk, sugar, and salt in a medium saucepan. Pour the cream into a large bowl and set a mesh strainer over the top.

In a separate medium bowl, whisk together the egg yolks. Slowly pour the warm milk into the egg yolks, whisking constantly, then scrape the warmed egg yolks back into the saucepan.

Stir the mixture constantly over medium heat with a heatproof spatula, scraping the bottom as you stir, until the mixture thickens and coats the spatula. Pour the custard through the strainer and stir it into the cream. Add the vanilla and stir until cool over an ice bath. Chill thoroughly in the refrigerator.

An hour or so before churning the ice cream, make the raspberry swirl by mashing the raspberries together with the sugar and vodka with a fork (if using frozen raspberries, let them thaw a bit first) until they're juicy but with nice-sized chunks of raspberries remaining. Chill until ready to use.

Freeze the ice cream custard in your ice cream maker according to the manufacturer's instructions. As you remove it from the machine, layer it in the container with spoonfuls of the chilled raspberry swirl mixture.

VARIATION: To make Blackberry Swirl Ice Cream, substitute blackberries for the raspberries and add 1 teaspoon freshly squeezed lemon juice to the mixture.

> PERFECT PAIRINGS: Sandwich Raspberry Swirl Ice Cream between Oatmeal Ice Cream Sandwich Cookies (page 226) or Chocolate Ice Cream Sandwich Cookies (page 223).

Raspberry Ice Cream

MAKES ABOUT 1 QUART (1 LITER)

Raspberry ice cream is one of life's most unabashed luxuries. I prefer to strain out the seeds, which interfere with the sublime smoothness and pleasure of this ice cream. To do this, purée the raspberries in a food processor, then press them through a mesh strainer with a flexible rubber spatula, or use a food mill. This recipe requires $1^{1}/_{2}$ cups (375 ml) of purée, so you'll need to begin with about 6 cups (750 g) of fresh or frozen raspberries.

> $1^{1}/_{2}$ cups (375 ml) half-and-half
>
> 1 cup (200 g) sugar
>
> $1^{1}/_{2}$ cups (375 ml) heavy cream
>
> 4 large egg yolks
>
> $1^{1}/_{2}$ cups (375 ml) strained raspberry purée
>
> 1 tablespoon freshly squeezed lemon juice

Warm the half-and-half and sugar in a medium saucepan. Pour the cream into a large bowl and set a mesh strainer over the top.

In a separate medium bowl, whisk together the egg yolks. Slowly pour the warm milk into the egg yolks, whisking constantly, then scrape the warmed egg yolks back into the saucepan.

Stir the mixture constantly over medium heat with a heatproof spatula, scraping the bottom as you stir, until the mixture thickens and coats the spatula. Pour the custard through the strainer and stir it into the cream. Mix in the raspberry purée and lemon juice, then stir until cool over an ice bath.

Chill thoroughly in the refrigerator, but to preserve the fresh raspberry taste, churn the ice cream within 4 hours after making the mixture.

> PERFECT PAIRING: Italians dip ice cream in pure, dark chocolate, creating Tartufi (page 230), truffles of ice cream. Serve Raspberry Tartufi with White Chocolate Sauce (page 167).

Passion Fruit Ice Cream

As a smart shopper, I like to outwit unsuspecting produce clerks who don't know any better and mark down passion fruits that are ugly and deeply wrinkled, which actually indicates that they're perfectly ripe and ready to use. I buy any and all, whether I need them right away or not, since the pulp freezes beautifully. You can find good-quality frozen passion fruit pulp in Latin markets as well (or see Resources, page 237). I like to add a drop or two of pure orange oil to augment the passion fruit flavor, but if unavailable, you can substitute a few swipes of freshly grated orange zest if you wish.

To extract the pulp, cut each passion fruit in half at the equator and scoop the pulp and seeds into a nonreactive strainer set over a bowl. Use a flexible rubber spatula to press and extract as much as the precious pulp as possible, until the seeds look rather dry. You can freeze the fragrant pulp or use it right away. But save a few of the seeds to add back to the ice cream just after it's churned.

> $1/2$ cup (125 ml) fresh or frozen passion fruit pulp (from 6 to 8 fresh passion fruits)
>
> 1 cup (250 ml) heavy cream
>
> 6 tablespoons (90 ml) whole milk
>
> 7 tablespoons (85 g) sugar
>
> Pinch of salt
>
> 3 large egg yolks
>
> A few drops pure orange oil, or grated zest of 1 small orange (optional)
>
> Spoonful of passion fruit seeds (optional)

Mix together the passion fruit pulp and $1/2$ cup (125 ml) of the cream in a large bowl. Set a mesh strainer over the bowl.

Warm the milk, sugar, salt, and the remaining $1/2$ cup (125 ml) cream in a medium saucepan. In a separate medium bowl, whisk together the egg yolks. Slowly pour the warm mixture into the egg yolks, whisking constantly, then scrape the warmed egg yolks back into the saucepan.

Stir the mixture constantly over medium heat with a heatproof spatula, scraping the bottom as you stir, until the mixture thickens and coats the spatula. Pour the custard through the strainer and stir it into the passion fruit and cream mixture. Mix in a few drops of orange oil, if using, then stir until cool over an ice bath.

Chill the mixture thoroughly in the refrigerator, then freeze it in your ice cream maker according to the manufacturer's instructions. Add a spoonful of passion fruit seeds to the custard during the last few minutes of churning, if you wish.

Avocado Ice Cream

I had a sheltered life growing up in staid New England and never tasted an avocado until I was a teenager and took my first trip to California. There I was served a salad loaded with chunks of avocado, squishy, pale, and icky green. I tried to spear the offending slices to get them off my plate, but they resisted my persistent jabs and kept eluding my grasp. Now I realize that those luscious tidbits were trying to tell me something, and I regret the loss of so many avocados that I could have loved.

If you're hesitant to try avocado ice cream, let my foolhardy prejudice be a lesson to you. The best avocados are the pebbly-skinned Hass variety. When ripe and ready, the flesh should give just a little when pressed. And be sure to try the Avocado Licuado con Leche in the Perfect Pairing at the end of the recipe. It is unbelievably delicious.

> 3 medium-sized ripe Hass avocados (about 1¹/₂ pounds, 675 g)
>
> ³/₄ cup (150 g) sugar
>
> 1 cup (240 g) sour cream
>
> ¹/₂ cup (125 ml) heavy cream
>
> 1 tablespoon freshly squeezed lime juice
>
> Big pinch of salt

Slice the avocados in half and pluck out the pits. Scoop out the flesh with a spoon and cut it into little pieces.

Purée the avocado pieces in a blender or food processor with the sugar, sour cream, heavy cream, lime juice, and salt until smooth and the sugar is dissolved.

Freeze immediately in your ice cream maker according to the manufacturer's instructions.

PERFECT PAIRING: A great summertime refresher is Avocado Licuado con Leche (or *batido*) milkshakes, popular in South and Central America. For each serving, put 2 scoops (4 ounces, 115 g) of Avocado Ice Cream in a blender along with ¹/₂ cup (125 ml) milk, 2 teaspoons sugar, 3 ice cubes, and a squirt of freshly squeezed lime juice. Blend until smooth, then pour into a glass. A shot of espresso can be added as well.

Toasted Coconut Ice Cream

I'll admit that my favorite selection from the shiny white Good Humor jalopy that cruised our neighborhood was simply called Toasted Coconut: vanilla ice cream on a stick, coated with lots of sugary-sweet coconut.

On the last fateful day that I'd ever see the Good Humor man, the bully next door decided to spray him with water from a hose as he slowly circled our block. He beat a hasty retreat and never came back. Being blackballed by the Good Humor man made that the worst summer of my life. I don't know what happened to the neighborhood bully, but now that I'm an adult I can have Toasted Coconut Ice Cream whenever I want. And I do. Opposite, this ice cream is pictured marbled with Mango Sorbet (page 108).

> 1 cup (70 g) dried shredded coconut, preferably unsweetened
>
> 1 cup (250 ml) whole milk
>
> 2 cups (500 ml) heavy cream
>
> ³⁄₄ cup (150 g) sugar
>
> Big pinch of salt
>
> 1 vanilla bean, split in half lengthwise
>
> 5 large egg yolks
>
> ¹⁄₂ teaspoon vanilla extract, or 1 teaspoon rum

Preheat the oven to 350°F (175°C). Spread the coconut on a baking sheet and bake for 5 to 8 minutes, stirring it frequently so it toasts evenly. Remove it from the oven when it's nice and fragrant and golden brown.

In a medium saucepan, warm the milk, 1 cup (250 ml) of the heavy cream, sugar, and salt and add the toasted coconut. Use a paring knife, and scrape all the vanilla seeds into the warm milk, then add the pod as well. Cover, remove from the heat, and let steep at room temperature for 1 hour.

Rewarm the coconut-infused mixture. Set a mesh strainer over another medium saucepan and strain the coconut-infused liquid through the strainer into the saucepan. Press down on the coconut very firmly with a flexible rubber spatula to extract as much of the flavor from it as possible. Remove the vanilla bean pieces (rinse and reserve them for another use), and discard the coconut.

Pour the remaining 1 cup (250 ml) heavy cream into a large bowl and set the mesh strainer on top. In a separate medium bowl, whisk together the egg yolks. Slowly pour the warm coconut-infused mixture into the egg yolks, whisking constantly, then scrape the warmed egg yolks back into the saucepan.

Stir the mixture constantly over medium heat with a heatproof spatula, scraping the bottom as you stir, until the mixture thickens and coats the spatula. Pour the custard through the strainer and stir it into the cream. Mix in the vanilla or rum and stir until cool over an ice bath.

Chill the mixture thoroughly in the refrigerator, then freeze it in your ice cream maker according to the manufacturer's instructions.

Green Pea Ice Cream

If you're lucky enough to snag a reservation at Le Grand Véfour, the restaurant that presides over the splendid Palais Royal in Paris, you'll be treated to a culinary tour de force. In this jewel box of a restaurant, my advice is to sit back and let chef Guy Martin and his staff pamper you like royalty, which they have elevated to an art.

When it comes time for dessert, you scan the menu, but... "Can that be right?" you think to yourself, trying to recall snippets of your high school French. Indeed, chef Martin is fond of using vegetables in unexpected ways, often in desserts. But if you've ever enjoyed a wedge of carrot cake, you'll know that it's not so strange.

This ice cream is inspired by a dessert I had at his restaurant: a small, crispy cone filled with bright green ice cream that had the dewy taste of tiny spring peas. At home, in addition to serving it for dessert, I've found that it makes a lovely garnish to a bowl of chilled summer soup.

> 1 pound (450 g) green peas, fresh or frozen
>
> ¾ cup (180 ml) whole milk
>
> ¾ cup (150 g) sugar
>
> 1½ cups (375 ml) heavy cream
>
> 6 large egg yolks
>
> ½ cup (20 g) lightly packed fresh mint leaves

Bring about 3 quarts (3 liters) of lightly salted water to a boil in a medium saucepan. Add the peas. While the peas are cooking, fill a large bowl half full with ice cubes and water. After 10 minutes of cooking, drain the peas and add them to the ice water right away. After 1 minute, drain the peas in a mesh strainer and remove any pieces of ice. (Hold on to the saucepan and strainer, since you'll use them again.)

Warm the milk and sugar in the saucepan. Pour the cream into a large bowl, add the drained peas, and set the mesh strainer over the top.

In a separate medium bowl, whisk together the egg yolks. Slowly pour the warm milk into the egg yolks, whisking constantly, then scrape the warmed egg yolks back into the pan.

Stir the mixture constantly over medium heat with a heatproof spatula, scraping the bottom as you stir, until the mixture thickens and coats the spatula. Pour the custard through the strainer and stir it into the cream and peas. Stir until cool over an ice bath.

Pour the mixture into a blender, add the mint leaves, and blend until smooth. Press the mixture through a coarse mesh strainer and discard any tough pea skins. You can also pass the mixture through a food mill fitted with a fine disk.

Chill the mixture thoroughly in the refrigerator, then freeze it in your ice cream maker according to the manufacturer's instructions.

PERFECT PAIRING: Use as a garnish for a cold summer soup, such as vichyssoise or cucumber-yogurt soup.

Fresh Mint Ice Cream

Standing in front of an immense, intricately carved wooden door in Fez, Morocco, my guide handed me a big bunch of fresh mint, shoving it firmly under my nose and telling me not to move it from there or I'd be sorry. Sure enough, when the gate swung open and we entered a tannery I kept my face deeply buried in the mint, as advised, and was happy for the good advice. Afterward I didn't want to part with it since I love the aroma of fresh mint so much.

I use mint for much more than an air freshener. It makes a wonderfully invigorating ice cream. I've planted mint in my garden against the warnings of friends, who say it'll take over before I know it, but I've never had a problem using it all. And they've never had a problem eating the ice cream I make from it either.

1 cup (250 ml) whole milk

¾ cup (150 g) sugar

2 cups (500 ml) heavy cream

Pinch of salt

2 cups (80 g) lightly packed fresh mint leaves

5 large egg yolks

Warm the milk, sugar, 1 cup (250 ml) of the cream, and salt in a small saucepan. Add the mint leaves and stir until they're immersed in the liquid. Cover, remove from the heat, and let steep at room temperature for 1 hour.

Strain the mint-infused mixture through a mesh strainer into a medium saucepan. Press on the mint leaves to extract as much of the flavor as possible, then discard the mint leaves. Pour the remaining 1 cup (250 ml) heavy cream into a large bowl and set the strainer on top.

Rewarm the mint-infused mixture. In a separate medium bowl, whisk together the egg yolks. Slowly pour the warm mint liquid into the egg yolks, whisking constantly, then scrape the warmed egg yolks back into the saucepan.

Stir the mixture constantly over medium heat with a heatproof spatula, scraping the bottom as you stir, until the mixture thickens and coats the spatula. Pour the custard through the strainer and stir it into the cream. Stir until cool over an ice bath.

Chill the mixture thoroughly in the refrigerator, then freeze it in your ice cream maker according to the manufacturer's instructions.

PERFECT PAIRINGS: Make Good Scout Ice Cream Sandwiches by using Chocolate Ice Cream Sandwich Cookies (page 223) to surround scoops of Fresh Mint Ice Cream. You can also get that same chocolate-mint cookie effect by layering the just-churned ice cream with a swirl of Fudge Ripple (page 210), Stracciatella (page 210), or crumbled bits of Chewy-Dense Brownies (page 221).

Basil Ice Cream

Italians will often serve a *Torta di Verdura* for dessert, a cross between a cake and a tart packed with leafy greens. The first time I tried it I was unsure if I'd like it, but I found it unusually delicious and devoured the slice offered. Italian basil, which has a slight aniselike scent, provides the base for this herbaceous ice cream. This is wonderful to make in the summer when large bunches of basil are abundantly available at the market.

> 1 cup (25 g) packed basil leaves
>
> ¾ cup (150 g) sugar
>
> 2 cups (500 ml) heavy cream
>
> 1 cup (250 ml) whole milk
>
> Pinch of salt
>
> 5 large egg yolks
>
> 1 lemon, preferably unsprayed

Using a blender or small food processor, grind the basil leaves with the sugar and 1 cup (250 ml) of the cream until the leaves are ground as fine as possible. Pour about half of the basil mixture into a large bowl and add the remaining 1 cup (250 ml) cream. Set a mesh strainer on top.

Warm the other half of the basil mixture in a medium saucepan along with the milk and salt. In a separate medium bowl, whisk together the egg yolks. Slowly pour the warm mixture into the egg yolks, whisking constantly, then scrape the warmed egg yolks back into the saucepan.

Stir the mixture constantly over medium heat with a heatproof spatula, scraping the bottom as you stir, until the mixture thickens and coats the spatula. Pour the custard through the strainer and stir it into the cream. Zest the lemon directly into the custard, then stir until cool over an ice bath.

Chill the mixture thoroughly in the refrigerator, then freeze it in your ice cream maker according to the manufacturer's instructions.

PERFECT PAIRING: Try Basil Ice Cream paired with Strawberries in Lemon Syrup. For 4 servings, combine 1 cup (250 ml) water and ¼ cup (50 g) sugar with the grated zest of 1 lemon in a small saucepan. Bring to a boil and cook, stirring, until the sugar is dissolved. Remove from the heat, pour into a bowl, and chill thoroughly.

Hull and quarter 1 pound (450 g) of strawberries. Add them to the lemon syrup and let macerate in the refrigerator for 1 to 4 hours. To serve, spoon the strawberries and some lemon syrup into shallow bowls and float a scoop of Basil Ice Cream in the center.

Parsley Ice Cream

This ice cream is very popular at a wine bar I frequent, where it's served floating in a fruit soup surrounded by fresh berries. The contrast between the parsley-flecked ice cream and the rosy red berries floating in pink syrup is almost too lovely to eat. But after a few glasses of wine, inhibitions are lost and you're more susceptible to sly attempts of culinary persuasion. Believe me, the combination sounds perfectly reasonable after a couple of glasses of Chablis.

I use only flat-leaf parsley, which has a subtle hint of anise flavor. It first gets blanched and then shocked in ice water to preserve its brilliant green color.

Note that this recipe makes only about a pint of ice cream, perfect for a small get-together. Double the amounts if you wish.

> 1 cup (25 g) packed flat-leaf parsley leaves
>
> 1 1/2 cups (375 ml) half-and-half
>
> 1/3 cup (65 g) sugar
>
> Pinch of salt
>
> 2 large egg yolks

Bring about 4 cups (1 liter) of water to a boil in a saucepan. Meanwhile, prepare an ice bath by filling a small bowl with cold water and adding a few ice cubes.

Once the water is boiling, add the parsley and let it boil for 10 seconds. Drain the parsley (keep the saucepan handy) and immediately drop it in the cold water to shock it. Remove the parsley and squeeze it very tightly in your hand to extract as much water as possible.

Purée the parsley on high speed in a blender with 3/4 cup of the half-and-half for 30 seconds, until the parsley is very finely ground.

In the saucepan, warm the remaining 3/4 cup half-and-half with the sugar and salt. Scrape the parsley mixture into a large bowl and set a mesh strainer on top.

In a separate medium bowl, whisk together the egg yolks. Slowly pour the warm mixture into the egg yolks, whisking constantly, then scrape the warmed egg yolks back into the saucepan.

Stir the mixture constantly over medium heat with a heatproof spatula, scraping the bottom as you stir, until the mixture thickens and coats the spatula. Pour the custard through the strainer and stir it into the parsley mixture. Stir until cool over an ice bath.

Chill the mixture thoroughly in the refrigerator, then freeze it in your ice cream maker according to the manufacturer's instructions.

PERFECT PAIRING: Serve with Strawberries in Lemon Syrup (page 100).

Black Pepper Ice Cream

Black pepper ice cream tastes spicy and lively, as you probably can imagine. I like it as a contrast to sweet summer berries, or pears roasted with a swirl of dark honey in autumn. If you don't have a mortar and pestle, crack the peppercorns in a heavy-duty plastic bag with a hammer.

$1/2$ cup (125 ml) whole milk

$1/3$ cup (65 g) sugar

1 tablespoon black peppercorns, coarsely cracked

Pinch of salt

1 cup (250 ml) heavy cream

3 large egg yolks

Warm the milk, sugar, peppercorns, salt, and $1/2$ cup (125 ml) of the cream in a medium saucepan. Cover, remove from the heat, and let steep at room temperature for 1 hour.

Rewarm the peppercorn-infused mixture. Pour the remaining $1/2$ cup (125 ml) cream into a large bowl and set a mesh strainer on top. In a separate medium bowl, whisk together the egg yolks. Slowly pour the warm mixture into the egg yolks, whisking constantly, then scrape the warmed egg yolks back into the saucepan.

Stir the mixture constantly over medium heat with a heatproof spatula, scraping the bottom as you stir, until the mixture thickens and coats the spatula. Pour the custard through the strainer, pressing the peppercorns gently to extract as much flavor as possible. Discard the peppercorns and stir the custard into the cream. Stir until cool over an ice bath.

Chill the mixture thoroughly in the refrigerator, then freeze it in your ice cream maker according to the manufacturer's instructions.

PERFECT PAIRING: Icy-cold Melon in Lime Syrup is the perfect accompaniment to Black Pepper Ice Cream. Zest 2 limes into a small saucepan. Add 1 cup (250 ml) water and $3/4$ cup (150 g) sugar, bring the mixture to a boil, and cook until the syrup is reduced to $3/4$ cup (180 ml). Remove from the heat, pour into a bowl, and chill thoroughly.

Peel, seed, and cut a cantaloupe or honeydew melon into 1-inch (3-cm) chunks, and add them to the syrup. Chill for at least 1 hour, then serve the melon pieces with some of the syrup, alongside the Black Pepper Ice Cream. Garnish with a few grains of cracked pink peppercorns.

Saffron Ice Cream

MAKES ABOUT 2 CUPS (500 ML)

After an exotic Indian or Moroccan feast, sprinkle this ice cream (and your guests) with a few drops of rosewater and top it all off (the ice cream, not your guests) with a few toasted pine nuts. For a stunning presentation, serve it on a platter with thinly sliced oranges dusted with cinnamon and scattered with candied French Almonds (page 189).

$^1\!/_2$ cup (125 ml) whole milk

1 cup (250 ml) heavy cream

$^1\!/_2$ cup (100 g) sugar

Scant $^1\!/_2$ teaspoon saffron threads

3 large egg yolks

Warm the milk, cream, and sugar in a small saucepan. Remove from the heat and add the saffron. Pour into a small bowl and steep in the refrigerator for 4 hours.

Strain the saffron-infused mixture into a medium saucepan. Rescue the threads of saffron and put them in a medium bowl. Set the strainer over the top.

Rewarm the saffron-infused mixture. In a separate medium bowl, whisk together the egg yolks. Slowly pour the warm saffron mixture into the egg yolks, whisking constantly, then scrape the warmed egg yolks back into the saucepan.

Stir the mixture constantly over medium heat with a heatproof spatula, scraping the bottom as you stir, until the mixture thickens and coats the spatula. Pour the custard through the strainer and stir to incorporate the saffron threads. Stir until cool over an ice bath.

Chill the mixture thoroughly in the refrigerator, then freeze it in your ice cream maker according to the manufacturer's instructions. Be sure to scrape off any saffron threads stuck to the dasher and stir them back into the frozen ice cream.

VARIATION: To make Saffron–Pine Nut Ice Cream, add $^1\!/_4$ cup toasted pine nuts (see page 13) to the ice cream during the last 5 minutes of churning.

PERFECT PAIRING: Serve Saffron Ice Cream with Vanilla-Poached Quince. To poach the quince, for 6 to 8 servings you need to start out with 3 quinces (2 pounds, 1 kg). Peel and quarter the quinces, then remove the seeds and cores with a melon baller. In a non-reactive saucepan, heat $1^1\!/_2$ cups (300 g) sugar, 4 cups (1 liter) water, and 1 vanilla bean, split lengthwise. While the syrup is heating, cut the quinces into 1-inch (3-cm) slices.

Add the quince slices to the syrup, cover with a round of parchment paper, and cook at a gentle simmer for about $1^1\!/_2$ hours, or until the quince slices are rosy and tender. Let cool to room temperature, then serve the quince slices with a scoop of Saffron Ice Cream and some of the delicious poaching liquid, which can be reduced to a thick syrup before serving.

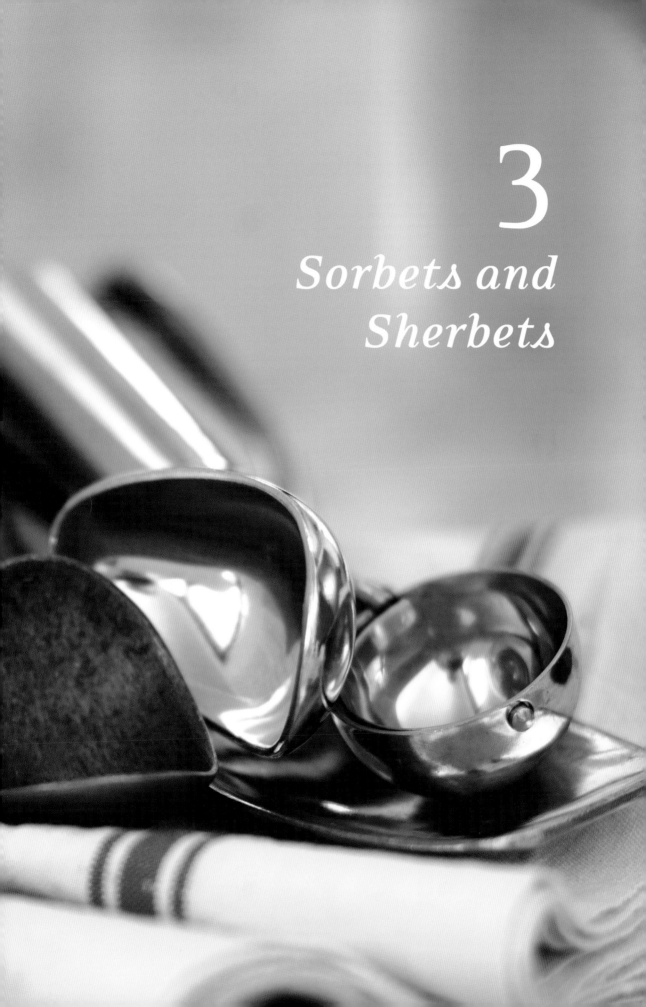

3
Sorbets and Sherbets

No matter how full I am, I'm always ready to dig into a bowl of icy-cool sorbet after dinner. There's something both cleansing and exhilarating about a spoonful of homemade sorbet; the pure flavor of spectacular fresh fruit cuts through any of the clutter beforehand and ends any meal on a perfect note. I like to think of fruit sorbets as a way to heighten the taste of fresh fruit, too. By adding just a touch of sweetness, a little bit of water, and perhaps a squeeze of lemon juice, you can brighten fruit flavors, making them "pop" with even more intensity than fresh fruit itself.

You'll find no better inspiration for churning out a superb fresh fruit sorbet than your local market. When I see spectacular fruits, like juicy, tree-ripened peaches, tart limes, or succulent tangerines, I can't resist turning them into sorbet, capturing the essence of the fruit itself. The best-tasting fruit sorbets are made from the most luscious, ripe, and fragrant fruit you can find.

You'll notice that most of my sorbets have just a few ingredients. Most are made with fresh fruit and just enough sugar to augment their natural sweetness and to keep them smooth once frozen. I use their simplicity as a springboard for ideas to dress them up for a special occasion. Most often I find myself serving a seasonal fruit compote in chilled soup bowls with a scoop of sorbet or sherbet resting in the middle. You can be creative and pair whatever fruits you like. But be sure to offer some nice cookies alongside, or dress it up with a tangle of Candied Citrus Peel (page 178) on top.

Why not present a scoop of citrusy sorbet in a pretty goblet with a splash of very cold Champagne and a few raspberries? It makes a quick yet sophisticated dessert. Or add a bit of indulgence in the form of a wispy dollop of Whipped Cream (page 170), an effortless and elegant counterpoint to zippy Tangerine Sorbet (page 119) or Lemon Sherbet (page 116).

The difference between a sorbet and a sherbet can be elusive. Technically, sorbets are never made with milk or cream, and sherbets often have milk or buttermilk added. (You may also see versions elsewhere with egg whites mixed in.) But these definitions are not set in stone, and I've seen the terms used interchangeably, even by professionals.

Most sorbets and sherbets will benefit by being taken out of the freezer at least 5 minutes before you plan to serve them, to soften them up to just the right serving temperature. Since fruit is composed primarily of water and sorbets have very little fat, they tend to freeze much harder than ice cream.

Mango Sorbet

MAKES ABOUT 1 QUART (1 LITER)

One day while wasting the afternoon flipping through the television channels (what did we do before the remote control?), I stopped when I came across a not-very-well-choreographed procession of statuesque, exotically beautiful women parading across a stage. After a few minutes of riveted attention, I realized that I'd happened upon the Miss Martinique pageant.

Once the glamorous gals had strutted their stuff wearing barely-there bikinis, teetering around precariously on steep high heels (it seemed the smaller the swimsuit, the higher the heels), the contest concluded with the host posing the all-important question about why the pageant was so vital for promoting world peace and understanding. One of the contestants flashed her big, bright smile, looked right into the camera, and responded, "Because beauty is the key to communication."

With a thought-provoking answer like that, awarding the crown to anyone else would have been a crime. And sure enough, she won. But maybe she got mixed up and was talking about mangoes, the other beauties of the tropics. Their vibrant red exterior and succulent orange pulp do indeed communicate beauty and good taste that are not just skin deep.

2 large, ripe mangoes (2 pounds, 1 kg)

$^2/_3$ cup (130 g) sugar

$^2/_3$ cup (160 ml) water

4 teaspoons freshly squeezed lime juice, plus more to taste

1 tablespoon dark rum, plus more to taste

Pinch of salt

Peel the mangoes and cut the flesh away from the pit. Cut the flesh into chunks and put them in a blender with the sugar, water, lime juice, rum, and salt. Squeeze the mango pits hard over the blender to extract as much of the pulp and juice as possible. Purée the mixture until smooth. Taste, then add more lime juice or rum if desired. Chill the mixture thoroughly, then freeze it in your ice cream maker according to the manufacturer's instructions.

PERFECT PAIRING: Mango Sorbet is terrific served along with a cool scoop of Toasted Coconut Ice Cream (page 96) or marbled and swirled together with Raspberry Sherbet (page 132).

Green Apple and Sparkling Cider Sorbet

MAKES ABOUT 3 CUPS (750 ML)

I was toiling away years ago in a restaurant kitchen when one day a celebrity chef stopped by who had a reputation for being rather, um, obnoxious. I was minding my own business, caught in a Zen-like state while peeling a case of apples and, naturally, generating a huge pile of peels, which I tossed into the garbage as I went. He walked by, looked in the garbage, and reprimanded me: "Don't you know you're throwing away the best part?"

My infamous sarcasm got the best of me, so I offered to wrap them up for him to take home. From the look on his face, I'm sure it was that moment that effectively killed my professional television cooking career. All kidding (and sarcasm) aside, the peelings do indeed have a lot of flavor, so I include the peels when infusing the apples in this sorbet. Hopefully, this recipe will make amends to the offended party and soon you'll see me peeling away on prime time.

> 4 Granny Smith or green pippin apples (2 pounds, 1 kg), preferably unsprayed
>
> 2 cups (500 ml) sparkling dry apple cider, with or without alcohol (see Note)
>
> 1/3 cup (65 g) sugar
>
> 1/2 cup (125 ml) water
>
> 1/2 teaspoon freshly squeezed lemon juice, or to taste

Quarter the apples and remove the cores and seeds. Cut the unpeeled apples into 1-inch (3-cm) chunks.

Combine the cider, sugar, and water and bring to a boil in a medium, nonreactive saucepan. Add the apples, reduce the heat to low, and cover. Simmer the apple chunks for 5 minutes, then turn off the heat and let the apples steep until the mixture is room temperature.

Pass the apples and their liquid through a food mill fitted with a fine disk, or use a coarse-mesh strainer and press firmly on the apples to extract their pulp and all the liquid into a container. Discard the apple peels—they've given up their flavor at this point. Add the lemon juice. Taste and add more if you wish, since sparkling apple ciders can vary in sweetness.

Chill the mixture thoroughly, then freeze it in your ice cream maker according to the manufacturer's instructions.

NOTE: California-produced nonalcoholic sparkling apple cider is available at most supermarkets in the fruit juice aisle. If using French sparkling cider, *brut* (dry) cider is preferable to *doux* (sweet).

> PERFECT PAIRING: Pour a good dose of Calvados, the powerful apple brandy from Normandy, over scoops of Green Apple and Sparkling Cider Sorbet, and serve it after dinner. Poire Williams, a pear eau-de-vie, also works well.

Apple-Ginger Sorbet

Few folks are as opinionated about all things apple as Frank Browning, whom I've dubbed the Apple Autocrat. Frank grew up on an apple farm in Kentucky, which nurtured his headstrong, southern-style convictions regarding apples. He offered this recipe from *An Apple Harvest*, which he cowrote with Sharon Silva, but absolutely insisted that I make it only in the fall, when good-tasting, red-skinned apples are in abundance. So wait I did.

Okay... I didn't wait. But please don't tell Frank. I made this during the spring using Jonagold apples, which worked great. And although Frank insisted I use Gewürztraminer, I made it with a dry Riesling instead (blame my rebellious Yankee spirit). So feel free to use any tasty, red-skinned apple, but don't use bland Red Delicious ones, or you might get yourself a Kentucky-style comeuppance.

> 4 red-skinned apples (2 pounds, 1 kg), preferably unsprayed
>
> 2 cups (500 ml) Riesling or Gewürztraminer
>
> 1/2-ounce (15-g) piece of fresh ginger, about 1 inch (3 cm)
>
> 2/3 cup (130 g) sugar

Cut the unpeeled apples, cores and all, into 1-inch (3-cm) chunks.

Put the apples and wine in a large, nonreactive saucepan. Crush the piece of ginger with the side of a cleaver and add it to the apples. Cover and bring to a boil. Reduce the heat and simmer the apple chunks for 15 minutes, stirring once or twice during cooking, until tender.

Remove the knob of ginger and pass the apples and their liquid through a food mill fitted with a fine disk, or use a coarse-mesh strainer and press firmly on the apples to extract their pulp and all the liquid into a container. Discard the peels and seeds.

Stir the sugar into the warm apple mixture until dissolved.

Chill the mixture thoroughly, then freeze it in your ice cream maker according to the manufacturer's instructions.

Pear Sorbet

Use fragrant pears that are buttery ripe and slightly soft to the touch. You'll be glad you did when you taste how good this simple sorbet is. Pears are one of the only fruits that ripen off the tree, so if your pears are rock hard when you buy them, chances are they'll transform into soft, luscious, sorbet-worthy fruits in a few days. When just right, pears exude a strong, unmistakable sweet pear fragrance at the end opposite the stem. Bartlett, Comice, and French butter pears are varieties that I recommend.

4 ripe pears (2$^1/_2$ pounds, 1$^1/_4$ kg), peeled and cored

1$^1/_4$ cups (305 ml) water

$^2/_3$ cup (130 g) sugar

1 teaspoon freshly squeezed lemon juice

Cut the pears into 1-inch (3-cm) chunks. Put them in a large, nonreactive saucepan along with $^1/_2$ cup (125 ml) of the water. Cover and cook over medium to high heat for 15 minutes, stirring occasionally, until the pears are cooked through and tender when poked with a paring knife.

Transfer the cooked pears to a blender (you should have 2 cups, 500 ml, of purée) and add the remaining $^3/_4$ cup (180 ml) water, sugar, and lemon juice. Purée until smooth.

Chill the mixture thoroughly, then freeze it in your ice cream maker according to the manufacturer's instructions.

VARIATION: For Pear-Ginger Sorbet, add $^1/_4$ cup (25 g) very finely chopped candied ginger to the sorbet during the last few minutes of churning.

PERFECT PAIRINGS: Serve Pear Sorbet with a scoop of Chocolate Sorbet (page 120) or Chocolate Ice Cream (pages 26 and 28).

Cantaloupe Sorbet

MAKES ABOUT 2 CUPS (500 ML)

My friend Susan Loomis says that finding a perfect melon is like finding love—you need to try many before you land just the right one. The best way to pick one (a melon, that is) is to find one that has lots of netting around the outside and a sweet and delicious smell. Follow those tips, and there's no doubt that you'll fall head over heels for this simple sorbet that makes excellent use of the fragrant melons that are available during the summer months.

One 2-pound (1-kg) ripe cantaloupe

$^1/_2$ cup (100 g) sugar

Pinch of salt

1 teaspoon freshly squeezed lime juice, plus more to taste

2 tablespoons dry or sweet white wine or Champagne (optional)

Peel the rind from the melon, removing any traces of green. Split the melon in half and scrape out the seeds.

Cut the melon into 1-inch (3-cm) pieces. Purée in a blender with the sugar, salt, and lime juice until smooth. Taste, and add additional lime juice if desired and the wine, if using.

Chill the mixture thoroughly, then freeze it in your ice cream maker according to the manufacturer's instructions.

Watermelon Sorbetto

I wouldn't dream of visiting the vast Central Market in Florence without my friend Judy Witts, known throughout town as the Divina Cucina. With Judy as my guide, butchers and cheese merchants greet us like given-up-for-lost family members, and everywhere we turn another oversized platter appears, heaped with Tuscan delights: sheep's-milk pecorino, candied fruits spiced with mustard seeds, fresh raspberries dotted with syrupy balsamic vinegar, and, gulp, juicy tripe sandwiches (which I haven't built up the courage to try). And because we're in Italy, it all ends with shots of grappa taken straight from little glass vials, *obbligatorio* after all that sampling.

This *sorbetto* is adapted from Judy's recipe. One of her favorite parts is the little chocolate "seeds" it contains. Since watermelons have a lot of water, take the *sorbetto* out of the freezer long enough ahead of serving to make it scoopable, 5 to 10 minutes. To pass the time, serve shots of grappa, and if there's any left by serving time, splash some over the *sorbetto* too.

> 3 cups (750 ml) watermelon juice (see Note)
>
> $^1/_2$ cup (100 g) sugar
>
> Big pinch of salt
>
> 1 tablespoon freshly squeezed lime juice
>
> 1 to 2 tablespoons vodka (optional)
>
> 1 to 2 tablespoons mini semisweet chocolate chips

In a small, nonreactive saucepan, heat about $^1/_2$ cup (125 ml) of the watermelon juice with the sugar and salt, stirring until the sugar is dissolved. Remove from the heat and stir the sugared syrup into the remaining $2^1/_2$ cups (625 ml) watermelon juice in a medium bowl. Mix in the lime juice and vodka, if using.

Chill the mixture thoroughly, then freeze it in your ice cream maker according to the manufacturer's instructions. During the last minute of churning, add the mini chocolate chips.

NOTE: I find that I get about 3 cups (750 ml) of watermelon juice from a 3-pound ($1^1/_2$-kg) chunk of watermelon. Cut away the rind, remove any seeds, and then cut the juicy, pink flesh into cubes and purée them in a blender or food processor. Any extra juice can be frozen for another use, such as watermelon margaritas.

PERFECT PAIRING: This *sorbetto* makes excellent Watermelon Popsicle (pictured opposite). Simply pour the mixture into plastic popsicle molds and freeze until very firm.

Grape Sorbet

MAKES ABOUT 1 QUART (1 LITER)

Grapes that are very robust, such as Concord or Muscat, make a fine, flavorful grape sorbet. These grapes are usually at their best in autumn. If you have access to wine grapes, they produce a wonderful sorbet as well. Don't use seedless table grapes, such as Thompson and Red Flame; these make a great snack, but not a very tasty sorbet.

> 3½ pounds (1¾ kg) grapes
>
> 3 tablespoons (45 ml) water
>
> ¼ cup (60 ml) light corn syrup
>
> 1 tablespoon vodka

Remove the grapes from the stems (see page 151) and cut them in half if they're large or have thick skins. Place them in a large, nonreactive pot, add the water, and cover. Cook the grapes over medium heat, stirring occasionally, until the skins have burst and the grapes are soft and cooked through.

Remove from the heat and pass the warm grapes through a food mill fitted with a fine disk, or press through a strainer with a flexible spatula if you wish to remove the grape solids. Stir the corn syrup and vodka into the grape juice.

Chill the mixture thoroughly, then freeze it in your ice cream maker according to the manufacturer's instructions.

PERFECT PAIRING: Serve Grape Sorbet alongside Peanut Butter Ice Cream (page 50).

Lime Sorbet

MAKES ABOUT 1 QUART (1 LITER)

Whenever I pass a bin of colorful limes at the market, I can't resist running my hands over their glossy, knobby, emerald skins. I don't know why, but I'm always hypnotized when I see big, overflowing bins of shiny limes, and I just love to touch them. Maybe it's because fresh limes transport us to somewhere far away, suggesting blazing hot beaches full of sexy, half-dressed locals lounging in the sun. If that doesn't give you the impetus to make this sorbet, I don't know what will.

> 2¼ cups (560 ml) water
>
> ¾ cup (150 g) sugar
>
> 1 lime, preferably unsprayed
>
> ¾ cup (180 ml) freshly squeezed lime juice (from about 9 limes)
>
> 6 tablespoons (90 ml) Champagne or sparkling wine (optional)

In a medium, nonreactive saucepan, mix 1 cup (250 ml) of the water with the sugar. Grate the zest of the lime directly into the saucepan. Heat, stirring frequently, until the sugar is completely dissolved. Remove from the heat and add the remaining 1¼ cups (310 ml) water, then chill thoroughly in the refrigerator.

Mix in the lime juice and the Champagne or sparkling wine, if using. Freeze in your ice cream maker according to the manufacturer's instructions.

PERFECT PAIRING: To make Lime Sorbet more festive, prepare the recipe but omit the Champagne. Serve scoops in frosty cocktail glasses with shots of tequila poured over them. Top each off with a few flecks of coarse salt.

Cranberry-Orange Sorbet

MAKES ABOUT 1 QUART (1 LITER)

One of the few fruits native to North America is the cranberry. They are hollow, which is why you can bounce them (go ahead, try it) and also explains why they float, which turns out to be an advantage at harvest time. Farmers flood the areas where cranberries are cultivated with water, causing the berries to rise to the surface, where it's a cinch to scoop 'em up.

Predictably, the majority of cranberries are purchased just before Thanksgiving, but I stock up the day after, when they're on sale, and freeze them to use during the rest of the year.

> 1½ cups (180 g) cranberries, fresh or frozen
>
> 1 cup (250 ml) water
>
> ¾ cup (150 g) sugar
>
> Grated zest of 1 orange
>
> 1½ cups (375 ml) freshly squeezed orange juice (from 5 or 6 oranges)
>
> 1 to 2 teaspoons Grand Marnier or Cointreau (optional)

Heat the cranberries, water, sugar, and zest in a medium, nonreactive saucepan until the liquid begins to boil. Boil for 1 minute, then remove from the heat, cover, and let stand for 30 minutes.

Pass the cranberries and their liquid through a food mill fitted with a fine disk, or purée them in a blender or food processor and then press the purée through a sieve to remove any large bits of cranberry skin. Stir in the orange juice and the liqueur, if using.

Chill the mixture thoroughly, then freeze it in your ice cream maker according to the manufacturer's instructions.

PERFECT PAIRING: Dress Cranberry-Orange Sorbet up by serving scoops nestled in Lemon–Poppy Seed Cookie Cups (page 228), topped with pieces of Candied Citrus Peel (page 178) made with orange zest.

Lemon Sorbet

Anyone who's been to New York City in August knows that one of the best ways to cool down is by spooning up the ubiquitous Italian ice sold by pushcart vendors all over town. Unfortunately, it's mostly disappointing and is never as good as what you can easily make at home. This sorbet captures the taste of fresh lemons better than anything you'll find on the street.

> 2$\frac{1}{2}$ cups (625 ml) water
>
> 1 cup (200 g) sugar (see Note)
>
> 2 lemons, preferably unsprayed
>
> 1 cup (250 ml) freshly squeezed lemon juice (from about 6 lemons)

In a medium, nonreactive saucepan, mix $\frac{1}{2}$ cup (125 ml) of the water and the sugar. Grate the zest of the 2 lemons directly into the saucepan. Heat, stirring frequently, until the sugar is completely dissolved. Remove from the heat and add the remaining 2 cups (500 ml) water, then chill thoroughly in the refrigerator.

Stir the lemon juice into the sugar syrup, then freeze the mixture in your ice cream maker according to the manufacturer's instructions.

NOTE: I like my Lemon Sorbet tangy. If you prefer it sweeter, you can add another $\frac{1}{4}$ cup (50 g) of sugar.

> PERFECT PAIRING: Freshly made Raspberry Granita (page 157) makes a lively partner and stands up well to the puckery lemon flavor.

Lemon Sherbet

If you're looking for a light, simple, lemony frozen dessert, here it is. It's a bit more substantial than the Lemon Sorbet (above) and every bit as good.

> 3 cups (750 ml) whole milk
>
> $\frac{3}{4}$ cup (150 g) sugar
>
> 1 lemon, preferably unsprayed
>
> 6 tablespoons (90 ml) freshly squeezed lemon juice
> (from 2 to 3 lemons)

In a medium, nonreactive saucepan, mix 1 cup (250 ml) of the milk with the sugar. Grate the zest of the lemon directly into the saucepan. Heat, stirring frequently, until the sugar is dissolved. Remove from the heat and add the remaining 2 cups (500 ml) milk, then chill thoroughly in the refrigerator.

Stir the lemon juice into the milk mixture. If it curdles a bit, whisk it vigorously to make it smooth again. Freeze in your ice cream maker according to the manufacturer's instructions.

PERFECT PAIRINGS: Lemon Sherbet is good with anything berry, including Raspberry Ice Cream (page 93) or Strawberry Sorbet (page 128). Or simply serve it with lots of lightly sweetened berries.

Lemon-Buttermilk Sherbet

MAKES ABOUT 1 QUART (1 LITER)

While teaching classes in the American heartland few years back, as I started to measure out some buttermilk, I stopped and gasped, horrified to see tiny yellow flecks floating on top. Being a city slicker, I figured there was something wrong with the buttermilk and thought I'd have to toss it. But on closer inspection, I noticed that those flecks were little bits of real, honest-to-goodness butter, something you don't see often anymore, since most buttermilk is cultured rather than a by-product of the butter-making process. The crowd got a good laugh at my startled reaction to my first encounter with real, old-fashioned buttermilk. And I promised them that I'd never dismiss the country's midsection as "flyover states" again, since there's very good buttermilk down there.

$^{1}/_{3}$ cup (80 ml) water

$^{2}/_{3}$ cup (130 g) sugar

1 lemon, preferably unsprayed

2 cups (500 ml) buttermilk

$^{1}/_{4}$ cup (60 ml) freshly squeezed lemon juice (from about 2 lemons)

In a medium, nonreactive saucepan, mix the water and sugar. Grate the zest of the lemon directly into the saucepan. Heat, stirring frequently, until the sugar is dissolved. Remove from the heat and let stand until the syrup reaches room temperature, then chill thoroughly in the refrigerator.

Whisk the buttermilk into the syrup, then whisk in the lemon juice. Freeze in your ice cream maker according to the manufacturer's instructions.

PERFECT PAIRING: Lemon-Buttermilk Sherbet is pretty and delicious resting on a pool of Creamy Caramel Sauce (page 170).

Pink Grapefruit-Champagne Sorbet

Way back when, long before svelte supermodels made it chic to do so, relatives of mine would make their annual winter pilgrimage to sunny Miami Florida for relaxation and, God willing, a bit of a *schvitz*. A week later we'd greet a deeply bronzed Uncle Myron and Aunt Sophie at the airport, and they'd invariably be schlepping mesh nylon sacks bulging with yellow-skinned grapefruits, a bit of sunshine for those of us without the chutzpah to escape the dreary Northeast winter.

Nowadays grapefruits are everywhere, but they're at their best during the dead of winter. Choose fruits that are heavy for their size, with ends that are a bit flat, an indication they'll be juicy and sweet.

1⅓ cups (330 ml) Champagne or sparkling wine

1 cup (100 g) sugar

2½ cups (625 ml) freshly squeezed pink grapefruit juice
(from about 3 grapefruits)

In a medium, nonreactive saucepan, heat about half of the Champagne with the sugar, stirring frequently, until the sugar is completely dissolved. Remove from the heat and stir in the remaining Champagne and the grapefruit juice.

Chill the mixture thoroughly, then freeze it in your ice cream maker according to the manufacturer's instructions.

PERFECT PAIRING: Although lots of other fruit granitas go well with Pink Grapefruit-Champagne Sorbet, Raspberry Granita (page 157) makes the most stunning complement.

Chocolate-Tangerine Sorbet

There are folks who can't imagine dessert without chocolate, while others aren't happy unless they get something with citrus. Sometimes I can't decide which I feel like. Am I in the mood for something citrusy? Or am I having a chocolate craving that needs to be satisfied? Here's a happy truce that marries the two flavors in perfect harmony and is guaranteed to please everyone.

1½ cups (375 ml) water

¾ cup (150 g) sugar

6 ounces (170 g) bittersweet or semisweet chocolate, finely chopped

1½ cups (375 ml) freshly squeezed tangerine juice
(from 6 to 8 tangerines, depending on variety)

In a medium, nonreactive saucepan, heat the water and sugar, stirring frequently, until the sugar is completely dissolved. Remove from the heat.

Add the chocolate and whisk until it's melted. Whisk in the tangerine juice. Purée the mixture in a blender until smooth.

Chill the mixture thoroughly, then freeze it in your ice cream maker according to the manufacturer's instructions.

PERFECT PAIRINGS: Almond Butterscotch Cookie Cups (page 227) are good vessels for Chocolate-Tangerine Sorbet. Drizzle a bit of Lean Chocolate Sauce (page 165) over the top, or serve with Candied Citrus Peel (page 178) made with orange zest.

Tangerine Sorbet

MAKES ABOUT 1 QUART (1 LITER)

It's easy to forget that citrus fruits do have a specific season, since they seem abundant all year round. The major exception is tangerines, which are rarely seen except during the winter. My favorite varieties for making this sorbet are the oddly shaped tangelos, whose juice is mischievously tart, and the mottled honey tangerines, whose coarse, funky exterior belies the bright-colored and exceptionally sweet juice within.

> 3 cups (750 ml) freshly squeezed tangerine juice
> (from about 12 to 15 tangerines, depending on size)
>
> ¾ cup (150 g) sugar
>
> 1 tangerine, preferably unsprayed

Mix about ½ cup (125 ml) of the tangerine juice with the sugar in a small, nonreactive saucepan. Warm over low heat until the sugar is dissolved, then stir the syrup into the remaining 2½ cups (625 ml) tangerine juice in a medium bowl. Zest the tangerine into the mixture.

Chill the mixture thoroughly, then freeze it in your ice cream maker according to the manufacturer's instructions.

PERFECT PAIRINGS: Mixed Berry Coulis (page 181) served alongside Tangerine Sorbet makes for a truly eye-popping, colorful dessert, or try the sorbet with a scattering of French Almonds (page 189).

Mocha Sherbet

MAKES ABOUT 1 QUART (1 LITER)

This frozen delight is perfect in the summer when you need a brisk perk-me-up. It combines two of my favorite flavors, coffee and chocolate, in one scoop.

2¼ cups (560 ml) strongly brewed coffee or espresso

¾ cup (150 g) sugar

6 tablespoons (50 g) unsweetened Dutch-process cocoa powder

Pinch of salt

¾ cup (180 ml) whole milk

Whisk together the coffee, sugar, cocoa powder, and salt in a large saucepan. Bring the mixture to a boil and allow it to boil for 30 seconds, whisking constantly. Remove from the heat and stir in the milk. Chill the mixture thoroughly, then freeze it in your ice cream maker according to the manufacturer's instructions.

PERFECT PAIRING: To make a Mocha Freeze (pictured opposite), for each serving put 2 scoops of Mocha Sherbet (4 ounces, 115 g) in a blender along with ½ cup (125 ml) very strongly brewed coffee or espresso, 1½ tablespoons sugar, and 3 ice cubes. Blend until almost smooth. Pour into a glass and top with Whipped Cream (page 170).

Chocolate Sorbet

MAKES ABOUT 1 QUART (1 LITER)

This is the perfect chocolate sorbet—very rich and full of bittersweet chocolate flavor. Use a top-quality cocoa powder; it will make a huge difference. And be sure to use a large saucepan, since the mixture will bubble up as it boils.

2¼ cups (555 ml) water

1 cup (200 g) sugar

¾ cup (75 g) unsweetened Dutch-process cocoa powder

Pinch of salt

6 ounces (170 g) bittersweet or semisweet chocolate, finely chopped

½ teaspoon vanilla extract

In a large saucepan, whisk together 1½ cups (375 ml) of the water with the sugar, cocoa powder, and salt. Bring to a boil, whisking frequently. Let it boil, continuing to whisk, for 45 seconds.

Remove from the heat and stir in the chocolate until it's melted, then stir in the vanilla extract and the remaining ¾ cup (180 ml) water. Transfer the mixture to a blender and blend for 15 seconds. Chill the mixture thoroughly, then freeze it in your ice cream maker according to the manufacturer's instructions. If the mixture has become too thick to pour into your machine, whisk it vigorously to thin it out.

Apricot Sorbet

I was twenty years old when I tasted my first fresh apricot. I was baking in a restaurant in upstate New York, and one day the produce person handed me a small paper sack of dewy orange orbs. I'd eaten many a dried apricot in my lifetime but had neither seen nor tasted a fresh one, and frankly, I didn't know what to do with them. Since I had just a handful, I made one singularly gorgeous apricot tart that I kept away from prying hands (the greatest hazard for the pastry chef in any professional kitchen), slicing it carefully so eight lucky customers were able to have a taste.

My first summer in California, I was amazed at how many fresh apricots there were and thought that the stacks of crates at the market were a one-time windfall. So I started hoarding them, making as many things as I could before they disappeared forever. Or so I thought.

When next year rolled around and the cases of apricots started stacking up again, I learned that they were actually quite common and rather prolific. But to this day, when they're in season I try to use as many as I can, still mindful of how precious each and every silky-soft apricot is. And don't be put off by apricots that are so ripe they feel like they're ready to burst. That's when they're at their best.

> 2 pounds (1 kg) squishy-ripe fresh apricots (10 to 15, depending on size)
>
> 1 cup (250 ml) water
>
> 1 cup (200 g) sugar
>
> 3 drops almond or vanilla extract

Split the apricots in half, remove the pits, and cut each apricot into sixths. Cook the apricot pieces with the water in a medium, nonreactive saucepan over medium heat, covered, stirring occasionally, until cooked through, about 10 minutes. Remove from the heat and stir in the sugar. Let cool to room temperature.

Purée the mixture in a blender or food processor until smooth. Taste a spoonful, and if there are any small fibers, press the purée through a mesh strainer. Stir in the almond or vanilla extract.

Chill the mixture thoroughly, then freeze it in your ice cream maker according to the manufacturer's instructions.

PERFECT PAIRING: Turrón Ice Cream (page 66), flavored with honey and nuts, goes very nicely with the tangy taste of Apricot Sorbet.

Had a Meltdown?

If neglected in the freezer for too long, sorbets can become icy and crystallized. If this happens, simply rechurn any of the fruit sorbets in your ice cream machine, which will make them taste as good as new.

Plum-Raspberry Sorbet

MAKES ABOUT 1 QUART (1 LITER)

Plums are the last of the summer fruits to arrive, and they stay around long enough to welcome in the fall. Having a batch of this sorbet in the freezer is the perfect way to extend the warm glow of summer just a few more weeks.

> 1 pound (450 g) plums (about 8)
>
> 1 cup (250 ml) water
>
> $^2/_3$ cup (130 g) sugar
>
> $^3/_4$ cup (90 g) raspberries, fresh or frozen
>
> 1 teaspoon kirsch

Slice the plums in half and remove the pits. Cut the plums into eighths and put them in a medium, nonreactive saucepan with the water. Cover and cook over medium heat, stirring occasionally, for 8 minutes, or until tender. Remove from the heat and stir in the sugar and raspberries. Let cool, to room temperature.

Once cool, purée the mixture in a blender or food processor until smooth. If you wish, press the purée through a mesh strainer to remove the seeds. Stir in the kirsch.

Chill the mixture thoroughly, then freeze it in your ice cream maker according to the manufacturer's instructions.

PERFECT PAIRING: Serve scoops of Plum-Raspberry Sorbet in Gingersnap Ice Cream Cones (page 230).

To Seed or Not to Seed

Normally I'm a fan of leaving things as close to their natural state as possible. Yet in many of the frozen desserts with berries, I choose to strain out the seeds. Why? Much of the pleasure of eating ice creams, sorbets, and sherbets is in the smooth, creamy mouthfeel, and crunching on seeds, or getting them stuck between your teeth, can be somewhat unpleasant if there are a lot of them. Especially if you don't have a toothpick handy afterward. If you do wish to keep the seeds in your mixtures, by all means do so. Or compromise a bit by straining out half of the seeds and leaving the rest in.

Nectarine Sorbet

MAKES ABOUT 1 QUART (1 LITER)

There's a curious custom in Gascony, a region in the southwest of France known for its full-bodied red wines (its famous neighbor is Bordeaux). When they've just about finished their soup, the locals tip a little bit of the red wine from their glass into their soup bowl, mingling the wine with the last few spoonfuls of the broth.

I later discovered that this custom is equally good with a goblet of sorbet when I was scrambling to figure out a way to make this rosy nectarine sorbet a bit more special for an impromptu dinner party. I simply scooped sorbet into my guests' wine glasses at the table and let them pour in as little (or as much) red wine as they wished. It was a big success. If you have time to think ahead, prepare a big bowl of sweet, juicy berries and sliced nectarines, and let your guests add some fruit to their sorbet too.

> 6 ripe nectarines (about 2 pounds, 1 kg)
>
> $2/3$ cup (160 ml) water
>
> $3/4$ cup (150 g) sugar
>
> 1 teaspoon kirsch, or $1/4$ teaspoon freshly squeezed lemon juice

Slice the nectarines in half and remove the pits. Cut the unpeeled nectarines into small chunks and cook them with the water in a medium, nonreactive saucepan, covered, over medium heat, stirring occasionally, until they're soft and cooked through, about 10 minutes. Add a bit more water if necessary during cooking.

Remove from the heat and stir in the sugar. Let cool to room temperature. When cool, purée the mixture in a blender or food processor until smooth. Stir in the kirsch or lemon juice.

Chill the mixture thoroughly, then freeze it in your ice cream maker according to the manufacturer's instructions.

VARIATION: For Peach Sorbet, substitute 7 large, ripe peaches for the nectarines. Remove the skins prior to cutting them into chunks.

PERFECT PAIRINGS: If you like the idea of red wine with Nectarine Sorbet, pair it with the Raspberry-Rosé Sorbet (page 130), or simply serve it in goblets and pass a bottle of fruity red wine, such as Beaujolais, Brouilly, or Merlot.

Blackberry Sorbet

When I moved into my first home in San Francisco, the backyard was teeming with blackberry bushes. Blinded by greed, I was thrilled at the prospect of having as many luscious blackberries as I wanted. But as I soon learned, blackberry bushes are a mixed blessing, and for the next few years I spent many thorny weekends working to thwart the persistent shrubs from advancing and taking over my entire yard.

Luckily, the bonus was indeed lots and lots of inky blackberries all summer long. But each and every one I picked was well earned, and I still have some battle scars to prove it.

> 4 cups (450 g) blackberries, fresh or frozen
>
> I cup (250 ml) water
>
> 2/3 cup (130 g) sugar
>
> 2 teaspoons freshly squeezed lemon juice

Purée the blackberries in a blender or food processor with the water and sugar. Press the mixture through a strainer to remove the seeds. Stir in the lemon juice.

Chill the mixture thoroughly, then freeze it in your ice cream maker according to the manufacturer's instructions.

PERFECT PAIRING: Fill Meringue Nests (page 234) with Blackberry Sorbet and top with Whipped Cream (page 170) and a flurry of crisp French Almonds (page 189).

Blackberry-Lime Sorbet

You can tell a lot about people by looking in their freezer. Next time you're at a friend's house, peek in theirs and you'll discover their most hidden desires. One secret I am willing to share is that I'm hopelessly frugal and it's impossible for me to throw anything away, no matter how trivial. One day when I had lots of blackberries on hand, I pulled out one of my buried treasures, a small container of frozen lime juice left over from an overanxious lime-buying spree. I was curious about how the tart lime juice would play against the sweet blackberries. Happily, it was a great combination, and it's one secret I don't need to keep to myself. Although I recommend that you use freshly squeezed juice, frozen lime juice that you've kept well concealed is the next best thing.

¾ cup (150 g) sugar

¾ cup (180 ml) water

4 cups (450 g) blackberries, fresh or frozen

¾ cup (180 ml) freshly squeezed lime juice (from about 9 limes)

In a small saucepan, bring the sugar and water to a boil, stirring, until the sugar is dissolved. Remove from the heat and set aside to cool.

Purée the blackberries in a blender or food processor with the sugar syrup. Press the mixture through a strainer to remove the seeds, then stir the lime juice into the sweetened purée.

Chill the mixture thoroughly, then freeze it in your ice cream maker according to the manufacturer's instructions.

PERFECT PAIRING: Serve Blackberry-Lime Sorbet with a heap of Lime Granita (page 153).

Cherry Sorbet

MAKES ABOUT 1 QUART (1 LITER)

I'm insatiable when it comes to fresh cherries, and I eat pounds and pounds of them right off the stem during their ridiculously brief season, which I'm convinced is one of nature's cruelest acts. But their characteristic flavor really becomes pronounced when warmed, so I sauté them first to deepen their luxurious flavor. Be sure to start with full-flavored, very dark cherries, like plump Burlat cherries or blackish red Bings.

2 pounds (1 kg) cherries

1 cup (250 ml) water

¾ cup plus 2 tablespoons (180 g) sugar

1 teaspoon freshly squeezed lemon juice

⅛ teaspoon almond extract, or 1 teaspoon kirsch

Stem the cherries and remove the pits. In a medium, nonreactive saucepan, warm the cherries over moderate heat with the water, sugar, and lemon juice until they start becoming juicy. Cook for 10 to 15 minutes, stirring occasionally, until the cherries are very soft and cooked through. Remove from the heat and let stand until they reach room temperature.

Purée the cherries and their liquid with the almond extract or kirsch in a blender until smooth.

Chill the mixture thoroughly, then freeze it in your ice cream maker according to the manufacturer's instructions.

PERFECT PAIRINGS: Any of the other summer fruit and berry sorbets make good partners for Cherry Sorbet, including Nectarine Sorbet (page 125), Cantaloupe Sorbet (page 111), or even Banana Sorbet (page 136).

Strawberry Sorbet

MAKES ABOUT 3 CUPS (750 ML)

If you've ever gone shopping at the Fairway Market on the Upper West Side of Manhattan, you've found that the simple act of buying a good basket of strawberries has become a full-contact sport. Never in my life have I left a market with so many bumps and bruises! Next time I go, I'm wearing football gear to protect myself from the combative shoppers who wield their carts like modern-day jousting vehicles, ready to take on any and all oncoming produce shoppers who might happen to be heading toward the basket of berries they've set their sights on.

If you think this is just an East Coast phenomenon, you should visit the Berkeley Bowl, in California, where people who've just parked their Volvos with fading "Make Love, Not War" bumper stickers are more than happy to hike up their drawstring pants and trample you with their Birkenstocks while homing in on their berries.

But no matter where you live, I recommend that you take the trouble and assume all risks to find good strawberries with which to make this intensely flavored sorbet at home, where you're safe and sound.

I pound (450 g) fresh strawberries, rinsed and hulled

¾ cup (150 g) sugar

I teaspoon kirsch (optional)

I teaspoon freshly squeezed lemon juice

Pinch of salt

Slice the strawberries and toss them in a medium bowl with the sugar and kirsch, if using, stirring until the sugar begins to dissolve. Cover and let stand for 1 hour, stirring every so often.

Purée the strawberries and their liquid with the lemon juice and salt in a blender or food processor until smooth. Press the mixture through a strainer to remove the seeds if you wish.

Chill the mixture thoroughly, then freeze it in your ice cream maker according to the manufacturer's instructions.

PERFECT PAIRING: Strawberry Sorbet goes well with Plum-Berry Compote. For 6 servings, slice I pound (450 g) purple-skinned plums in half and remove the pits. Cut each plum into 8 slices. Bring I cup (250 ml) water and ¼ cup (50 g) sugar to a boil in a medium, nonreactive saucepan. Add the plum slices, reduce the heat, and simmer for 5 minutes. Remove from the heat and add I cup (115 g) fresh or frozen raspberries, blackberries, or blueberries. Cover and let stand until cooled to room temperature. Serve the compote with a scoop of Strawberry Sorbet.

Strawberry-Rhubarb Sorbet

One of the funniest (albeit most excruciating) things I've ever seen was a video-taped appearance of a cookbook author making a rhubarb pie on a live morning television show. Just as the cameras began rolling, the cocky, self-assured host looked at his guest and blurted out, "I hate rhubarb. I mean, I *really* hate it."

The poor dear continued to make her rhubarb pie, but it was easy to see that his constant grousing was taking its toll on her as she baked, bantered, and defended her delicious-looking pie for a few painful on-air minutes.

If it were me, I would have taken a different approach. With the cameras rolling, I would have ordered him out of the studio and pulled another person into the kitchen who looked forward to the first rhubarb in the spring with the same anticipation that I do. Look for stalks that are bright red, which will make the most enticingly colored sorbet. The flavor of the gently stewed ruhubarb with fresh strawberries will remind you why this combination is so beloved by almost everyone, including me.

12 ounces (325 g) rhubarb

²/₃ cup (160 ml) water

¾ cup (150 g) sugar

10 ounces (280 g) fresh strawberries, rinsed and hulled

½ teaspoon freshly squeezed lemon juice

Wash the rhubarb stalks and trim the stem and leaf ends. Cut the rhubarb into ½-inch (2-cm) pieces.

Place the rhubarb, water, and sugar in a medium, nonreactive saucepan and bring to a boil. Reduce the heat, cover, and simmer for 5 minutes, or until the rhubarb is tender and cooked through. Remove from the heat and let cool to room temperature.

Slice the strawberries and purée them with the cooked rhubarb mixture and lemon juice in a blender or food processor until smooth.

Chill the mixture thoroughly, then freeze it in your ice cream maker according to the manufacturer's instructions.

PERFECT PAIRING: To make a lovely Red Wine-Poached Rhubarb Compote that goes beautifully with this sorbet, use cookbook author Susan Loomis's recipe: for 6 servings, cut 1 pound (450 g) rhubarb into green bean–sized strips. In a nonreactive saucepan, combine 2 cups (500 ml) red wine, ½ cup (100 g) sugar, 1 tablespoon honey, 1 cinnamon stick, and a pinch of ground cloves. Bring to a boil, then simmer until the wine is reduced by about one-third. Serve a scoop of Strawberry-Rhubarb Sorbet in the middle.

Raspberry-Rosé Sorbet

Creating a whole book with lots of recipes for sorbets means that you run the risk of using the word "refreshing" too often. But this sorbet is truly the most refreshing of them all, so I saved that word to describe it. Each bite is pure, frosty bliss.

I use a rosé wine that's not too sweet, with a touch of fruitiness. You could use almost any blush wine that leans toward the dry side as well, though in saying so I risk losing cred in the eyes of wine lovers and oenophiles. Because of the quantity of wine in this sorbet, it will not freeze very firmly in your ice cream machine and will be somewhat soft when you scrape it out. But don't worry. When you go to serve it a few hours later, you'll find that it's the perfect texture, and yes, very refreshing.

> 2 cups (500 ml) rosé wine
>
> 2/3 cup (130 g) sugar
>
> 3 cups (340 g) raspberries, fresh or frozen

In a medium, nonreactive saucepan, bring the rosé and sugar to a boil. Remove from the heat, add the raspberries, and let cool to room temperature. Pass the mixture through a food mill fitted with a fine disk, or purée in a blender or food processor and then press the purée through a strainer to remove the seeds.

Chill the mixture thoroughly, then freeze it in your ice cream maker according to the manufacturer's instructions.

VARIATION: To make Strawberry-Rosé Sorbet, substitute 1 pound (450 g) fresh strawberries, rinsed, hulled, and sliced, for the raspberries. Press the mixture through a strainer to remove the seeds.

PERFECT PAIRING: Raspberry-Rosé Sorbet is so perfect on its own that you should resist serving it with anything except a handful of luscious raspberries.

Raspberry Sherbet

MAKES ABOUT 1 QUART (1 LITER)

The flavor of raspberries is so intense that they can simply be blended with milk and sugar and made into this sumptuous, full-flavored sherbet. The mixture is best frozen right after you've blended together the ingredients, which preserves the vivid taste of the raspberries.

  4 cups (450 g) raspberries, fresh or frozen

  2 cups (500 ml) whole milk

  1 cup (200 g) sugar

  1¹/₂ teaspoons freshly squeezed lemon juice

Put the raspberries in a blender or food processor, along with the milk and sugar. Purée until smooth, then strain the mixture to remove the seeds. Stir in the lemon juice.

Freeze the mixture in your ice cream maker according to the manufacturer's instructions.

PERFECT PAIRING: White Chocolate Ice Cream (page 31) or Fresh Apricot Ice Cream (page 76) make good partners for Raspberry Sherbet.

Raspberry-Champagne Sorbet

MAKES ABOUT 2 CUPS (500 ML)

Although the official title of this recipe is Raspberry-*Champagne* Sorbet, I invite you to improvise, and economize, by substituting a sparkly cava from Spain or a prosecco from Italy, which provide an equally lively sparkle. Have a tasting (and invite me!) and find one that you like. Here's a tip: The one in the black bottle is a good budget option.

Note that this recipe makes a small quantity, as the sorbet is better when it's soft and freshly churned, and doesn't improve with age. If you're expecting lots of guests or just have a big appetite, simply double the recipe.

  1¹/₄ cups (310 ml) Champagne or sparkling wine

  ¹/₄ cup (60 ml) water

  ¹/₂ cup (100 g) sugar

  2 cups (220 g) raspberries, fresh or frozen

Mix the Champagne, water, and sugar in a medium, nonreactive saucepan. Bring to a boil. Add the raspberries, remove from the heat, and cover. Let stand for 10 minutes.

Pass the mixture through a food mill with a fine disk, or press it firmly through a mesh strainer with a flexible rubber spatula. Discard the seeds.

Chill the mixture thoroughly, then freeze it in your ice cream maker according to the manufacturer's instructions.

PERFECT PAIRINGS: A pool of White Chocolate Sauce (page 167) underneath makes Raspberry-Champagne Sorbet a bit more festive. You also can't go wrong pairing it with colorful Peach Ice Cream (page 89) or Passion Fruit Ice Cream (page 94).

Fleur de Lait

MAKES ABOUT 1 QUART (1 LITER)

My lifelong dream is to own an ice cream shop. But rather than start from scratch, there's one in Paris that I used to dream of taking over: Raimo. The interior was a perfectly preserved midcentury ice cream parlor, with curved, undulating ceilings, shiny leather-and-chrome swivel chairs, and a truly contemporary touch for a city as old as Paris—a machine dispensing ice water. *Très moderne.*

In spite of an unfortunate recent remodel, Raimo still serves an unusual frozen *glace* called *fleur de lait*, which means "flower of milk." Although they once invited me into the workshop for a tasting, I was too intimidated to ask for the recipe. So I played around in my kitchen and got it just right by using cornstarch instead of eggs, which not only preserves the milky whiteness of the cream and milk but also adds a pleasing richness that's not overwhelming. If you ever come to Paris, stop in at Raimo. And if you see me behind the counter churning away, you'll know I'm no longer just a contented customer but a happier *glacier*.

> 2 cups (500 ml) whole milk
>
> ¾ cup (150 g) sugar
>
> Pinch of salt
>
> 3 tablespoons (25 g) cornstarch
>
> 1 cup (250 ml) heavy cream

Warm the milk with the sugar and salt in a medium saucepan. Whisk together the cornstarch and cold heavy cream until dissolved, and stir it into the milk.

Heat the mixture, stirring constantly, until it begins to boil and bubble up. Reduce the heat and simmer for 2 minutes, continuing to stir. Remove from the heat and scrape it into a bowl. Chill thoroughly in the refrigerator, stirring the mixture occasionally as it cools. Once well-chilled, whisk to remove any lumps, then freeze the mixture in your ice cream maker according to the manufacturer's instructions.

PERFECT PAIRING: Try sandwiching Fleur de Lait between Oatmeal Ice Cream Sandwich Cookies (page 226).

Leche Merengada

Should you ever find yourself in Spain, withering away during the fierce heat of summer, rejuvenate with the locals at one of the many *heladerías* that make the country a top destination for any ice cream aficionado. I always order *leche merengada*, a cinnamon-and-lemon-flavored frozen meringue. To make it more invigorating, I sometimes ask for a shot of high-strength *café exprés* poured over.

> 2 cups (500 ml) whole milk
>
> 1/2 cup (100 g) sugar
>
> Pinch of salt
>
> Two 3-inch cinnamon sticks, or 1/8 teaspoon ground cinnamon
>
> 1 lemon, preferably unsprayed
>
> 2 large egg whites, at room temperature (see Note)

Heat the milk in a medium, nonreactive saucepan with 6 tablespoons (75 g) of the sugar, salt, and the cinnamon sticks or ground cinnamon. Zest the lemon directly into the saucepan. Once the mixture is warm and the sugar has dissolved, remove from the heat, transfer to a bowl, and chill thoroughly.

In a large metal or glass bowl, beat the egg whites with an electric mixer or by hand until they form soft peaks. Whip in the remaining 2 tablespoons sugar and continue to beat until the whites are stiff and glossy. Remove the cinnamon sticks, if using, and fold the cold milk mixture into the meringue, using a flexible rubber spatula.

Freeze in your ice cream maker according to the manufacturer's instructions. Leche Merengada will take longer to freeze than a traditional ice cream or sorbet. You can also simply freeze it in the mixing bowl, checking it after an hour in the freezer and beating it with a flexible rubber spatula occasionally while it's freezing.

NOTE: This recipe calls for uncooked egg whites. Most supermarkets now carry pasteurized egg whites, which you may wish to use if you have health concerns. Be sure to read the packaging, since some pasteurized egg whites aren't suitable for whipping.

PERFECT PAIRINGS: Pour a shot of very strong espresso over the top, or serve Leche Merengada with Espresso Granita (page 146) shaved over the top (pictured opposite).

Banana-Blueberry Sorbet

MAKES ABOUT 1 QUART (1 LITER)

When I was a professional baker, foodies would walk into the kitchen, look down their noses at my gorgeous flats of cultivated blueberries, and sneer, "Oh, I only like wild blueberries." Then they'd stand there making idle chat while grabbing fistfuls of domestic blueberries and gobbling them up.

Wild blueberries are indeed wonderful, but they can be hard to find (unlike annoying food snobs), so you can use any kind of blueberry here. Just don't gobble them all up, or let anyone else do so, before you get a chance to use them.

> 1 medium-sized ripe banana, peeled
>
> 2 cups (360 g) blueberries, fresh or frozen
>
> ¾ cup (180 ml) water
>
> ½ cup (100 g) sugar
>
> 1 tablespoon freshly squeezed lemon or lime juice

Cut the banana into chunks and purée in a blender or food processor with the blueberries, water, sugar, and lemon or lime juice until smooth and few discernible bits of blueberry skins remain.

Chill the mixture thoroughly, then freeze it in your ice cream maker according to the manufacturer's instructions.

VARIATION: To make Banana-Blackberry Sorbet, substitute 2 cups (240 g) fresh or frozen blackberries for the blueberries.

PERFECT PAIRING: Make a fruit salad combining pineapple, tangerines, bananas, and any available berries, tossing the fruits with a bit of sugar and dark rum. Serve with a scoop of Banana-Blueberry Sorbet.

Banana Sorbet

MAKES ABOUT 1 QUART (1 LITER)

This sorbet should be frozen right after it's mixed to preserve the fresh flavor and color of the bananas. They should be very ripe. If you want to add a spoonful or more of dark rum to taste, feel free to do so. One of my testers, Joanna, mentioned that this was the most budget-friendly dessert she'd ever made.

> 4 medium-sized ripe bananas, peeled
>
> 1 cup (250 ml) water
>
> ¾ cup (150 g) sugar
>
> 2 teaspoons freshly squeezed lime juice

Cut the bananas into chunks and purée them in a blender or food processor with the water, sugar, and lime juice until smooth.

Freeze in your ice cream maker according to the manufacturer's instructions.

PERFECT PAIRINGS: Icy Espresso Granita (page 146) or Mocha Sherbet (page 120) is an excellent accompaniment, as is a garnish of Candied Pineapple (page 177).

Pineapple Sorbet

MAKES ABOUT 3 CUPS (750 ML)

Once upon a time, before the advent of mass transportation, only the rich were privileged enough to taste pineapples. They became a status symbol, meaning that one had great wealth and enjoyed much prosperity if one was able to afford them. Nowadays, fresh pineapples are available just about everywhere, and few of us have to deprive ourselves of enjoying a juicy, sweet pineapple whenever we want. Now that's my idea of progress.

To peel a fresh pineapple, use a knife to lop off the bottom and the top. Cut away the skin and pry out any "eyes" with the tip of a vegetable peeler. Then cut the pineapple flesh into quarters and remove the tough inner core.

$^1/_2$ pineapple, peeled and cored (2 cups, 500 ml purée)

8 to 10 tablespoons (100 to 130 g) sugar

$^1/_2$ cup (125 ml) water

Cut the pineapple into chunks and purée in a blender with 8 tablespoons (100 g) sugar and the water until smooth. Taste, then add up to 2 tablespoons additional sugar, if desired.

Chill the mixture thoroughly, then freeze it in your ice cream maker according to the manufacturer's instructions.

PERFECT PAIRING: You can make Pineapple Popsicles by reducing the sugar to 2 tablespoons, pouring the mixture into plastic popsicle molds, and freezing until firm.

Can I Use Canned?

Although fresh pineapples are readily available, some people prefer the convenience of using canned pineapple. If you wish to do so, choose a brand that's unsweetened and packed in its own juice, not in heavy or light sugar syrup. Purée the fruit and the juice in a blender until smooth, then simply measure out the amount of pineapple purée called for in the recipe.

Pineapple-Champagne Sorbet

I'll bet Dom Pérignon, the monk who is often given credit for inventing Champagne, would be turning over in his grave if he knew I had mixed his fizzy elixir with pineapple. But I'm sure I'd have his blessing if he tasted how good this combination is.

> ½ pineapple, peeled and cored (2 cups, 500 ml purée)
>
> 6 tablespoons (75 g) sugar
>
> ½ cup (125 ml) Champagne or sparkling wine

Cut the pineapple into chunks and purée in a blender with the sugar until smooth. Stir in the Champagne.

Chill the mixture thoroughly, then freeze it in your ice cream maker according to the manufacturer's instructions.

PERFECT PAIRING: Serve in goblets, with a festive pour of Champagne or sparkling wine.

Piña Colada Sherbet

MAKES ABOUT 1½ QUARTS (1½ LITERS)

If I was stranded on a deserted tropical island and could have only one dessert, this would be my choice. Admittedly, it would likely be my only choice, since all the ingredients are native to the tropics.

> 1 pineapple, peeled and cored (4 cups, 1 liter purée)
>
> 1 cup (200 g) sugar
>
> 1 cup (250 ml) Thai coconut milk (see Note)
>
> 1 tablespoon dark rum
>
> 1 teaspoon freshly squeezed lime juice

Cut the pineapple into chunks. Purée in a blender with the sugar, coconut milk, rum, and lime juice until smooth. Chill the mixture thoroughly, then freeze it in your ice cream maker according to the manufacturer's instructions.

NOTE: Thai coconut milk can be found in well-stocked supermarkets or Asian markets. Do not substitute Coco López, which is heavily sweetened.

Tropical Fruit Sorbet

MAKES ABOUT 1 QUART (1 LITER)

If you don't have fresh passion fruit or pulp, make do by adding more tangerine juice. But I do advise looking around for it (see Resources, page 237), since its unmistakable flavor gives this sorbet an authentic taste of the tropics.

> 2 medium-sized ripe bananas, peeled
>
> 1/2 pineapple, peeled and cored (2 cups, 500 ml purée)
>
> 3/4 cup (180 ml) freshly squeezed tangerine or orange juice (from about 4 to 6 tangerines or oranges)
>
> 1/4 cup (60 ml) passion fruit juice or pulp (or substitute tangerine juice)
>
> 1 cup (200 g) sugar
>
> 4 teaspoons dark rum
>
> 1 teaspoon freshly squeezed lime juice

Cut the bananas and pineapples into small chunks. Purée the fruit in a blender, along with the orange or tangerine juice, passion fruit juice or pulp (if using), sugar, rum, and lime juice until very smooth.

Chill the mixture thoroughly, then freeze it in your ice cream maker according to the manufacturer's instructions.

Kiwifruit Sorbet

MAKES ABOUT 1 QUART (1 LITER)

Kiwis are people from New Zealand. Kiwifruits are the emerald green fruits that we consume. The difference is important to New Zealanders, who are apt to look somewhat terrified if you present them with a bowl of sorbet and proudly tell them is made from fresh kiwis.

> 2 pounds (1 kg) ripe kiwifruits (10 to 15)
>
> 3/4 cup (150 g) sugar
>
> 1 1/3 cups (330 ml) water

Peel the kiwifruits and pluck out the woody nubbins within the stem ends, using the point of a paring knife. Cut the kiwifruits into chunks and purée them in a blender or food processor (you'll should have 2 cups, or 500 ml, of purée). Add the sugar and water and blend until smooth. Chill the mixture thoroughly, then freeze it in your ice cream maker according to the manufacturer's instructions.

Papaya-Lime Sorbet

Cutting up a papaya can be a rather messy affair, with the dark, slippery seeds spilling all over the place. I always eat a few of them, which I call the caviar of the fruit world. Try a few; you'll find they're quite spicy and peppery.

If possible, choose a brilliant orange variety of papaya. I find Latin American markets usually have the widest selection, with the best coming from Central America or Hawaii. Sometimes you'll find giant papayas cut into small pieces, which gives you a good chance to check out the color of the flesh beforehand.

> 2 pounds (1 kg) papayas (about 2 small papayas)
>
> 2/3 cup (130 g) sugar
>
> 1/4 cup (60 ml) water
>
> 1/4 cup (60 ml) freshly squeezed lime juice (from about 3 limes)
>
> Pinch of salt

Cut the papayas in half and remove the seeds with a spoon. Peel the papayas and cut them into chunks. Put the papaya pieces in a blender along with the sugar, water, lime juice, and salt, and purée the mixture until completely smooth.

Chill the mixture thoroughly, then freeze it in your ice cream maker according to the manufacturer's instructions.

PERFECT PAIRING: Add lots of shavings of Lime Granita (page 153) to a dish of Papaya-Lime Sorbet, drizzle with a bit of dark rum, and top with shaved Pineapple Granita (page 153).

Chocolate-Coconut Sorbet

MAKES ABOUT 1 QUART (1 LITER)

I once wanted to try my hand at making coconut milk and read that the best way to crack open a coconut is to mimic the way monkeys do it. So I went out to my driveway, lifted my coconut high above my head, and sent it crashing down to the pavement.

Suddenly, I began to feel rather wet from my knees down, and I realized that the watery liquid had splashed everywhere, saturating my shoes and trousers. I suppose I should have followed those instructions more literally. Since monkeys don't wear clothing, I probably should have removed mine first. So if you see a scantily clad man hurling coconuts around in your neighborhood, don't call the police. It's probably me preparing the ingredients for this really delicious sorbet, which combines two of my favorite flavors: dark, bittersweet chocolate and sweet coconut.

On second thought, maybe I should just stick to store-bought coconut milk from now on....

> 1 cup (250 ml) water
>
> 1 cup (200 g) sugar
>
> Pinch of salt
>
> 8 ounces (230 g) bittersweet or semisweet chocolate, finely chopped
>
> 2 cups (500 ml) Thai coconut milk (see Note)
>
> $\frac{1}{2}$ teaspoon vanilla extract

Warm the water, sugar, and salt in a medium saucepan, stirring, until the sugar is dissolved. Remove from the heat. Add the chocolate pieces and whisk until the chocolate is melted. Whisk in the coconut milk and vanilla. Chill the mixture thoroughly, then freeze it in your ice cream maker according to the manufacturer's instructions. If a layer of coconut milk has firmed up on top, simply whisk in it before churning.

NOTE: Thai coconut milk can be found in well-stocked supermarkets or Asian markets. Do not substitute Coco López, which is heavily sweetened.

PERFECT PAIRINGS: Serve Chocolate-Coconut Sorbet atop a Blondie (page 222), topped with a spoonful of Dulce de Leche (page 171) or Cajeta (page 173) and some toasted shredded coconut.

4

Granitas

Italians just never seem to get enough granita. In fact, they're so fanatical about it that Sicilians are known to split open yeasted rolls during their sweltering summers and pile it inside...for breakfast! But if you want to see Italians really in a frenzy from granita, no matter what time of day, whatever the season, head to Tazza d'Oro in Rome, just across from the Pantheon. The long, curving counter is constantly abuzz with activity. Muscle your way to the front as baristas pack take-away cups full of industrial-strength espresso granita made from slick, dark espresso beans hand-roasted in the rear of the shop, often moments before brewing. It's obligatory to top if off with a big, sweet dollop of whipped cream, *con panna*, a necessary foil to the hair-raisingly strong caffeinated crystals.

Just a few blocks away is Giolitti, where locals and tourists press their noses against the overloaded freezer displaying rows and rows of stainless steel tubs filled with granitas in a hallucinogenic hodgepodge of hues and colors. There's *fragole*, made from lush, ripe strawberries, and *arancia*, made of astonishingly red blood orange pulp. Although both are tempting, there's also *frutti di bosco*, a mixture of red berries, to consider, and exotic *fichi d'India*, made from prickly pear cactus fruits. Once you elbow your way through the mob swarming the counter (a necessary skill if you expect to get served in any Roman *gelateria*), you can watch as they heap the icy crystals into a cup, top it off with an equivalent-sized drift of *panna*, and send you back out into the fray of Rome.

Granita is simply a shaved ice, made from a lightly sweetened fruit purée or another liquid. Of all the frozen desserts, granita is the simplest to make, requiring nothing more than a dish, a freezer, and a fork. Forming fine-grained icy crystals is the goal.

I find that flat plastic containers are the easiest to use for making granita, since they're lightweight and unbreakable, although you can use containers made of earthenware, porcelain, or stainless steel, as long as they're approximately 8 to 12 inches (20 to 30 cm) across, with a 2-quart (2-liter) capacity. I recommend a dish with sides that are about 2 inches (5 cm) high, to contain all the crystals.

To freeze granita, pour the mixture into the dish and place in the freezer. Begin checking it after about 1 hour. Once it begins to freeze around the edges, take a fork and stir the mixture, breaking up the frozen parts near the edges into smaller chunks and raking them toward the center.

Return the dish to the freezer, then check the mixture every 30 minutes afterward, stirring each time and breaking up any large chunks into small pieces with a fork, until you have beautiful, fine crystals of homemade granita. If at any time the granita freezes too hard, simply leave it out at room temperature for a few minutes until it softens enough to be stirred again with a fork, and rake it back into crystals. Then return it to the freezer.

Once frozen, the icy crystals are delightfully good spooned over any kind of ice cream or sorbet that you find makes an appealing combination. Or simply pile crystals of granita into a cup, top it off with sweetened whipped cream, as much as you dare, and dig in.

Most of the recipes in this chapter make about 1 quart (1 liter) of granita. But unlike ice creams or sorbets, which tend to be more compact and richer, a quart of granita will serve only about four people for dessert. Feel free to increase the recipes if you're having more guests.

Espresso Granita

This granita is a favorite in Italy, where they top it with what seems like an unspeakable amount of whipped cream, which I see many Americans scraping off just after they walk out the door—to the shock of passing Italians. You don't need to heap it on quite as high, but a dollop of Whipped Cream (page 170) is always a welcome, and sometimes necessary, counterpoint to the strong coffee.

4 cups (1 liter) warm espresso or very strongly brewed, top-quality coffee

1½ cups (300 g) sugar

Mix the warm espresso with the sugar until the sugar is dissolved. Freeze according to the instructions for freezing granita on page 145.

Chocolate Granita

If you're looking for a chocolate dessert that's fudgy and festive without being fussy and filling, here it is. Using a top-quality cocoa powder and just the right amount of dark chocolate ensures that this granita will satisfy any and all chocolate lovers.

4 cups (1 liter) water

1 cup (200 g) sugar

Pinch of salt

⅔ cup (70 g) unsweetened Dutch-process cocoa powder

4 ounces (115 g) bittersweet or semisweet chocolate, chopped

1 teaspoon vanilla extract

In a large saucepan, whisk together the water, sugar, salt, and cocoa powder. Bring to a full boil and continue to boil, stirring occasionally, for 15 seconds. Remove from the heat and add the chocolate. Stir the mixture until the chocolate is completely melted, then add the vanilla. Freeze according to the instructions for freezing granita on page 145.

PERFECT PAIRINGS: Spoon crystals of Chocolate Granita over White Chocolate Ice Cream (page 33) or in contrast to a dish of Tangerine Sorbet (page 119).

Plum Granita

MAKES ABOUT 1 QUART (1 LITER)

One of the best-tasting plums for cooking and eating is the Santa Rosa plum. Their meaty, succulent yellow flesh contrasts in color and flavor with the tangy purple skin. When cooked together, the sweet-tart flavors meld perfectly to make a heavenly granita. If you find it a bit too tart, serve it with a dollop of Whipped Cream (page 170).

> 1½ pounds (675 g) plums (about 12)
>
> 1¾ cups (430 ml) water
>
> ½ cup (100 g) sugar

Slice the plums in half and remove the pits. Cut each plum into 8 pieces and put them in a medium, nonreactive saucepan with the water. Cover and cook over medium heat, stirring occasionally, for 8 minutes, or until tender. Remove from the heat and stir in the sugar until dissolved. Let cool to room temperature.

Once the mixture is cool, purée it in a blender or food processor until smooth. Freeze according to the instructions for freezing granita on page 145.

Nectarine Granita

MAKES ABOUT 1 QUART (1 LITER)

Nectarines make a particularly enticing summertime granita that definitely merits precious freezer space as the temperature climbs. I patiently wait and wait for the first of the sweetest-smelling nectarines to appear, and then *bang*—I hit the markets, buying as many as I can. Try serving this granita surrounded by a mixture of raspberries, blueberries, and sliced strawberries sweetened with a touch of honey.

> 6 ripe nectarines (about 2 pounds, 1 kg)
>
> 1⅓ cups (330 ml) water
>
> ½ cup (100 g) sugar

Slice the nectarines in half and remove the pits. Cut the unpeeled nectarines into small chunks and cook them with 1 cup (250 ml) of the water in a medium, nonreactive saucepan over medium heat, covered, stirring occasionally, until they're soft and cooked through, about 10 minutes.

Remove from the heat and stir in the sugar. Let cool to room temperature. When cool, purée the mixture in a blender or food processor with the remaining ⅓ cup (80 ml) water until smooth. Freeze according to the instructions for freezing granita on page 145.

VARIATION: To make Peach Granita, substitute 6 large peaches for the nectarines. Peel the peaches before cooking.

Champagne-Cassis Granita

Inspired by the classic Kir Royale, this granita (pictured opposite) makes a similarly elegant after-dinner dessert. Because of the quantity of Champagne in this recipe, it takes bit longer to freeze than other granitas.

$^1/_2$ cup (100 g) sugar

1$^1/_2$ cups (375 ml) water

2 cups (500 ml) Champagne or sparkling wine

$^1/_3$ cup (80 ml) crème de cassis (black currant liqueur)

In a medium, nonreactive saucepan, heat the sugar and water until the sugar is completely dissolved. Remove from the heat and add the Champagne. Stir in the crème de cassis. Freeze according to the instructions for freezing granita on page 145.

NOTE: Since this granita may melt rapidly, I suggest spooning it into chilled goblets and letting them rest in the freezer until you're ready to serve.

PERFECT PAIRING: Although Champagne-Cassis Granita is delicious just as it is, a scoop of Raspberry-Champágne Sorbet (page 132) at the bottom of the glass is an elegant touch.

Strawberry Granita

Serve the delicate, rosy crystals of this granita with a pour of sparkling wine, making a rather sophisticated slushie. Or perfume it with a few drops of fragrant rosewater sprinkled over to transform it into something curiously exotic and a bit elusive.

2 pounds (1 kg) fresh strawberries, rinsed and hulled

6 tablespoons (75 g) sugar

1 cup (250 ml) water

A few drops freshly squeezed lemon juice

Slice the strawberries and toss them in a large bowl with the sugar, stirring until the sugar begins to dissolve. Cover and let stand at room temperature for 1 hour, stirring every so often.

Combine the strawberries and their liquid with the water and a few drops of lemon juice in a blender or food processor and purée until smooth. Press the mixture though a strainer to remove any seeds. Freeze according to the instructions for freezing granita on page 145.

Pear Granita

MAKES ABOUT 1 QUART (1 LITER)

Choose a fragrant, tasty variety of pear for this granita, such as Comice, Bartlett, or French butter. Few people think of pairing pears with chocolate, but it's a surprisingly good combination, and once you taste it, you'll wish you'd known about it sooner. Don't hesitate to use one of my Perfect Pairings that follow the recipe to make up for lost time.

6 ripe pears (3 pounds, 1½ kg)

1 cup (250 ml) water

6 tablespoons (75 g) sugar

Quarter the pears, peel them, and remove the cores. Dice the pears into 1-inch (3-cm) pieces. Put them in a medium-sized, nonreactive saucepan with the water and sugar and cook over medium heat, covered, stirring occasionally, until completely soft, about 8 minutes. A knife inserted into a pear chunk should meet no resistance.

Cool to room temperature, then purée the pears and their liquid in a blender or food processor until smooth. Freeze according to the instructions for freezing granita on page 145.

PERFECT PAIRINGS: Serve Pear Granita with Chocolate Sorbet (page 120) or Chocolate Ice Cream, Philadelphia-Style (page 28).

Cranberry Granita

MAKES ABOUT 1 QUART (1 LITER)

The arrival of cranberries in the fall magically coincides with the holiday food shopping frenzy. A wonder of nature? Or just good timing? Regardless, I'm happy whenever I find cranberries in abundance. Their flavor is invigorating and restorative, which is probably why they're so popular around the time of year when many of us could use help after overindulging in copious holiday feasts.

3 cups (340 g) cranberries, fresh or frozen

1 cup (250 ml) water

1 cup (200 g) sugar

½ cup (125 ml) freshly squeezed orange juice (from about 2 oranges)

Put the cranberries, water, sugar, and orange juice in a medium, nonreactive saucepan and bring to a boil. Cover, remove from the heat, and let stand for 30 minutes.

Purée the mixture in a blender or food processor until smooth, then press through a mesh strainer to remove the bits of cranberry skin. Freeze according to the instructions for freezing granita on page 145.

PERFECT PAIRINGS: Serve with Tangerine Sorbet (page 119) or spicy Cinnamon Ice Cream (page 38).

No Separation Anxiety

To quickly separate grapes from their stems, put bunches of grapes in the bowl of a standing electric mixer. Fit the mixer with the dough hook and turn it on at the lowest speed. The hook will separate the stems easily from the grapes.

Grape Granita

MAKES ABOUT 1 QUART (1 LITER)

The best grapes to use for making this granita are bold-tasting varieties. Full-flavored dark Muscat grapes are perfect, as are Concord grapes, sometimes referred to by winemakers as tasting "foxy." Speaking of winemakers, just about any grapes used for winemaking make excellent granita. Don't use the common seedless grapes found in supermarkets, though, since they don't have much flavor once cooked.

The amount of water will depend on the type of grapes you use. Before adding the water, taste the mixture. Add the smaller amount of water, and then taste it again to see if it needs more.

> 2 pounds (1 kg) fresh grapes
>
> $2/_3$ cup (130 g) sugar
>
> $1/_2$ to 1 cup (125 to 250 ml) water
>
> A few drops freshly squeezed lemon juice

Rinse the grapes and remove them from the stems. Cut them in half if the skins are thick and tough. Cook the grapes with the sugar and $1/_2$ cup (125 ml) water in a medium-sized, nonreactive saucepan over medium heat, covered, stirring occasionally until the skins have burst and the grapes are soft and cooked through.

Pass the grapes through a food mill or press through a mesh strainer to separate the skins from the pulp. Add the lemon juice and taste, adding some or all of the remaining water if you wish. Freeze according to the instructions for freezing granita on page 145.

PERFECT PAIRINGS: Grape Granita is lovely with Mascarpone Ice Cream (page 59) or Pear Sorbet (page 110).

Lemon Granita

A few years back, while I was making a chocolate dessert during a cooking demonstration, I noticed a woman sitting in the third row was watching me with what I thought was disdain. Attempting to win her over, while everyone ate their samples I asked what she thought, and she responded matter-of-factly, "I don't really like chocolate." So smart-aleck me shot back, "You're probably one of those lemon people!" To which she sheepishly nodded yes.

I kept on baking and finished the class. But my accusatory words "one of those lemon people" stuck in my mind, and I worried for a long time that she might have been affronted by my comment.

Years later, there she was again in my audience! I was happy to see her, since experts advocate finding resolution to traumatic events in your life (like meeting someone who doesn't like chocolate). Attempting reparation, I asked if I had offended her several years back. She was surprised that I even remembered and said that no, she wasn't offended in the least. In fact, she even brought me a tasty gift (not chocolate...but I'm letting *that* go) and then slipped off into the night. So this is my gift back to her, the mysterious lemon lover, whoever and wherever you are.

2¹/₂ cups (625 ml) water

1 cup (200 g) sugar

2 lemons, preferably unsprayed

1 cup (250 ml) freshly squeezed lemon juice (from about 6 lemons)

In a medium, nonreactive saucepan, mix ¹/₂ cup (125 ml) of the water with the sugar. Grate the zest of the 2 lemons directly into the saucepan. Heat, stirring frequently, until the sugar is completely dissolved. Remove from the heat, add the remaining 2 cups (500 ml) water, and then chill in the refrigerator.

Stir the lemon juice into the sugar syrup, then freeze according to the instructions for freezing granita on page 145.

PERFECT PAIRING: Smooth and silky White Chocolate Ice Cream (page 33) makes a great counterpoint to tangy Lemon Granita.

Most of the granita recipes make excellent popsicles too (except the Champagne-Cassis Granita on page 148, which doesn't freeze quite so firmly). Simply pour the mixture into plastic popsicle molds and freeze until very firm. To remove, run the molds very briefly under warm water, then carefully slide the popsicles from the molds.

Lime Granita

Try this granita drizzled with a shot of tequila and sprinkled with a pinch of coarse salt for a Mar*granita.*

> 3 cups (750 ml) water
>
> 1 cup (200 g) sugar
>
> 2 limes, preferably unsprayed
>
> 1 cup (250 ml) freshly squeezed lime juice (from about 12 limes)

In a medium, nonreactive saucepan, mix $1/2$ cup (125 ml) of the water with the sugar. Grate the zest of 2 limes into the saucepan. Heat, stirring frequently, until the sugar is completely dissolved. Remove from the heat, add the remaining $2 1/2$ cups (625 ml) water, and then chill in the refrigerator. Stir the lime juice into the sugar syrup, then freeze according to the instructions for freezing granita on page 145.

PERFECT PAIRINGS: Lime Granita is a tropical treat with Mango Sorbet (page 108) or Avocado Ice Cream (page 95).

Pineapple Granita

Curiously, this granita really comes alive when a few grains of coarse salt are flecked over each serving. When I had friends over for a taste, they were surprised to see me salting their granita, but they quickly changed their minds when they tasted it. Try fleur de sel, hand-harvested salt crystals from France, or whisper-thin squares of Maldon salt, from England.

> 1 pineapple, peeled and cored (4 cups, 1 liter purée)
>
> 1 cup (250 ml) water
>
> $1/2$ cup (100 g) sugar
>
> 2 teaspoons freshly squeezed lime juice
>
> Pinch of salt

Cut the pineapple into small chunks and purée them in a blender or food processor with the water, sugar, lime juice, and salt until completely smooth. If you wish, press the mixture through a mesh strainer for a more fine-textured granita. Freeze according to the instructions for freezing granita on page 145.

PERFECT PAIRINGS: Serve Pineapple Granita alongside either Toasted Coconut Ice Cream (page 96) or another tropical flavor, such as Roasted Banana Ice Cream (page 72).

Mojito Granita

There's a good reason mojitos have become all the rage. Made with rum and lots of fresh mint and lime juice, this lively Cuban cocktail practically begs to be made into a terrific granita. To make it more adult, drizzle a bit of extra rum over each serving and garnish with fresh mint sprigs.

2$^1/_2$ cups (625 ml) water

$^1/_2$ cup (100 g) sugar

2 limes, preferably unsprayed

1 cup (40 g) lightly packed fresh mint leaves

$^1/_2$ cup (125 ml) freshly squeezed lime juice (from about 6 limes)

3 tablespoons (45 ml) white or light rum

Add the water and sugar to a small, nonreactive saucepan, then grate the zest from the 2 limes directly into the saucepan. Bring the mixture to a boil and cook, stirring occasionally, until the sugar is dissolved. Reserve 5 of the mint leaves, add the remaining mint to the saucepan, and remove from the heat. Cover and let stand for 8 minutes, then remove the cover and let cool to room temperature.

Once cool, strain the mixture into the container you plan to freeze the granita in, pressing firmly on the leaves to extract all the flavorful liquid. Discard the mint leaves. Stir in the lime juice and rum, then finely chop the reserved 5 mint leaves and add them as well. Freeze according to the instructions for freezing granita on page 145.

PERFECT PAIRING: If you love the refreshing taste of mint as much as I do, pair this with a scoop of Fresh Mint Ice Cream (page 99).

Pink Grapefruit Granita

MAKES ABOUT 1 QUART (1 LITER)

I know people who are grapefruit dependent. They're addicted to starting their day with half a pink grapefruit. They absolutely have to have one, and frankly, that's a little odd to me. It's not that I don't like grapefruits, and I often buy them with the intention of following in the healthy footsteps of my grapefruit-dependent friends. But the next morning I wake up and honestly can't seem to face anything but a much-needed, soothing pot of coffee and a couple of nonconfrontational slices of buttered toast.

Later in the day, those pink grapefruits become more and more appealing though, and I'll slice one in half and greedily attack the sections, slurping up the plentiful juice while perched over the sink to contain the mess from my assault. So perhaps I do have some grapefruit issues of my own, but I wait until later in the day before I succumb and take my tumble off the citrus wagon.

> 4 cups (1 liter) freshly squeezed pink grapefruit juice
> (from about 4 or 5 grapefruits)
>
> ³/₄ cup plus 2 tablespoons (180 g) sugar

In a small, nonreactive saucepan, warm ¹/₂ cup (125 ml) of the grapefruit juice with the sugar, stirring until the sugar is dissolved. Stir the syrup back into the grapefruit juice, then freeze according to the instructions for freezing granita on page 145.

PERFECT PAIRING: Serve Pink Grapefruit Granita in tall Champagne flutes with a rather dry Champagne or sparkling wine poured over the top, along with a few fresh raspberries or wild strawberries.

Blood Orange Granita

MAKES ABOUT 1 QUART (1 LITER)

I love the word *spremuta*, which means "freshly pressed orange juice" in Italian. At any *caffè*, if you order one, you'll be brought a tall, vivid red glass of juice served with a few packets of sugar and a long, slender spoon alongside. Although years ago Americans were astonished when confronted with blood orange juice, this colorful citrus fruit has become common stateside and can be found in many supermarkets and farmer's markets. When sliced open, they reveal a brilliantly colored interior, and like snowflakes, each one intrigues me, since no two seem to be colored alike. The Moro variety of blood oranges is the most intensely colored, but other varieties, like Sanguinelli and Tarocco, make remarkably colorful granita as well.

³/₄ cup plus 2 tablespoons (180 g) sugar

4 cups (1 liter) freshly squeezed blood orange juice
(from about 14 to 16 blood oranges)

4 teaspoons Grand Marnier or Triple Sec

Warm the sugar with 1 cup (250 ml) of the orange juice in a medium, nonreactive saucepan. Stir until the sugar is dissolved. Remove from the heat and add the remaining 3 cups (750 ml) orange juice and the Grand Marnier or Triple Sec. Freeze according to the instructions for freezing granita on page 145.

PERFECT PAIRINGS: Think Italian, pairing this with Rice Gelato (page 70) or Anise Ice Cream (page 36), a flavor that goes very well with this deeply flavored Blood Orange Granita.

Raspberry Granita

MAKES ABOUT 2 CUPS (500 ML)

Perhaps the most eye-popping of all the granitas, this one has a color that perfectly matches the dazzling flavor of the raspberries. If using frozen raspberries, let them thaw before you purée them.

4 cups (480 g) raspberries, fresh or frozen

1 cup (250 ml) water

¹/₄ cup (50 g) sugar

Pass the raspberries through a food mill, or purée in a food processor and press through a sieve to remove the seeds. Stir in the water and sugar, stirring until the sugar is dissolved. Freeze according to the instructions for freezing granita on page 145.

PERFECT PAIRINGS: Super Lemon Ice Cream (page 85) and Lemon-Buttermilk Sherbet (page 117) are two of my favorite pairings with Raspberry Granita.

Melon Granita

Either cantaloupe or honeydew melon makes a wonderful granita. Use the best you find at the market. Be sure to heft a few and take a sniff to find the sweetest specimen.

> 1 medium-sized melon (2 pounds, 1 kg)
>
> $^2/_3$ cup (130 g) sugar
>
> 1 teaspoon freshly squeezed lemon or lime juice
>
> $^1/_4$ cup (60 ml) water
>
> Pinch of salt

Peel the melon, split it in half, and scoop out the seeds. Cut the melon into chunks and purée in a blender or food processor with the sugar, lemon or lime juice, water, and salt until completely smooth. Freeze according to the instructions for freezing granita on page 145.

PERFECT PAIRINGS: Raspberry Ice Cream (page 93) and Raspberry Sherbet (page 132) make nice counterpoints to Melon Granita.

Kiwifruit Granita

To make the tastiest and most colorful granita, be sure to select kiwifruits that are tender and soft to the touch. They'll have the most vibrant green flesh and the fullest, most tropically tinged flavor.

> 2 pounds (1 kg) ripe kiwifruits (about 10 to 15 kiwi)
>
> $1^1/_3$ cups (330 ml) water
>
> $^3/_4$ cup (150 g) sugar

Peel the kiwifruits and remove the tough nubbins just inside the stem ends. Cut the kiwifruits into small pieces and purée in a blender or food processor with the water and sugar until smooth. Freeze according to the instructions for freezing granita on page 145.

PERFECT PAIRING: Serve Kiwifruit Granita with Tangerine Sorbet (page 119).

5

Sauces and Toppings

What would a book on ice cream be like without lots of recipes for sauces and toppings of all kinds? A perfect scoop of ice cream is great on its own, but add a ladle of sauce and you've got a full-fledged dessert. Whether you'll be serving a classic hot fudge sundae or a scoop of fresh fruit sorbet resting on a pool of vividly colored berry coulis, the recipes in this chapter are designed to give you lots of options for customizing any ice cream or sorbet as you wish.

One of life's great pleasures is spooning a homemade topping over mounds of ice cream and watching it ooze down the sides before digging in. Is there anything better than scraping warm, rich Classic Hot Fudge (page 164) off your spoon and while it mingles with cool, creamy ice cream? Is there anyone out there who doesn't like a good hot fudge sundae? But in case you're not in the mood for a full-blown sundae extravaganza, you'll also find plenty of other chocolate sauces to choose from, including a Lean Chocolate Sauce (page 165) that's so chocolaty you'll feel deprived of nothing. And if you're looking for a chocolate topping with a kick, espresso-fueled Mocha Sauce (page 166) will turbocharge any dish of ice cream into something stratospherically good.

Anyone who knows me is aware that I, as a pastry chef, hold a singular, puffy marshmallow in the same high esteem that a savory cook reserves for a rare, pricey truffle. There's nothing I enjoy more than anything made with marshmallows, and in my headstrong youth I would insist that ice cream parlors replace the whipped cream they normally served on ice cream sundaes with sticky marshmallow sauce on mine. (Unfortunately, I could never convince them to give me both.) I'm sorry, but there's no substitute for the sweet sensation of diving into billowy Marshmallow Sauce (page 168).

Because we Americans are famous for our love of butterscotch and gooey caramel, there's a Pecan-Praline Sauce (page 176) loaded with toasted nuts, and a Creamy Caramel Sauce (page 170) as well. With a nod to ice cream lovers around the world, I've also gone global, with recipes such as Candied Red Beans (page 183), Cajeta (page 173), and Dulce de Leche (page 171). I think you'll enjoy making and eating them all, no matter where you call home.

Classic Hot Fudge

A chef once asked me if all pastry chefs were crazy. To be honest, we do have that reputation, since many of us are indeed crazed perfectionists. If we get something in our minds, we're not satisfied until it's just right. When I imagined the perfect hot fudge sauce, I envisioned it being gooey, shiny, silky smooth, and full of deep, dark chocolate flavor. So I tinkered around until I came up with the perfect version of this sauce.

³/₄ cup (180 ml) heavy cream

¹/₄ cup (60 g) packed dark brown sugar

¹/₄ cup (25 g) unsweetened Dutch-process cocoa powder

¹/₂ cup (125 ml) light corn syrup

6 ounces (170 g) bittersweet or semisweet chocolate, chopped

1 tablespoon (15 g) salted butter

¹/₂ teaspoon vanilla extract

Mix the cream, brown sugar, cocoa powder, and corn syrup in a large saucepan. Bring to a boil and cook, stirring frequently, for 30 seconds.

Remove from the heat and add the chocolate and butter, stirring until melted and smooth. Stir in the vanilla. Serve warm.

STORAGE: This sauce can be stored in the refrigerator for up to 2 weeks. Rewarm it gently in a microwave or by stirring in a saucepan over very low heat.

Semisweet Hot Fudge

This sauce is very rich and very thick. If you prefer your hot fudge on the sweeter side, this is the one for you.

1 cup (250 ml) heavy cream

6 tablespoons (85 g) unsalted butter, cut into pieces

2 tablespoons light corn syrup

²/₃ cup (130 g) sugar

8 ounces (230 g) bittersweet or semisweet chocolate, chopped

1 teaspoon vanilla extract

Heat the cream, butter, corn syrup, and sugar in a large saucepan until it begins to boil. Boil for 3 minutes, stirring occasionally, making sure it doesn't boil over.

Remove from the heat and add the chocolate pieces, stirring until melted and smooth. Stir in the vanilla. Serve warm.

STORAGE: This sauce can be stored in the refrigerator for up to 2 weeks. Rewarm it gently in a microwave or by stirring in a saucepan over very low heat.

Lean Chocolate Sauce

MAKES 3 CUPS (750 ML)

This is my favorite all-purpose chocolate sauce. Although the name says lean, it tastes anything but. It's a wonderful alternative to richer chocolate sauces spiked with cream or butter, and gets its flavor from lots of chocolate and cocoa powder (an important reason to use the best you can find). This sauce gets gloriously thicker the longer it sits, which I find makes a reasonable excuse for keeping a batch on hand in the refrigerator at all times.

> 2 cups (500 ml) water
>
> 1 cup (100 g) unsweetened Dutch-process cocoa powder
>
> 1 cup (250 ml) light corn syrup
>
> 4 ounces (115 g) bittersweet or semisweet chocolate, chopped

Whisk the water, cocoa powder, and corn syrup together in a saucepan and bring to a boil. Reduce the heat to very low and simmer for 3 minutes, stirring frequently. Remove from the heat and add the chocolate pieces, stirring until melted and smooth. Serve warm.

STORAGE: This sauce can be stored in the refrigerator for up to 2 weeks. Rewarm it gently in a microwave or by stirring in a saucepan over very low heat.

Mocha Sauce

MAKES 2 CUPS (500 ML)

The coffee craze shows no sign of slowing down. And fueled by all that caffeine, it probably never will. This sauce combines coffee and chocolate into mocha, named after an Arabian port famous for its coffee. Somewhere along the line, chocolate got added, and "mocha" nowadays means coffee fortified with a good dose of chocolate.

1 cup (250 ml) espresso or strongly brewed coffee

3/4 cup (150 g) sugar

1/2 cup (50 g) unsweetened Dutch-process cocoa powder

2 ounces (60 g) bittersweet or semisweet chocolate, chopped

4 tablespoons (60 g) butter, salted or unsalted, cut into pieces

Whisk the espresso, sugar, and cocoa powder together in a medium saucepan and bring to a boil. Let the sauce cook at a low boil for 30 seconds without stirring.

Remove from the heat and whisk in the chocolate pieces and butter, stirring until melted and smooth. Let the sauce stand for at least 1 hour before serving.

STORAGE: This sauce can be stored in the refrigerator for up to 2 weeks. Rewarm it gently in a microwave or by stirring in a saucepan over very low heat.

Marshmallow-Hot Fudge Sauce

MAKES 2 CUPS (500 ML)

This decadently thick sauce is perfect if you're nostalgic for the incredibly thick hot fudge sauce served in old-fashioned ice cream parlors, many of which are disappearing. I was inspired to use airy marshmallows (which hopefully won't be disappearing anytime soon) as a foundation by the sauce served at Edy's, a well-loved ice cream fountain in Berkeley, California, that (sadly) no longer exists.

Warning: This sauce is very, very thick!

2/3 cup (160 ml) milk (whole or low-fat)

2 tablespoons (30 g) salted butter

30 large marshmallows (185 g)

8 ounces (230 g) bittersweet or semisweet chocolate, finely chopped

1/4 teaspoon vanilla extract

Warm the milk and butter in a medium saucepan. Add the marshmallows and cook over low heat, stirring constantly, until they've melted. Remove from the heat and add the chocolate pieces. Let stand for 30 seconds, then stir until smooth. Add the vanilla. Serve warm.

STORAGE: This sauce can be stored in the refrigerator for up to 2 weeks. Rewarm it gently in a microwave or by stirring in a saucepan over very low heat. If the sauce becomes too thick, stir in a few spoonfuls of milk.

White Chocolate Sauce

MAKES 2 CUPS (500 ML)

This sauce is easy to put together and is lovely served with any of the dark chocolate ice creams or sorbets in this book. I appreciate it for its creamy sweetness, and it rarely fails to impress. Be sure to use top-quality, real white chocolate, which is actually ivory colored, due to an abundance of pure cocoa butter.

1¼ cups (310 ml) heavy cream

10 ounces (280 g) white chocolate, finely chopped

Warm the cream in a small saucepan. Once it's hot but not boiling, remove it from the heat and stir in the white chocolate until it is completely melted and the sauce is smooth. Serve warm or at room temperature.

STORAGE: This sauce can be stored in the refrigerator for up to 5 days. Rewarm it gently in a double boiler or in a microwave oven. If the sauce gets too thick, thin it out with a tablespoon or two of whole milk.

VARIATIONS: For White Chocolate and Vanilla Bean Sauce, stir in 3/4 teaspoon ground vanilla beans or 1 teaspoon vanilla bean paste.

To make White Chocolate-Chartreuse Sauce, add 1 tablespoon green Chartreuse liqueur.

Marshmallow Sauce

I love sticky marshmallow sauce perhaps more than anything else on earth. When it's spooned over a hot fudge sundae, the combination sends me skyward to heaven. Make it for yourself and see what all the fuss is about.

This sauce must be made just before serving, as it doesn't hold well. But it never lasts long around my house, and I don't think you'll have any trouble finding someone to help you finish it all up rather quickly either.

$3/4$ cup (185 ml) cold water

1 envelope ($1/4$ ounce, 10 g) unflavored powdered gelatin

$1/4$ cup (50 g) sugar

$1/2$ cup (125 ml) light corn syrup

1 large egg white

Big pinch of salt

1 teaspoon vanilla extract

Pour $1/2$ cup (125 ml) of the cold water into a small bowl and sprinkle the gelatin over the top; set aside. In a small, heavy-duty saucepan fitted with a candy thermometer, mix the remaining $1/4$ cup (60 ml) water with the sugar and corn syrup. Put the egg white in the bowl of an electric stand mixer.

Bring the sugar syrup to a boil. When the syrup reaches about 225°F (110°C), begin beating the egg white with the salt. Once the syrup reaches 240°F (116°C) and the egg white is stiff, pour the hot syrup into the mixer bowl in a slow stream while beating on medium-high speed. (Aim the syrup between the whip and the side of the bowl to keep the syrup from clinging to the whip.)

Once you've added all the syrup, scrape the softened gelatin into the warm saucepan and stir, allowing the heat of the pan to melt the gelatin. Pour the gelatin into the egg white mixture while whipping, as you did with the sugar syrup. Continue to beat until the mixture cools to room temperature, then whip in the vanilla. Serve this sauce as soon as possible after it's made.

Whipped Cream

MAKES 2 CUPS (500 ML)

Successful whipped cream means starting with the best-tasting, freshest cream you can find. Buy heavy or whipping cream that hasn't been ultrapasteurized, if you can.

Before you start whipping, make sure your cream is very cold. If you chill the bowl and whisk beforehand, the cream will whip much faster, which is especially important in warmer weather.

> 1 cup (250 ml) heavy cream
>
> 1 to 2 tablespoons sugar
>
> $1/2$ teaspoon vanilla extract

With an electric mixer, or by hand with a whisk and stainless steel bowl, whip the cream until it begins to mound and hold its shape. Whisk in 1 tablespoon sugar and the vanilla. Taste, then add the additional tablespoon of sugar if you wish. Whip until the cream forms soft, droopy peaks.

NOTE: You can rescue overwhipped cream by gently folding in additional liquid cream with a rubber spatula until smooth.

STORAGE: If you whip the cream in advance and store it in the refrigerator, it may separate as it sits. A light whisking will bring it back.

Creamy Caramel Sauce

MAKES 1$1/2$ CUPS (375 ML)

There's nothing that beats the taste of darkly caramelized sugar transformed by a pour of cream into a suave, velvety caramel sauce. If you've never made caramel before, it's simple, but do take care, since the sugar gets very hot as it liquefies. Wear an oven mitt when stirring in the cream, and resist the temptation to gaze too closely into the pot while it's bubbling and boiling away.

> 1 cup (200 g) sugar
>
> 1$1/4$ cups (310 ml) heavy cream
>
> $1/4$ teaspoon coarse salt
>
> $1/2$ teaspoon vanilla extract

In a large, deep, heavy-duty saucepan or Dutch oven, spread the sugar in an even layer. Cook the sugar over low to medium heat, watching it carefully. When it begins to liquefy and darken at the edges, use a heatproof spatula to very gently stir it to encourage even cooking.

Tilt the pan and stir gently until all of the sugar is melted and the caramel begins to smoke and turns a deep amber color. Immediately remove from the heat and whisk in half of the cream, which will steam and bubble up furiously. Carefully stir until the sugar is dissolved, then gradually whisk in the remaining cream and the salt and vanilla. If there are any bits of hardened sugar, whisk the sauce over low heat until smooth. Serve warm.

STORAGE: This sauce can be stored in the refrigerator for up to 2 weeks. Rewarm it gently in a microwave or by stirring in a saucepan over very low heat. If the sauce is too thick, you can thin it by adding a small amount of milk or additional cream.

Dulce de Leche

MAKES 1 CUP (250 ML)

This is an oven-baked version of Cajeta (page 173). It's a superb sauce for ice cream when slightly warm, as well as being excellent when layered in ice cream. Baking it in the oven means you don't need to watch it carefully while it cooks, but do make sure there's sufficient water in the outer pan while it's cooking. You can also add a vanilla bean at the beginning or stir in a tablespoon of sherry at the end.

> One 14-ounce (397 g) can sweetened condensed milk
>
> Pinch of salt

Preheat the oven to 425°F (220°C).

Pour the condensed milk into a 9-inch (23-cm) glass or nonreactive metal pie plate, or a similar-sized baking dish and sprinkle the salt over it. Cover snugly with foil and set the baking dish within a larger pan, such as a roasting pan. Add hot water until it reaches halfway up the side of the pie plate.

Bake for 1 to 1$\frac{1}{4}$ hours, checking a few times during baking and adding warm water to the roasting pan if it needs more. Once the milk is the color of dark butterscotch, remove it from the oven. Remove the foil and let it cool to room temperature, then whisk until smooth.

STORAGE: This sauce can be stored in the refrigerator for up to 2 months. Rewarm it gently in a microwave or by stirring in a saucepan over very low heat. If it seems too thick, you can thin it with a small amount of milk.

Cajeta

I think of *cajeta* as the risotto of dessert sauces, since it's made on the stovetop and requires vigilant attention while it simmers and transforms itself from ordinary ingredients (milk and sugar) into a deeply browned, sticky-sweet paste. The first *cajeta* I tasted was made in Mexico from goat's milk, and it was absolutely the best thing I'd ever tasted. Since you might not be able to find goat's milk, or it may not be to your taste, cow's milk makes yummy *cajeta* as well.

Begin your *cajeta* in a very large pot, with a capacity of at least 8 quarts (8 liters), since the mixture can bubble up unexpectedly. It should be a heavy-duty pot with a thick bottom. Be sure to pay attention while you're cooking it, especially during the last 20 minutes, when it's vital to keep watch. If you don't stir it constantly during that final stage of cooking, it's likely to scorch on the bottom. If it does, simply strain it to remove any browned bits.

> 4 cups (1 liter) whole milk (cow's milk or goat's milk)
>
> 1 cup (200 g) sugar
>
> 2 tablespoons light corn syrup
>
> ¼ teaspoon baking soda
>
> 1 cinnamon stick, or ½ vanilla bean
>
> Big pinch of salt

In a large, heavy-duty Dutch oven or stockpot, heat the milk, sugar, corn syrup, baking soda, cinnamon stick or vanilla bean, and salt until the mixture comes to a boil. As the milk begins to foam up, begin stirring it with a heatproof spatula or wooden spoon.

Reduce the heat so the milk is at a low, rolling boil and continue to cook, stirring frequently and scraping the bottom, allowing it to reduce.

After about 20 minutes, the milk will begin to thicken and turn a light beige color. At this point, lower the heat as much as possible (if you have a flame tamer, you may wish to use it), and be vigilant, scraping the bottom constantly as it cooks.

Continue to cook for about 15 minutes more, stirring vigilantly, until the milk is the color of coffee with a touch of cream. Remove from the heat and allow the Cajeta to cool before serving.

Cajeta can be layered into ice cream like Fudge Ripple (page 210), in generous spoonfuls as you remove the just-churned ice cream from the machine. This is easiest to do when the cajeta is at room temperature and not chilled.

STORAGE: Cajeta can be stored in the refrigerator for up to 2 months. Rewarm it gently in a microwave or by stirring it in a saucepan over very low heat to serve as an accompaniment to ice cream. If it's too thick, you can thin it with a little milk.

Salted Butter Caramel Sauce

We all need heroes in life. Someone to look up to, whom you idolize, and who does something that radically alters your life forever.

For me, that person is Henri Le Roux, who makes caramel-butter-salt caramels (nicknamed CBS) in the seaside town of Quiberon, on the Atlantic coast of France. The residents of Brittany are famous for consuming shocking amounts of butter, most of it heavily flecked with coarse sea salt to preserve and complement its buttery goodness. When Monsieur Le Roux unwrapped one of his buttery, meltingly tender salted caramels and popped it in my mouth, I knew I'd found my hero.

To get the same flavor, be sure to use a good-quality kosher or coarse sea salt, such as fleur de sel (see Resources, page 237), recognizable by its delicate, shimmering crystals. It makes quite a difference.

> 6 tablespoons (85 g) butter, salted or unsalted
>
> ¾ cup (150 g) sugar
>
> 1 cup (250 ml) heavy cream
>
> ½ teaspoon vanilla extract
>
> 1¼ teaspoons coarse salt

Melt the butter in a large, deep heavy-duty saucepan or Dutch oven. Stir in the sugar and cook, stirring frequently, until the sugar is a deep golden brown and starts to smoke.

Remove from the heat and immediately whisk in half of the cream until smooth (wear an oven mitt, since the mixture will steam and splatter and may bubble up furiously). Stir in the rest of the cream, then the vanilla and salt. If there are any lumps of caramel, whisk the sauce gently over low heat until they're dissolved. Serve warm.

STORAGE: This sauce can be stored in the refrigerator for up to 2 weeks. Rewarm it gently in a microwave or by stirring in a saucepan over very low heat.

Lemon Caramel Sauce

Do you have OSD? When you see something in a saucepan, do you find that you can't stop yourself from giving it a stir? If so, you've probably got obsessive stirring disorder, and you need to curb that kind of behavior to caramelize sugar properly.

Mix the sugar as little as possible, just enough to keep it from burning. Stirring encourages the jagged little crystals to join together and crystallize, which you want to avoid. If crystallization does start to happen, remove the pan from the heat and tenderly stir it to dissolve the crystals before adding the water and lemon juice. This lemony sauce is superb when drizzled over any lemon-flavored ice cream served in Profiteroles (page 232), or along with ice cream-filled Crêpes (page 233).

> 1 cup (200 g) sugar
>
> 1 cup (250 ml) water
>
> 2 to 3 tablespoons freshly squeezed lemon juice

In a large, heavy-bottomed saucepan or skillet, spread the sugar in an even layer. Pour $^1/_2$ cup (125 ml) of the water over it, along with a few drops of the lemon juice. Heat the sugar, *without stirring*, over medium heat until the mixture begins to bubble and the sugar starts to dissolve. Tilt the pan gently if the sugar is cooking unevenly, or use a heatproof utensil to ever so gently stir the syrup.

Once the sugar begins to smoke and becomes a deep amber color, remove it from the heat and add the remaining $^1/_2$ cup (125 ml) water. Let the steam subside, then whisk the caramel until smooth (wear an oven mitt, as the hot caramel can splatter).

Stir in 2 tablespoons lemon juice and let the mixture cool to room temperature. Strain it if there are any bits of undissolved sugar. Once the caramel reaches room temperature, taste it and add the additional lemon juice if you wish. Serve at room temperature or warm.

STORAGE: This sauce can be stored in the refrigerator for up to 1 month. Rewarm it gently in a microwave or by stirring in a saucepan over very low heat.

VARIATION: To make Whiskey (or Rum) Caramel Sauce, replace the lemon juice with 1 tablespoon of whiskey (or rum). Once the mixture reaches room temperature, taste and add more liquor if desired.

Pecan-Praline Sauce

Although I like to make this chunky sauce all year long and I use it to top everything from Super Lemon Ice Cream (page 85) in the winter to Fresh Apricot Ice Cream (page 76) in the summer, you can make it more winter-holiday-friendly by adding a handful of dried cranberries in place of some of the pecans, using the variation at the end of the recipe. Then try it ladled over Cinnamon Ice Cream (page 38) for a real treat. If possible, make this sauce in advance and let it sit for a few hours, so all the ingredients have a chance to mingle and meld together deliciously.

    4 tablespoons (60 g) butter, salted or unsalted, cut into pieces

    $3/4$ cup (150 g) sugar

    2 tablespoons light corn syrup

    $1/2$ cup (125 ml) water

    $1/4$ cup (60 ml) heavy cream

    $1^1/4$ cups (125 g) pecans, toasted (page 13) and coarsely chopped

    $1/8$ teaspoon coarse salt

    3 tablespoons (45 ml) whiskey

    $1/2$ teaspoon vanilla extract

In a medium, heavy-duty saucepan, melt the butter. Stir in the sugar and corn syrup and cook, stirring regularly, until the mixture becomes deep amber, the color of coffee with a touch of cream.

Remove from the heat and whisk in the water. Since the mixture can splatter, you may wish to wear an oven mitt. (The sugar might seize when you add the water, but it will smooth out as you stir it.) Bring the sauce to a low boil, whisking, until the sugar is dissolved and the sauce is smooth.

Remove from the heat and stir in the cream, pecans, salt, whiskey, and vanilla. Serve warm.

STORAGE: This sauce can be stored in the refrigerator for up to 2 weeks. Rewarm it gently in a microwave or by stirring in a saucepan over very low heat.

VARIATION: To make Pecan, Cranberry, and Praline Sauce, substitute $1/4$ cup (30 g) of chopped dried cranberries for $1/4$ cup (30 g) of the pecans.

Candied Pineapple

The sweet-tart taste of candied pineapple spiked with real vanilla makes a lovely accompaniment paired with any tropical fruit–flavored ice cream or sorbet. Be sure to cook the pineapple long enough so the juices and sugar mingle together and caramelize to a dark amber color for maximum flavor.

> 1 large pineapple, peeled, cored, and eyes removed
>
> $3/4$ cup (150 g) sugar
>
> 1 vanilla bean, split in half lengthwise

Dice the pineapple into $1/2$-inch (2-cm) pieces. Mix with the sugar and the vanilla bean in a large, nonstick saucepan or skillet. Cook over medium heat until the sugar dissolves and the pineapple becomes very juicy and shiny.

Continue cooking the pineapple until most of the liquid is gone; this will take about 20 minutes. Continue to cook, stirring and turning the pineapple constantly at this point, until the pineapple becomes sticky and the syrup thickens.

Remove from the heat and let the pineapple cool in the pan. Remove the vanilla bean before serving (it can be rinsed and saved for another use). Serve warm or at room temperature.

STORAGE: Candied Pineapple can be stored in the refrigerator up to 1 week. Let it come to room temperature before serving, or rewarm it in a microwave or a saucepan over very low heat.

NOTE: If you wish to use canned pineapple, use 4 cups (600 g) of diced pineapple, drained, from unsweetened pineapple packed in its own juice.

Candied Citrus Peel

Not only does this chewy candied peel make a tasty tangle atop a scoop of citrus-flavored sorbet or ice cream, but it's also terrific drained, finely chopped, and folded into just-churned Super Lemon Ice Cream (page 85), Fresh Ginger Ice Cream (page 43), or Cheesecake Ice Cream (page 62).

If you don't have a candy thermometer, simply cook the peel until most of the liquid has boiled away and the fine threads of peel are shiny and translucent.

4 large lemons or oranges, preferably unsprayed

2 cups (500 ml) water

1 cup (200 g) sugar

1 tablespoon light corn syrup

Pinch of salt

With a vegetable peeler, remove stirps of peel 1 inch (3 cm) wide from the lemons or oranges, cutting lengthwise down the fruit. Remove just the colorful outer peel, leaving behind the bitter white pith. Using a very sharp chef's knife, slice the peel lengthwise into very thin strips no wider than a toothpick.

Put the strips of peel in a small, nonreactive saucepan, add enough water to cover them by a few inches, and bring to a boil. Reduce to a gentle boil and cook for 15 minutes. Remove from the heat, strain the peel, and rinse with fresh water.

Combine the 2 cups (500 ml) water, sugar, corn syrup, and salt in the saucepan. Fit the pan with a candy thermometer and bring to a boil. Add the blanched peel, reduce the heat, and cook at a very low boil for about 25 minutes, until the thermometer reads 230°F (110°C). Turn off the heat and let the peel cool in the syrup.

Once cool, lift the peel out of the syrup with a fork, letting the syrup drain away, and serve atop ice cream or sorbet.

STORAGE: Store the peel in the syrup. Candied Citrus Peel can be stored in the refrigerator for up to 2 months.

Strawberry Sauce

When I see the first gorgeous baskets of strawberries at the markets, I know that spring has truly arrived and winter is a thing of the past. Since their season lasts throughout summer, you'll find that this sauce goes perfectly well with any of the summer fruit and berry ice creams, sorbets, or frozen yogurts in this book.

> 1¹/₂ pounds (675 g) fresh strawberries, rinsed and hulled
>
> ¹/₄ cup (50 g) sugar
>
> 1 teaspoon freshly squeezed lemon juice

Purée the strawberries with the sugar and lemon juice in a food processor until smooth. Press the purée through a strainer to remove the seeds. Serve chilled or at room temperature.

STORAGE: This sauce can be stored in the refrigerator for up to 3 days.

Smooth Raspberry Sauce

This sauce is so intensely flavored that just a minimum amount is needed for maximum impact. It goes particularly well over anything sharp and lemony, such as Super Lemon Ice Cream (page 85) or Lemon Sherbet (page 116).

> 2 cups (225 g) raspberries, fresh or frozen
>
> 2 tablespoons sugar
>
> ¹/₄ cup (60 ml) water
>
> A few drops freshly squeezed lemon juice

Purée the raspberries in a blender or food processor with the sugar and water until smooth. Press the mixture through a mesh strainer to remove any seeds. Mix in the lemon juice. Serve chilled or at room temperature.

STORAGE: This sauce can be stored in the refrigerator for up to 3 days.

Chunky Raspberry Sauce

MAKES 1 CUP (250 ML)

All raspberry sauces need not be created equal. Unlike the previous sauce, this one is loaded with big, chunky raspberries. It was inspired by a sauce that baking guru Nick Malgieri whizzed up during a cooking demonstration, and I've been making it ever since.

> 2 cups (225 g) raspberries, fresh or frozen
>
> 3 to 4 tablespoons (45 to 60 g) sugar
>
> A few drops freshly squeezed lemon juice

Purée 1 cup (115 g) of the raspberries with 3 tablespoons (45 g) sugar in a food processor until smooth. Put the remaining raspberries in a bowl. Set a mesh strainer over the bowl and press the purée through the strainer over the raspberries. Stir the purée together with the whole raspberries, mashing the berries just a bit as you stir. Add the lemon juice. Taste, then add the additional tablespoon of sugar if you wish. Serve chilled or at room temperature.

STORAGE: This sauce can be stored in the refrigerator for up to 3 days.

Mixed Berry Coulis

MAKES 2 CUPS (500 ML)

Coulis is a fancy word that simply means a sauce made with fresh, uncooked ingredients. Feel free to change the mix of berries as you wish, depending on what's available. If you find fresh red currants at your market, the tangy little berries are a wonderful addition.

> 8 ounces (230 g) fresh strawberries, rinsed and hulled
>
> 1 cup (115 g) raspberries, fresh or frozen
>
> 1 cup (115 g) blackberries, fresh or frozen
>
> 3 to 4 tablespoons (45 to 60 g) sugar

Slice the strawberries and toss them in a bowl with half of the raspberries and half of the blackberries. Purée the remaining berries in a blender or food processor with 3 tablespoons (45 g) of sugar. Mix the berry purée with the sliced berries. Taste, then add the remaining tablespoon of sugar if you wish. Serve chilled or at room temperature.

STORAGE: This sauce can be stored in the refrigerator for up to 3 days.

VARIATION: Add a splash of liqueur, such as Grand Marnier, Cognac, or kirsch to the sauce.

Blueberry Sauce

I'm a big fan of the all-American blueberry, and why not? They're so easy to transform into a versatile sauce that's equally at ease atop Philly-friendly Cheesecake Ice Cream (page 62) or alongside Hollywood–healthy Vanilla Frozen Yogurt (page 49).

Or forge a Franco-American alliance by adding crème de cassis, the deep, dark black currant liqueur from Dijon (see the Variation at the end of the recipe).

2 cups (225 g) blueberries, fresh or frozen

$1/4$ cup (50 g) sugar

$1^1/_2$ teaspoons cornstarch

1 tablespoon cold water

1 tablespoon freshly squeezed lemon juice

2 teaspoons kirsch

In a medium, nonreactive saucepan, heat the blueberries and sugar until the blueberries begin to release their juices. Mix the cornstarch with the cold water and lemon juice until lump free, then stir the slurry into the blueberries.

Bring to a boil, then reduce the heat to a simmer and cook for 1 minute. Remove from the heat and stir in the kirsch. Serve chilled or at room temperature.

STORAGE: This sauce can be stored in the refrigerator for up to 3 days.

VARIATION: To make Blueberry-Cassis Sauce, increase the amount of cornstarch to 2 teaspoons. After you mix the cornstarch into the cooked blueberries, stir in $1/4$ cup (60 ml) crème de cassis, then simmer as indicated in the recipe.

Candied Red Beans

One of my great pleasures in life is stopping at one of the "shave ice" stands (as the locals call them, inexplicably dropping the "d") in Hawaii. I watch as they tuck sweet red beans in the bottom of a paper cone and then pile on the shaved ice. I always choose *lilikoi*, or passion fruit syrup, to be drizzled over the ice. It has remarkable complexity and tastes as if every possible tropical flavor has been packed together into one intensely flavored fruit. Then a shot of sweet milk is poured over it all. I slurp the whole thing down, then I'm ready to tackle the surf again. Or, more likely, just take a snooze under the shade of a palm tree.

The inspiration likely came from Japan, where red beans are spooned over ice cream or puréed for beautifully intricate pastries called *wagashi*. You can easily make them at home from adzuki beans, available in well-stocked supermarkets and natural food stores. Their sweet-starchy flavor is justifiably popular and is especially good paired with Asian-inspired ice creams, like Green Tea Ice Cream (page 40) and Toasted Coconut Ice Cream (page 96). I find chewing on these sticky little beans positively addictive.

½ cup (100 g) dried adzuki beans, rinsed

4 cups (1 liter) water

Pinch of baking soda

½ cup (100 g) sugar

½ cup (125 ml) light corn syrup

Sort the beans and discard any foreign matter, then rinse them in a colander. Put them in a large saucepan and cover with plenty of water. Soak for at least 4 hours, or overnight.

Drain the beans in a colander, then return them to the saucepan and add the 4 cups (1 liter) water and the baking soda. Bring the beans to a boil, then reduce the heat and simmer for 1 hour. (If the water boils away too quickly, add another ½ cup (125 ml) to keep the beans submerged.)

When the beans are cooked through, add the sugar and corn syrup. Continue to cook the beans, stirring constantly, for 10 minutes, until the liquid is thick and syrupy. Serve warm or at room temperature.

STORAGE: These beans will keep in the refrigerator for up to 1 week.

Sour Cherries in Syrup

MAKES 2 CUPS (600 G)

If you're as wild about sour cherries as I am, you'll be as happy as I was to discover that big jars of them are available in Eastern European markets and specialty grocers (see Resources, page 237). They come packed in light syrup and are a fraction of the cost of their pricey Italian counterparts, and they're simple to candy yourself.

Once cooked and cooled, if you wish to mix the cherries into ice cream, drain them of their syrup completely (until they feel dry and sticky), and then fold them into your favorite flavor. I recommend White Chocolate Ice Cream (page 33), or try the Toasted Almond and Candied Cherry Ice Cream (page 60). Or simply use one, or more, to top off an ice cream sundae. (Save any leftover syrup to mix with sparkling water to make homemade sour cherry soda.) This recipe calls for 3 cups of cherries, which includes their syrup.

> 3 cups sour cherries from a jar, with their light syrup,
> about 1½ pounds (675 g)
>
> 1 cup (200 g) sugar

Mix the cherries with their syrup and the sugar in a large, nonreactive saucepan. Fit the pan with a candy thermometer and cook over medium heat, stirring infrequently, until the syrup reaches 230°F (110°C). Remove from the heat and let cool to room temperature. Serve a few cherries with their thick, ruby-colored syrup over ice cream.

STORAGE: These cherries can be kept in the refrigerator for up to 1 month. Allow them to come to room temperature before serving.

Honey Crunch Granola

MAKES 5 CUPS (600 G)

I can't say I make it a habit of, or admit to, meeting women online. But luckily for me, my first time was the charm. I fell for Heidi Swanson, who entices men (and women) with her gorgeous web site, www.101cookbooks.com. An accomplished photographer and cookbook author, her recipes are tried-and-true and are always accompanied by stunning photos and clever commentary.

When we actually met, she was just as charming in person as online—which I hear makes me luckier than most of the other fellows out there. Here's a recipe I've adapted from her site. It makes a healthy, delightfully crunchy topping for ice cream or frozen yogurt for dessert, and since the recipe makes a bit more than you might need, you can keep some on hand for a great breakfast treat as well.

3 cups (300 g) rolled oats (not instant)

$1/2$ cup (70 g) raw sunflower seeds

$1/2$ cup (40 g) sliced almonds

$1/2$ cup (40 g) dried shredded coconut, unsweetened or sweetened

2 tablespoons sesame seeds

Big pinch of salt

6 tablespoons (90 ml) good-flavored honey

2 tablespoons vegetable oil

$1/2$ cup (80 g) diced dried fruit (see Note)

Preheat the oven to 300°F (150°C).

In a large bowl, mix together the oats, sunflower seeds, almonds, coconut, sesame seeds, and salt.

In a small saucepan, warm the honey and vegetable oil. Pour the warm honey mixture over the dry ingredients and stir until they're well coated. Spread evenly on a baking sheet and bake for 30 minutes, or until golden brown, stirring occasionally. Remove from the oven and cool. Once the granola is completely cool, stir in the dried fruit.

NOTE: Use any combination of raisins, date pieces, apricots, cherries, cranberries, pineapple, and papaya (cut larger fruits into $1/2$-inch [2-cm] dice).

STORAGE: Store in an airtight container at room temperature for up to 2 months.

Honeyed Cashews

These cashews are simple to make and can be sprinkled over ice cream sundaes. Be sure to keep them in an airtight container at room temperature to keep them as crisp as possible.

> 2¹/₂ tablespoons good-flavored honey
>
> Big pinch of coarse salt
>
> 1 cup (150 g) whole cashews, lightly toasted (see page 13)

Very lightly grease a baking sheet with vegetable oil, or line it with a silicone baking mat.

Heat the honey and salt in a 10-inch (25-cm) skillet, preferably nonstick. Once the honey starts to bubble, mix in the cashews. Cook over moderate heat, stirring frequently, for 3 to 3¹/₂ minutes, until the cashews are thickly glazed with the honey (take care not to let them burn).

Tip the cashews onto the prepared baking sheet and gently stir the nuts as they cool, scraping up the excess honey that collects beneath them on the baking sheet and basting the cashews with it for about 30 seconds. Let cool completely.

Once cool, break the clumps of cashews apart and immediately store in an airtight container.

STORAGE: Store in an airtight container at room temperature. Serve the same day.

Salt-Roasted Peanuts

MAKES 2 CUPS (400 G)

There are really simple to make and will make you feel like an accomplished candy maker with minimal effort, and they're very good too. I like these crunchy, salty peanuts liberally scattered all over the top of a towering hot fudge sundae.

You'll notice that I use raw peanuts, not ones that have been previously salted and roasted. If you wish, you can use unsalted preroasted peanuts (which, amusingly, are often called cocktail peanuts) and reduce the baking time to 15 minutes.

2 cups (300 g) raw (unroasted) peanuts

$^1/_4$ cup (60 ml) light corn syrup

2 tablespoons packed light or dark brown sugar

$1^1/_2$ teaspoons coarse salt

Preheat the oven to 350°F (175°C). Very lightly oil a baking sheet with peanut or vegetable oil, or line it with a silicone baking mat.

In a bowl, mix together the peanuts, corn syrup, and light brown sugar until the peanuts are sticky and coated with syrup. Sprinkle the salt over the peanuts and stir a few times.

Spread the nuts evenly on the baking sheet and bake for 25 to 30 minutes, stirring three times during baking, until the nuts are deep golden brown and glazed. Cool completely, then store in an airtight container to preserve their crispness.

STORAGE: Store in an airtight container at room temperature for up to 1 week.

French Almonds

MAKES 2 CUPS (200 G)

After dinner at the marvelous L'Os à Moelle in Paris, I finished up with a dessert of housemade ice cream topped with the most perfect, crispy caramelized almonds I'd ever imagined.

After leaving, I passed the kitchen window, where chef Thierry Faucher was leaning outside taking a break. I waved, and he waved back. So I got up the nerve to ask him how he made those fabulous almonds. He hefted a pitcher of liquid, and told me they were simply coated with equal parts water and sugar. The next morning, I immediately started tinkering around and came up with just the right proportions for making these incredibly addictive crispy flakes of almonds.

> 2 tablespoons water
>
> 2 tablespoons sugar
>
> 2 cups (160 g) sliced almonds, blanched or unblanched

Preheat the oven to 350°F (175°C).

In a small skillet, heat the water and sugar, stirring a bit, just until it begins to boil. Remove from the heat and stir in the almonds to coat them with the syrup.

Spread the almonds on a nonstick baking sheet, or a baking sheet lined with a silicone baking mat. Bake for 20 minutes, stirring twice during baking and separating any clumps.

Remove from the oven when the almonds are a medium golden brown. Cool completely.

STORAGE: Store French Almonds in an airtight container for up to 1 week.

VARIATION: For Candied Oats, toast 1 cup (100 g) rolled oats in a small baking pan in a 350°F (175°C) oven for 7 minutes. Heat $1^1/_2$ tablespoons of water, $1^1/_2$ tablespoons of sugar, and a big pinch of cinnamon in a small saucepan. Mix the syrup with the oats, spread the mixture on a nonstick baking sheet, and bake for 30 minutes, stirring a few times during baking.

6
Mix-Ins

There is something quintessentially American about mixing things into ice cream. Perhaps it's because we like to have our cake (and cookies and brownies) and eat them too. Especially if they're smashed into ice cream! Like the previous American Revolution a couple centuries back, the mix-in revolution took hold in Boston in the 1970s, when an ice cream shop came up with the idea of offering a panoply of popular candies, toasted nuts, nuggets of cake, and hunks of cookies—just about anything you could think of—and patrons were faced with that all-important decision of how to customize their scoops.

Once customers decided (I always seemed to be stuck behind the ones who couldn't), the brawny young folks behind the counter would slap a mound of ice cream onto the cool, hard slabs of marble and layer on whatever treats had been chosen. With brute force, they'd go to work, smashing and mashing the jumble of ingredients until everything came together into a messy, schizophrenic, wildly cohesive mass. Then they'd heap the impossibly large mound into a cone and off you'd go. For insurance purposes, I always requested my scoop in a cup, since as a regular, I'd seen all too many accidents where, after just a couple of licks, gravity would triumph and the oversized mound of ice cream would go tumbling downward, prompting a collective sigh of sympathy across the sidewalk.

The great thing about homemade ice cream is that it gives you the freedom to mix in whatever you want, in any quantity you want. You can really load it up. If you're anything like me, you like lots of stuff in your ice cream. Big chunks of Dark Chocolate Truffles (page 211) in White Chocolate Ice Cream (page 33)? Permission granted. Glistening, ruby red Candied Cherries (page 215) embedded in Toasted Almond and Candied Cherry Ice Cream (page 60)? Be my guest.

So here's your chance to unleash your own creativity and customize your ice cream as you like. I've given guidelines throughout the book, called Perfect Pairings, that are meant to plant the seeds of possibility. In general, I find that about $1^1/_2$ to 2 cups (375 to 500 ml) of goodies makes a good mix-in for 1 quart (1 liter) of ice cream. But this is just a suggestion; some people prefer less stuff added to their ice cream, while others like the extravagance of lots (and lots) of stuff, so by all means take some personal liberties here. All of the mix-in recipes can easily be doubled and any leftovers can be stored in the freezer in a zip-top bag and used for the next batch. And remember, if you're adding mix-ins to your ice cream, you'll want to have a big enough container, larger than 1 quart (1 liter), for the ice cream along with your mix-ins.

When adding mix-ins, speed is vital since you don't want your just-churned ice cream to melt. To start, scatter a few of the mix-ins in the bottom of your storage container, then put it in the freezer; some of the mix-ins, especially the larger pieces as well as the Peanut Butter Patties (page 204) and the Chocolate Chip Cookie Dough (page 209), will be much easier to add if they're chilled first.

As soon as your ice cream is churned, add the rest of the mix-ins, stirring quickly to disperse them evenly, then transfer the ice cream to the storage container. Put a lid on it, then get the container right into the freezer without delay.

If the mix-ins are in small pieces, I add them directly into the machine during the last minute of churning so they get mixed evenly. Larger mix-ins are best folded in after you're done churning, since they can get stuck and may cause the motor to rebel. A good rule is that anything larger than a chocolate chip is probably best folded in after the ice cream has been churned completely.

As for ripples and swirls, resist the temptation to *over*mix them into the just-frozen custard. You don't want a big, muddy mess. Instead, you want to end up with wide, distinct layers. The best way to get these is to begin with a big spoonful of the swirl mixture at the bottom of the storage container, since there's nothing worse than getting to the bottom and finding plain ice cream. Continue to layer the mixture, alternating ice cream, swirl mixture, some more ice cream, and then more swirl. If you're a lily gilder, add chunks of nuts or any of the other mix-ins in as you go.

One final word: If a mixture doesn't come out as you think it should or if you mess something up, go ahead and use it; it will likely taste delicious in the ice cream and no one will be the wiser. And feel free to crumble any cookies or bits of cake you may have left over into freshly churned ice cream. I'm positive many of the things that have gotten mixed into ice cream in the past were mistakes or leftovers that someone was trying to use up. And why am I so sure? I've done it myself...and no one was the wiser.

Buttered Pecans

I used to cringe every time someone would start a sentence with, "When I was your age…," knowing that I was in for a lecture, heavy with nostalgia for days gone by.

Nowadays, though, I find I'm doing the same a little too often for comfort. But it's true, when I was younger (perhaps your age), my local ice cream parlor would serve, alongside their gloriously overloaded ice cream sundaes, little paper cups filled way up to the brim with buttered pecans roasted in real, honest-to-goodness butter, for just five cents. *Five cents!*

Yikes! I think I'm becoming my parents.

1½ tablespoons (25 g) butter, salted or unsalted

1½ cups (150 g) pecan halves

¼ teaspoon coarse salt

Preheat the oven to 350°F (175°C).

Melt the butter in a skillet. Remove from the heat and toss the pecans with the melted butter until well coated, then sprinkle with the salt. Spread evenly on a baking sheet and toast in the oven for 10 to 12 minutes, stirring once during baking.

Remove from the oven and let cool completely.

MIXING THEM IN: Chop the Buttered Pecans coarsely, then add them to them to 1 quart (1 liter) of ice cream in the machine during the last minute of churning, or sprinkle them over when serving ice cream.

STORAGE: Buttered Pecans can be stored for up to 2 days in an airtight container at room temperature.

In a Hurry? Cheat.

If you don't have time to make your own ice cream, take a pint of your favorite store-bought premium vanilla ice cream and soften it in an electric stand mixer, using the paddle attachment.

Once it's softened slightly, add whatever flavorings you want. You can add mint or citrus oil (start with ⅛ teaspoon per pint, then taste and add more if desired), a favorite liqueur (1 to 2 tablespoons per pint), or any of the crunchy mix-ins in this chapter. Return the ice cream to the freezer and chill firmly before you serve it.

Another tip: To make instant crème anglaise, melt down some premium vanilla ice cream. *Voila!*

Pralined Almonds

This is one of my all-time favorite and most requested recipes. These nuts are lots of fun to make, and you'll feel like a real candy maker as you triumphantly tilt your first batch out of the pan. Whole almonds get cooked in a syrup, simmering until the sugar crystallizes and clings to them, creating a crackly caramelized coating. This recipe can easily be doubled.

> $^1/_4$ cup (60 ml) water
>
> $^1/_2$ cup (100 g) sugar
>
> 1 cup (135 g) whole almonds, unblanched and untoasted
>
> $^1/_8$ teaspoon coarse salt, preferably fleur de sel

Mix the water, sugar, and almonds in a large, heavy-duty skillet. Put the pan over medium to high heat and cook, stirring constantly with a wooden spoon, until the sugar dissolves and the liquid boils.

Lower the heat to medium and continue cooking and stirring for just a few minutes, until the liquid crystallizes and becomes sandy. Very soon the crystals of sugar on the bottom of the pan will begin to liquefy. Stir the dark syrup at the bottom of the pan over the nuts to coat them. Continue to stir the nuts and scrape the syrup over them until the almonds are glazed and become a bit glossy and shiny. (Sometimes I remove the pan from the heat while they're cooking to better control the glazing, so they don't get burned.) Remove the pan from the heat and sprinkle the almonds with the salt. Tip them onto an ungreased baking sheet and allow them to cool completely. As they cool, break up any clusters that are stuck together.

MIXING THEM IN: Chop the Pralined Almonds coarsely, then add them to 1 quart (1 liter) of ice cream in the machine during the last minute of churning.

STORAGE: Pralined almonds can be stored for up to 1 week in an airtight container at room temperature.

VARIATION: Substitute 1 cup raw (unroasted and unsalted) peanuts for the almonds to make Pralined Peanuts.

Spiced Pecans

It's often said that when selling your home, you should bake something aromatic and spicy to entrance potential buyers with the homey scent wafting from the kitchen.

These pecans are simple enough to make in the mad scramble before opening your house to strangers, and there's no better way to fill your home with a heady mix of spices. I recommend folding them into Bourbon Ice Cream (see Variation, page 24), which you can happily eat to celebrate the closing of the deal.

2 tablespoons egg whites (see Note)

1/4 cup (60 g) packed light brown sugar

2 teaspoons ground cinnamon

1/2 teaspoon ground ginger

1/4 teaspoon ground cloves

A few grinds black pepper

1/2 teaspoon coarse salt

1/4 teaspoon ground chile

I teaspoon vanilla extract

2 cups (200 g) pecan halves

Preheat the oven to 300°F (150°C). Spray a baking sheet with nonstick spray.

Whisk the egg whites in a medium bowl for about 15 seconds, until loose and foamy. Stir in the brown sugar, spices, vanilla, and pecans. Spread the coated nuts evenly on the baking sheet.

Bake for 30 minutes, stirring twice during baking, until the coating has hardened onto the pecans and they're nice and dry. Remove from the oven and let cool completely.

MIXING THEM IN: Chop the Spiced Pecans coarsely, then add them to 1 quart (1 liter) of ice cream in the machine during the last minute of churning. They can also be sprinkled over ice cream when serving.

NOTE: To measure the egg whites, beat them vigorously with a fork for a few seconds, until they're loose and slightly foamy. The whites will then be easy to pour and measure.

STORAGE: The pecans can be stored for up to 2 weeks in an airtight container at room temperature.

VARIATION: Make Spiced Walnuts by substituting untoasted walnut halves for the pecans.

Wet Walnuts

I was going to call these "Walnuts Gone Wild" but took a less seamy route and decided on simply Wet Walnuts. You can draw your own conclusions. But there's nothing indecent about these maple-glazed walnuts, except how good they taste.

½ cup plus 1 tablespoon (140 ml) dark amber maple syrup

1½ cups (150 g) walnuts, toasted (see page 13) and very coarsely chopped

Big pinch of salt

Heat the maple syrup in a small skillet or saucepan until it just begins to come to a full boil. Stir in the walnuts, then cook until the liquid comes to a full boil once again. Stir the nuts for 10 seconds, then remove them from the heat and let cool completely. The nuts will still be wet and sticky when cooled.

MIXING THEM IN: Chop the Wet Walnuts coarsely and add them to 1 quart (1 liter) of ice cream in the machine during the last minute of churning.

STORAGE: Wet Walnuts can be stored for up to 1 day in an airtight container at room temperature, but they'll lose a bit of their crispness overnight, so it's best to prepare them shortly before using them.

VARIATION: To make Wet Pecans, substitute toasted pecans for the walnuts.

Chocolate-Covered Peanuts

MAKES 1½ CUPS (265 G)

These easy-to-make peanuts will make you feel like a chocolatier assembling a world-class candy bar. If you're anything like me, you can't keep chocolate bars around the house without breaking off a hunk every time you pass by, so by all means double the recipe if you want, just to make sure there's enough for folding into the ice cream later on.

> 4 ounces (115 g) semisweet or bittersweet chocolate, chopped
>
> 1 cup (150 g) roasted, unsalted peanuts

Put the pieces of chocolate in an absolutely dry heatproof bowl. Set the bowl over a saucepan of simmering water to melt the chocolate, stirring until smooth. In the meantime, stretch a piece of plastic wrap over a dinner plate.

Once the chocolate is melted, remove it from the heat and stir in the peanuts, coating them with the chocolate. Spread the mixture on the plastic-lined plate and chill.

MIXING THEM IN: Use a chef's knife to chop the chocolate-covered block of peanuts into bite-sized pieces, then mix them into 1 quart (1 liter) of ice cream as you remove it from the machine.

STORAGE: Chocolate-Covered Peanuts can be stored for several months in an airtight container, refrigerated or at room temperature.

VARIATION: You can substitute Salt-Roasted Peanuts (page 188) or Pralined Peanuts (page 196) for the roasted peanuts in this recipe.

Buttercrunch Toffee

MAKES 2 CUPS (400 G)

When I put this recipe on my web site, I wasn't prepared for the onslaught of comments and accolades. It seems I'm not the only one out there who craves toffee—especially this buttery-crisp candy enrobed in dark chocolate and showered with lots of toasted almonds. It's very good folded into ice cream, and although the recipe makes a bit more than you'll need, I don't think you'll have any problem finding something to do with the rest.

I cup (135 g) almonds, toasted (see page 13) and finely chopped

I tablespoon water

4 tablespoons (60 g) butter, salted or unsalted, cut into pieces

$1/_2$ cup (100 g) granulated sugar

2 tablespoons packed light or dark brown sugar

$1/_8$ teaspoon baking soda

$1/_2$ teaspoon vanilla extract

$1/_2$ cup (80 g) chocolate chips, or 3 ounces (85 g) bittersweet or semisweet chocolate, chopped

Using half of the chopped almonds, form an 8-inch (20-cm) circle in an even layer on an ungreased baking sheet.

Fit a small, heavy-duty saucepan with a candy thermometer, then add the water, butter, granulated sugar, and brown sugar, mixing them together. Have the baking soda and vanilla measured and ready.

Cook the mixture over medium heat, stirring as little as possible. When the mixture reaches 300°F (150°C), remove the pan from the heat and immediately stir in the baking soda and vanilla. Mix just until combined; don't overstir.

Right away, pour the hot toffee mixture over the circle of almonds on the baking sheet. Using as little movement as possible, spread the toffee to cover the circle.

Scatter the chocolate pieces over the toffee and wait 2 minutes to allow them to melt. Use a spatula to spread the chocolate into an even layer, then scatter the remaining chopped almonds on top, pressing them into the chocolate. Cool completely, until the chocolate is firm. Depending on the temperature of your kitchen, you may need to cool it in the refrigerator. Remove it once the chocolate has hardened.

MIXING IT IN: Chop the Buttercrunch Toffee into coarse chunks, then fold the pieces into 1 quart (1 liter) of ice cream as you remove it from the machine.

STORAGE: Buttercrunch Toffee can be stored in an airtight container for up to 2 weeks in the freezer or at room temperature.

VARIATION: Feel free to substitute toasted hazelnuts or pecans for the almonds. I also like to fleck a few grains of coarse salt over the chocolate before adding the nuts. You can substitute milk chocolate for the dark chocolate if you wish.

Peanut Brittle

In spite of what you might see on television or read in cooking magazines, restaurant cooking is demanding, hectic work. Luckily, I baked professionally with Mary Jo Thoresen for many years, and although we worked really hard, we survived by finding humor in the craziest things, which would make no sense to anyone but us. We did everything from making up movie titles by substituting with the word "quince" in them (*A Room with a Quince, Quince on a Hot Tin Roof*, etc.) to writing a rap song about baking. At perhaps the depths of our silliness, we became obsessed with all things Scoopy, the clown on the box of ice cream cones you buy from the supermarket. Soon I started finding little pictures of him stuck in the oddest places in the pastry area where we worked. (I even discovered one on the windshield of my car one night after work.) Naturally, my nickname became Scoopy.

Now that we've both become grown-ups, Mary Jo (aka Scary Jo) is the pastry chef at Jojo restaurant, which she co-owns, in Piedmont, California. Here's her recipe for Peanut Brittle, which she crushes into brickly bits and adds to Vanilla Ice Cream (pages 24 and 25), dousing it with warm chocolate sauce for a wonderfully over-the-top peanut brittle sundae that should make sense to anyone. If you want to get creative, try mixing Peanut Brittle bits into Fresh Ginger Ice Cream (page 43) or Peanut Butter Ice Cream (page 50), and top it off with chocolate sauce as well. Whatever you mix it into, I'm sure you'll find the result absolutely scoop-endous.

> $^{1}/_{2}$ cup (125 ml) light corn syrup
>
> $^{1}/_{2}$ cup (100 g) sugar
>
> 2 tablespoons water
>
> $1^{1}/_{2}$ cups (225 g) salted cocktail peanuts or
> Salt-Roasted Peanuts (page 188)
>
> $^{1}/_{2}$ teaspoon baking soda

Line a baking sheet with a silicone baking mat, or grease it lightly with peanut or vegetable oil.

In a medium, heavy-duty saucepan fitted with a candy thermometer, mix together the corn syrup, sugar, and water. Bring the syrup to a full boil, then add the peanuts. Cook, stirring frequently with a heatproof spatula, making sure the peanuts aren't burning as the syrup cooks (some like to hide behind the thermometer, so keep an eye out for that). Have the baking soda measured and ready.

Cook until the temperature reaches between 300° and 305°F (149° and 151°C). Remove from the heat and immediately stir in the baking soda. Working quickly, pour the mixture onto the prepared baking sheet and spread it as thinly as possible with the spatula. Let cool completely. Once cool, break the brittle into bite-sized pieces.

MIXING IT IN: Fold the crumbled peanut brittle into 1 quart (1 liter) of ice cream as you remove it from the machine; Mary Jo likes to reserve a few extra pieces for scattering over the top.

STORAGE: Peanut Brittle can be stored in an airtight container at room temperature for up to 2 weeks.

Croquant

Croquant is French for "crunchy," and this version certainly lives up to its name and reputation. This simple mix-in of toasted nuts enrobed in glossy caramel is wonderful when crushed and added to ice cream. You can crack it as fine, or as coarse, as you want. One tip: Adding the nuts to the caramel while they're still warm will make them easier to mix.

> 1 cup (200 g) sugar
>
> 1½ cups (150 g) whole almonds, pecans, walnuts, hazelnuts, or peanuts, toasted (see page 13)

Cover a baking sheet with aluminum foil.

Spread the sugar in a heavy-bottomed skillet and cook over medium heat, watching it carefully. When it begins to liquefy and darken at the edges, use a heat-proof spatula to stir it very gently, encouraging the heat of the liquefied sugar around the edges to moisten and melt the sugar crystals in the center.

Add the nuts and stir gently but quickly, coating them with the caramel. Scrape the nuts onto the foil-lined baking sheet and spread as evenly as possible. Let cool completely.

Once cool, break the Croquant up in a food processor, or place it in a zip-top freezer bag and use a mallet or rolling pin to crush it.

MIXING IT IN: I like a lot of croquant in my ice cream and use the entire batch, but you may use less if you want. Add 1 to 2 cups (175 to 350 g) of crushed Croquant to 1 quart (1 liter) of ice cream in the machine during the last minute of churning.

STORAGE: Croquant can be stored for up to 1 week in an airtight container in the freezer or at room temperature.

Honey-Sesame Brittle

MAKES 1 CUP (270 G)

This delicate but highly flavored brittle may lose its appealing crispness after it cools, so I recommend baking it just an hour or so before adding it to just-churned ice cream. I like it mixed into ice creams that are exotically flavored, such as Anise Ice Cream (page 36) or Lavender-Honey Ice Cream (page 64). Sesame seeds are very flavorful, and you'll find that a small amount of this brittle will provide lots of flavor to any ice cream you chose to mix it into. Feel free to add a little freshly grated orange zest to the honey as well.

> 3 tablespoons (45 ml) good-flavored honey
>
> 1$^1/_2$ cups (210 g) sesame seeds

Preheat the oven to 350°F (175°C). Line a baking sheet with aluminum foil or a silicone baking mat.

In a skillet, warm the honey. Remove from the heat and stir in the sesame seeds, coating them with the honey until they're moist.

Spread the mixture evenly on the prepared baking sheet and bake for 25 minutes. Remove from the oven and let cool completely.

MIXING IT IN: Break the Honey-Sesame Brittle into little pieces, then add them to 1 quart (1 liter) of ice cream in the machine during the last minute of churning.

STORAGE: Use soon after it's cooled, preferably within an hour or so.

Peanut Butter Patties

MAKES FORTY $^1/_2$-INCH (2-CM) PATTIES

You don't need me to tell you that Peanut Butter Patties are *the best* when embedded in any chocolate-flavored ice cream. Use a commercial brand of peanut butter when making these since natural-style peanut butter will make them too runny. If you want tinier pieces in your ice cream, simply shape the mixture into smaller patties. And although they're rich, if you want more to add to your ice cream, it's easy to double the recipe.

> 6 tablespoons (90 g) peanut butter (smooth or crunchy)
>
> 2 tablespoons confectioners' sugar

Mix together the peanut butter and sugar in a small bowl. Line a dinner plate with plastic wrap. Pinch off small pieces of the peanut butter mixture, about $^1/_2$ teaspoon each, and drop them onto the dinner plate. Once you've used all of the mixture, freeze the patties.

MIXING THEM IN: Fold the Peanut Butter Patties into 1 quart (1 liter) of ice cream as you remove it from the machine.

STORAGE: Peanut Butter Patties can be stored in the freezer, well wrapped, for up to 1 month.

Oatmeal Praline

MAKES 1 CUP (175 G)

If you take a bite of the finished Oatmeal Praline (which I don't recommend, however tempting), you'll find that it's stubbornly hard. But don't worry. Once you've smashed it into bits, folded it into your favorite ice cream, and left it in the freezer a bit, the pieces will soften up perfectly and become toothsome nuggets.

> ¾ cup (75 g) rolled oats (not instant)
>
> ½ cup (100 g) sugar
>
> Pinch of coarse salt

Preheat the oven to 350°F (175°C).

Line a baking sheet with foil, spread the oats evenly on the sheet, and bake for 10 minutes, stirring once or twice while baking, until the oats are fragrant and nicely toasted. Remove from the oven.

Spread the sugar in a medium, heavy-bottomed skillet and cook over medium heat, watching it carefully. When it begins to liquefy and darken at the edges, use a heatproof spatula to stir it very gently, encouraging the heat of the liquefied sugar around the edges to moisten and melt the sugar crystals in the center.

Tilt the pan and stir gently until all the sugar is melted and the caramel begins to smoke. Once the mixture is deep golden, remove it from the heat and immediately add the oats to the skillet (lift the foil to guide them in quickly). Return the foil to the baking sheet.

Stir the oats gently but quickly, coating them with the caramel. Scrape the oats onto the foil-lined baking sheet and spread them as well as possible. Sprinkle with the salt and let cool completely. Once firm, break the pralined oats into small pieces by pulsing them in a food processor or placing the pieces in a heavy-duty plastic bag and smacking them with a mallet or rolling pin.

MIXING IT IN: Fold the Oatmeal Praline pieces into 1 quart (1 liter) of ice cream as you remove it from the machine.

STORAGE: The Oatmeal Praline can be stored for up to 1 week in an airtight container in the freezer or at room temperature.

Peppermint Patties

These mint disks are adapted from a recipe passed on to me by Elizabeth Falkner, the owner of San Francisco's deservedly popular Citizen Cake bakery. The mixture is simple to put together, and you can adjust the mint flavor to your liking. Taste a bit and add more if you wish, as mint extracts and oils vary. I make my Peppermint Patties very minty, which is especially important when they're crumbled into deep, dark chocolate ice cream, a combination I call "The Girl Scout Cookie Effect."

2 cups (225 g) confectioners' sugar

3 tablespoons (45 ml) light corn syrup

2 teaspoons water

Scant $1/8$ teaspoon peppermint extract or oil

6 ounces (170 g) bittersweet or semisweet chocolate, chopped

Line a baking sheet with plastic wrap or parchment paper and dust it with about 1 tablespoon of the confectioners' sugar.

In a bowl, mix the corn syrup, water, and mint extract or oil. Gradually stir in the remaining confectioners' sugar. As the mixture thickens, knead it with your hands until it forms a smooth ball (it will seem dry at first, but it will come together).

Pat the dough out onto the sugar-dusted baking sheet about $1/3$ inch (1 cm) thick and let it dry, uncovered, for at least 8 hours or overnight.

Melt the chocolate in a clean, absolutely dry bowl set over simmering water, stirring until smooth. Remove from the heat. Line a dinner plate with plastic wrap. Cut the mint disk into 6 triangular wedges, as if cutting a pie, and brush off any excess powered sugar. Using 2 forks, dip each wedge in the chocolate, turning it over to coat both sides, then transfer each piece to the plastic-lined dinner plate. (Since they're going to be chopped up, don't worry if they're not museum quality.)

Chill in the refrigerator or freezer until the chocolate has firmed up, then chop into bite-sized pieces.

MIXING THEM IN: Fold the Peppermint Patty pieces into 1 quart (1 liter) of ice cream as you remove it from the machine.

STORAGE: Peppermint Patties can be stored in the freezer or refrigerator, well wrapped, for up to 1 month.

Speculoos

These cookie chunks are inspired by the famous spiced cookies from Belgium, which are zippier than American gingersnaps. Soft-baked Speculoos meld wonderfully when folded into ice cream, but if you'd like to make them crunchier, break the cookies into little bite-sized nuggets and toast them in a low oven (325°F, 165°C) for about 10 minutes, until dry and crispy. Cool completely, then fold the crunchy bits into your ice cream.

> 2 tablespoons (30 g) salted butter, at room temperature
>
> 3 tablespoons (45 g) packed light or dark brown sugar
>
> 1 tablespoon molasses
>
> 1 large egg yolk
>
> ½ cup (70 g) flour
>
> ¼ teaspoon baking soda
>
> 2 teaspoons ground cinnamon
>
> 1 teaspoon ground ginger
>
> 1 teaspoon ground allspice

Preheat the oven to 350°F (175°C) and line a baking sheet with parchment paper or a silicone baking mat.

Beat together the butter and brown sugar in a medium bowl until smooth. Stir in the molasses and egg yolk.

In a separate small bowl, stir together the flour, baking soda, and spices. Stir the dry ingredients into the butter mixture and mix until smooth. Using your hands, pat the batter onto the baking sheet in a circle about 5 inches (12 cm) in diameter, then bake for 18 minutes. Remove from the oven and let cool. Once cool, break the Speculoos into bite-sized chunks.

MIXING THEM IN: Fold bits of Speculoos into 1 quart (1 liter) of ice cream as you remove it from the machine.

STORAGE: Once baked, Speculoos can be stored for up to 3 days at room temperature, well wrapped, or in the freezer for up to 1 month. The unbaked dough can also be stored in the freezer for the same amount of time.

Chocolate Chip Cookie Dough

I was an early trendsetter. I was snitching bites of raw cookie dough long before any-one else, way back in the sixties, so I would like to take credit for starting the craze.

Okay, maybe I wasn't the first kid to snitch a bit of raw cookie dough. But who-ever came up with the idea for adding cookie dough to ice cream rightly deserves the accolades from ice cream lovers across the United States. (I'm not sure the idea of raw cookie dough in ice cream has international appeal.)

This dough is packed with crunchy nuts and lots of chocolate chips, all embed-ded in a soft brown sugar dough. I debated with myself that this may be too much cookie dough for the average person to add to ice cream. Then, after much nibbling (while thinking about it), I decided that it was just not possible to have too much cookie dough!

5 tablespoons (70 g) salted butter, melted

$1/3$ cup (70 g) packed light brown sugar

$1/4$ cup (35 g) flour

$1/2$ teaspoon vanilla extract

$1/2$ cup (50 g) walnuts, pecans, or hazelnuts, toasted (see page 13) and coarsely chopped

$3/4$ cup (120 g) semisweet or bittersweet chocolate chips

In a medium-sized mixing bowl, stir together the butter and sugar until smooth. Stir in the flour, then the vanilla, nuts, and chocolate chips.

Form the dough into a disk about $1/2$ inch (1 cm) thick, wrap it in plastic wrap, and refrigerate until firm. Once chilled, unwrap the disk and chop the dough into bite-sized pieces, then store the pieces in the freezer until ready to mix in.

MIXING IT IN: Fold pieces of Chocolate Chip Cookie Dough into 1 quart (1 liter) of ice cream as you remove it from the machine.

STORAGE: This dough can be stored for up to 5 days in the refrigerator or up to 2 months in the freezer, well wrapped.

Stracciatella

Just about every *gelateria* in Italy features a bin of *stracciatella*, vanilla ice cream with chocolate "chips." It results from a technique that clever Italians devised for pouring warm, melted chocolate into cold ice cream. The flow of chocolate immediately hardens into streaks, which get shredded (*stracciato*) into "chips" as the ice cream is stirred.

The trick to *stracciatella* is to pour it into your ice cream maker in a very thin stream during the last moment of churning. If your aim isn't very good, or your ice cream machine has a small opening, transfer the melted chocolate into a measuring cup with a pouring spout. (If you're using a microwave to melt the chocolate, simply melt the chocolate in the measuring cup.) The trick is to pour it not on the turning dasher (mixing blade) but into the ice cream itself.

You can also drizzle it over the ice cream as you layer it into the storage container, stirring it very slightly while you're pouring.

> 5 ounces (140 g) bittersweet or semisweet chocolate, finely chopped
> (do not use chocolate chips)

In a clean, absolutely dry bowl set over a saucepan of simmering water, melt the chocolate, stirring it until it's completely smooth.

MIXING IT IN: Drizzle a very thin stream of the warm chocolate into 1 quart (1 liter) of ice cream during the last possible moment of churning. If the chocolate clings too much to the dasher, remove the ice cream from the machine and drizzle the chocolate into the frozen ice cream by hand while you layer it into the storage container, breaking up any chunks as you stir.

Fudge Ripple

This has the authentic taste of that old-fashioned ripple of fudge. You can swirl it through just about any ice cream you like. Try it in Fresh Mint Ice Cream (page 99) or as a contrasting swirl through White Chocolate Ice Cream (page 33).

> $^1/_2$ cup (100 g) sugar
>
> $^1/_3$ cup (80 ml) light corn syrup
>
> $^1/_2$ cup (125 ml) water
>
> 6 tablespoons (50 g) unsweetened Dutch-process cocoa powder
>
> $^1/_2$ teaspoon vanilla extract

Whisk together the sugar, corn syrup, water, and cocoa powder in a medium saucepan. Heat over medium heat, whisking constantly, until the mixture begins to bubble at the edges.

Continue to whisk until it just comes to a low boil. Cook for 1 minute, whisking frequently. Remove from the heat, stir in the vanilla, and let cool. Chill in the refrigerator before using.

MIXING IT IN: The Fudge Ripple should be thoroughly chilled, as it's easiest to use when very cold. Just before you remove the ice cream from the machine, spoon some of the Fudge Ripple onto the bottom of the storage container. As you remove the ice cream from the machine, layer generous spoonfuls of the sauce between layers of ice cream. Avoid stirring the Fudge Ripple, as it will make the ice cream muddy looking.

STORAGE: Fudge Ripple can be stored for up to 2 weeks, covered, in the refrigerator.

VARIATION: To make Mocha Ripple, substitute strongly brewed espresso for the water in the recipe, or stir in 1 tablespoon of best-quality instant coffee granules after you boil the mixture.

Dark Chocolate Truffles

MAKES FORTY $1/_2$-INCH (2-CM) TRUFFLES

These truffles will stay slightly soft in frozen ice cream. You can make them smaller or larger than indicated.

$1/_2$ cup plus 1 tablespoon (140 ml) heavy cream

3 tablespoons (45 ml) light corn syrup

6 ounces (170 g) bittersweet or semisweet chocolate, chopped

1 teaspoon Cognac, rum, or other liquor or liqueur

Heat the cream with the corn syrup in a small saucepan until it just begins to boil. Remove from the heat and add the chocolate, stirring until it's melted and the mixture is smooth. Mix in the Cognac. Scrape the mixture into a small bowl and freeze until firm, about 1 hour.

Line a dinner plate with plastic wrap. Form little $1/_2$-inch (2-cm) truffles using two small spoons. Scoop up a teaspoonful of truffle mixture, then scrape it off with the other spoon onto the dinner plate. Repeat, using all the truffle mix. Freeze the truffles until ready to mix in.

MIXING THEM IN: Fold the Dark Chocolate Truffles into 1 quart (1 liter) of ice cream as you remove it from the machine. If you wish, break or chop the chilled truffles into smaller pieces first.

STORAGE: Dark Chocolate Truffles can be refrigerated or frozen, well wrapped, for up to 2 weeks.

White Chocolate Truffles

White truffles are especially fun to fold into Chocolate Ice Cream (pages 26 and 28) for both color contrast and taste.

> $1/2$ cup plus 1 tablespoon (140 ml) heavy cream
>
> 9 ounces (255 g) white chocolate, finely chopped

In a small saucepan, heat the cream until it just begins to boil. Remove from the heat and stir in the white chocolate until it's melted and the mixture is smooth. Scrape the truffle mixture into a small bowl and freeze until firm, about 1 hour.

Line a dinner plate with plastic wrap. Form little $1/2$-inch (2-cm) truffles using two small spoons. Scoop up a teaspoonful of truffle mixture and scrape it off with the other spoon onto the dinner plate. Repeat, using all of the truffle mix. Freeze the truffles until ready to mix in.

MIXING THEM IN: Fold the White Chocolate Truffles into 1 quart (1 liter) of ice cream as you remove it from the machine. If you wish, break or chop the chilled truffles into smaller pieces first.

STORAGE: White Chocolate Truffles can be refrigerated or frozen, well wrapped, for up to 2 weeks.

Marshmallows

These marshmallows are chewy and compact, designed to be folded into ice cream. They are indispensable in Rocky Road Ice Cream (page 26) but can be deliciously added to lots of other flavors as well. To measure powdered gelatin, open the envelopes and measure the granules with a tablespoon. These are best made in a heavy-duty stand mixer.

> $1/4$ cup plus 2 tablespoons (90 ml) cold water
>
> 1 tablespoon unflavored gelatin powder
>
> $2/3$ cup (130 g) sugar
>
> $1/4$ cup (60 ml) light corn syrup
>
> Pinch of salt
>
> $1/2$ teaspoon vanilla extract
>
> About $1^1/2$ cups (180 g) confectioners' sugar, plus more for tossing with the marshmallows

Pour $1/4$ cup (60 ml) of the cold water into the bowl of an electric stand mixer and fit the mixer with the whip attachment. Sprinkle the gelatin over the top to soften.

In a small, heavy-duty saucepan fitted with a candy thermometer, combine the remaining 2 tablespoons water with the sugar, corn syrup, and salt.

Cook the syrup over medium-high heat until it reaches 250°F (121°C), tilting the saucepan to make sure the bulb of the thermometer is submerged in the syrup to get an accurate reading.

When the syrup is ready, turn the mixer on to medium-high speed and begin slowly begin pouring the syrup into the mixer bowl in a thin stream, aiming the hot syrup near the side of the mixer bowl (if you pour it over the beaters, the syrup will just get splattered onto the sides of the bowl, rather than into the gelatin).

Continue slowly pouring the syrup into the gelatin in a steady, threadlike stream. Once you've added all the syrup, turn the mixer to high speed and whip for 8 minutes, until the mixture is a stiff foam. Whip in the vanilla extract.

Sift $1/2$ cup (60 g) of the confectioners' sugar over a baking sheet, in an area roughly 8 by 10 inches (20 by 25 cm). Scrape the marshmallow mixture from the mixer bowl and the beaters and spread it over the sugar-dusted area of the baking sheet so that it is about $1/2$ inch (2 cm) thick. Very lightly dampening the spatula makes it easier to spread. Let stand, uncovered, for at least 2 hours.

Put about a cup (120 g) of confectioners' sugar into a large bowl and dust a pair of kitchen shears with the sugar. Working in batches, snip the marshmallow into strips, then dust the strips with some confectioners' sugar. Cut the strips into little pieces, dropping them directly into the confectioners' sugar as you cut. Once you're halfway through, toss the marshmallows with the confectioners' sugar to coat them, and then place them in a sieve and shake off the excess sugar. Set the marshmallows to dry in an even layer on a baking sheet. Continue until all the marshmallows are cut, adding more confectioners' sugar as needed.

MIXING THEM IN: Fold the marshmallows into 1 quart (1 liter) of ice cream as you remove it from the machine.

STORAGE: Marshmallows will keep for up to 1 week. Once dry, store them in an airtight container at room temperature.

Candied Lemon Slices

When I was at culinary school in France, my instructor advised adding a bit of salt when candying citrus peel. When I asked why, he said that for some reason it made the peel soften, but he couldn't explain why. So although it may be just a culinary superstition, I've added salt ever since. If you aren't superstitious, simply toss the salt over your shoulder and candy the lemons without it.

Although it's not required equipment, a candy thermometer will show you when the lemon slices are done. Fit the saucepan with the thermometer before starting. When the peel is candied, it should read 225°F (107°C).

> 3 lemons, preferably unsprayed
>
> 1 cup (250 ml) water
>
> 1½ cups (300 g) sugar
>
> Big pinch of salt

Cut the lemons crosswise into very thin slices. Pick out and discard any seeds.

Put the lemon slices in a heavy-duty, nonreactive saucepan and add enough water to cover them by a few inches. Bring to a boil, turn down the heat to a low boil, and cook for 15 minutes, turning the slices with a spoon occasionally.

Drain the lemon slices, return them to the saucepan, add more water, and blanch them again for 15 minutes.

Drain the lemon slices again. Return them to the saucepan and add the 1 cup (250 ml) water, sugar, and salt. Bring to a boil, then turn down the heat to reduce to a very low boil and cook for 20 minutes, or until the liquid is reduced to a thick syrup.

If the syrup is too frothy to gauge whether the slices are done, remove the pan from the heat and let it cool for a moment. The lemons should be translucent and the syrup should be thick and shiny. Remove from the heat and let the lemon slices cool in their syrup.

MIXING THEM IN: Place the Candied Lemon Slices in a strainer and drain off as much of the syrup as possible. Chop the lemon slices into small pieces, then fold them into 1 quart (1 liter) of ice cream as you remove it from the machine.

STORAGE: Candied Lemon Slices will keep for 2 to 3 weeks in the refrigerator.

VARIATION: To make Candied Orange Slices, substitute 2 oranges for the lemons.

Candied Cherries

This is a terrific recipe for preserving fresh cherries during their relatively short season. As they cook, their ruby red juices gush out and continue to deepen in color until they thicken to a flavorful syrup. Before folding them into ice cream, you'll want to make sure they're dry, since the liquid will muddy the ice cream. Drain the cherries in a strainer for at least 1 hour first, until they are sticky and dry (save the syrup for drizzling over ice cream). Then coarsely chop the cherries, or fold them into the ice cream whole as you remove it from the machine. Candied cherries are excellent on top of Lemon Sherbet (page 116) or Olive Oil Ice Cream (page 83), and on any homemade ice cream sundae you make as well.

    1 pound (450 g) cherries, fresh or frozen

    1 1/2 cups (375 ml) water

    1 cup (200 g) sugar

    1 tablespoon freshly squeezed lemon juice

    1 drop almond extract

Remove the stems and pit the cherries. Heat the cherries, water, sugar, and lemon juice in a large, nonreactive saucepan or skillet until the liquid starts to boil.

Turn down the heat to a low boil and cook the cherries for 25 minutes, stirring frequently during the last 10 minutes of cooking to make sure they are cooking evenly and not sticking.

Once the syrup is reduced to the consistency of maple syrup, remove the pan from the heat, add the almond extract, and let the cherries cool in their syrup.

MIXING THEM IN: Drain the cherries in a strainer for about 1 hour (reserve the syrup for another use). Coarsely chop the drained cherries and fold them into 1 quart (1 liter) of ice cream as you remove it from the machine.

STORAGE: Candied Cherries can be kept in the refrigerator for up to 2 weeks.

Everything in the world deserves a proper, final nesting place, and you won't find any better ways to present your homemade ice creams and sorbets than perched atop or tucked within the delicious vessels in this chapter.

The most famous, and surely most popular, way to eat ice cream is undoubtedly the Ice Cream Cone (page 228). Its origins are rife with controversy. One story goes that a Middle Eastern man invented the cone when he ran out of dishes for serving ice cream at the St. Louis World's Fair in 1904 and rolled up one of the Persian wafers he was baking. Conflicting accounts give credit to an Italian who evidently patented a mold for creating cones a decade before. Whoever came up with the idea, there's no denying that cones have become universally popular everywhere you go.

If you've never made your own cones, it's really quite simple and well worth trying. Although you can bake them on cookie sheets, electric waffle cone makers are affordable fun, and I can't think of anything more enjoyable than peeling a freshly baked, buttery-crisp cone off the griddle, rolling it up, and then piling a few scoops of homemade ice cream inside.

Brownies (pages 220 and 221) and Blondies (page 222) have also become the rage for accompanying ice cream. And why not? Top a chocolate brownie with a melting scoop of Butterscotch Pecan Ice Cream (page 44), spoon lots of Whiskey Caramel Sauce (page 175) over it, and add a handful of Spiced Pecans (page 197) to top it all off. What's not to like? And should you have leftovers, chocolate brownies are wonderful when crumbled into little fudgy bits and folded into ice cream.

Speaking of leftovers, a wonderful use for an overabundance of egg whites is Meringue Nests (page 234), or *vacherins*, as the French call them. These sweetly simple dessert shells can be used to cradle any ice cream or sorbet in a flavorful foil that's shatteringly crisp. These feather-light nests turn any frozen dessert into an elegant event, making them suitable for a simple dinner party or a swanky soirée. We also have the French to thank for giving us Profiteroles (page 232). Americans have happily adopted these eggy little cream puffs, filling them with ice creams of all kinds, and you'll find they're as good when doused with slick Mocha Sauce (page 166) as they are when floating in a pool of summer-fresh Mixed Berry Coulis (page 181).

But I don't know of any country other than America that can take credit for the ice cream sandwich: two oversized, soft cookies enveloping ice cream and then mellowed in the freezer. It's a perfect partnership, undoubtedly the result of good old American ingenuity. But there's more to cookies and ice cream than ice cream sandwiches. Cookie cups can be downright upscale, like lacy and delicate Lemon–Poppy Seed Cookie Cups (page 228), with crackly poppy seeds and lemon zest, or Almond Butterscotch Cookie Cups (page 227), rich with brown sugar and crackly almonds.

Cakelike Brownies

If you like your brownies airy and not too dense, these are the ones for you.

$^1/_2$ cup (115 g) unsalted butter, cut into pieces

6 ounces (170 g) bittersweet or semisweet chocolate, finely chopped

$^1/_4$ cup (25 g) unsweetened Dutch-process cocoa powder

1 cup (200 g) sugar

3 large eggs

1 teaspoon vanilla extract

1 cup (140 g) flour

$^1/_8$ teaspoon salt

1 cup (100 g) pecans or walnuts, toasted (see page 13) and coarsely chopped (optional)

Preheat the oven to 350°F (175°C).

Line an 8-inch (20-cm) square pan with a long sheet of aluminum foil that covers the bottom and reaches up two sides. Cross another sheet of foil over it, making a large cross with edges that overhang the other two sides. Grease the bottom and sides of the foil with butter or nonstick spray.

Melt the butter in a medium saucepan. Add the chocolate pieces and stir constantly over very low heat until the chocolate is melted. Remove from the heat and whisk in the cocoa powder until smooth. Mix in the sugar, then whisk in the eggs one at a time, then the vanilla. Stir in the flour, salt, and nuts, if using.

Scrape the batter into the prepared pan, smooth the top, and bake for 35 to 40 minutes. The brownies are done when the center feels just slightly firm. Remove from the oven and cool completely. Serve topped with ice cream and sauce.

STORAGE: Wrap the pan of brownies with foil and store at room temperature. These brownies are actually better the second day and will keep well for up to 3 days.

VARIATIONS: To make Chocolate–Dulce de Leche Brownies, use 1 cup (250 ml) Dulce de Leche (page 171) or Cajeta (page 173). Spread half of the brownie batter in the pan. Take $^1/_3$ cup (80 ml) of the Dulce de Leche and drop 5 spoonfuls of it, evenly spaced, over the brownie batter. Cover with the remaining brownie batter, then drop tablespoonfuls of the remaining Dulce de Leche in dollops over the top of the brownie batter. Drag a knife through the batter three or four times to swirl the Dulce de Leche slightly. Be careful not to overswirl it or the brownies won't bake properly. Bake for 45 to 50 minutes, or until the brownies feel slightly firm in the center.

To make Peppermint Brownies, crumble $1^1/_2$ cups (350 g) of crumbled Peppermint Patties (page 206) or store-bought thin mint pieces into the batter, and substitute $^3/_4$ teaspoon mint extract for the vanilla extract.

Chewy-Dense Brownies

These are the best brownies for crumbling into ice cream, since they'll stay nice and chewy even after they're frozen.

$^1/_2$ cup (115 g) unsalted butter, cut into pieces

4 ounces (115 g) unsweetened chocolate, cut into small pieces

$1^1/_4$ cups (250 g) sugar

2 large eggs

1 teaspoon vanilla extract

$^1/_2$ cup (70 g) flour

$^1/_8$ teaspoon salt

$^1/_2$ cup (80 g) semisweet or bittersweet chocolate chips

$^3/_4$ cup (75 g) hazelnuts, pecans, almonds, or walnuts, toasted (see page 13) and chopped (optional)

Preheat the oven to 350°F (175°C).

Line an 8-inch (20-cm) square pan with a long sheet of aluminum foil that covers the bottom and reaches up the sides. If it doesn't reach all the way up all four sides, cross another sheet of foil over it, making a large cross with edges that overhang the sides. Grease the bottom and sides of the foil with butter or nonstick spray.

Melt the butter in a medium saucepan. Add the chocolate pieces and stir constantly with a whisk over very low heat until the chocolate is melted.

Remove from the heat and stir in the sugar, then the eggs one at a time, and the vanilla. Stir in the flour and the salt. Beat the batter vigorously for 30 seconds, until it begins to form a smooth ball. Stir in the chocolate chips and nuts, if using.

Scrape the batter into the prepared pan, smooth the top, and bake for 30 minutes, until the center feels just about set. Remove from the oven and let cool. Serve topped with ice cream and sauce. To mix brownies into ice cream, chop or crumble them into bite-sized pieces and fold them into the frozen ice cream as you remove it from the machine.

STORAGE: Wrap the pan of brownies with foil and store at room temperature. These brownies will keep for up to 3 days.

Brownies

It seems that the entire world—well, my world—is divided into two camps. On one side are the folks who like cakelike brownies, and on the other side are those who like chewy-dense brownies. To keep the peace, I'm giving you two recipes. Because both types of brownies can be somewhat sticky once baked, it's best to line the pan with aluminum foil that goes up and overhangs all sides of the pan. After baking, you'll be able to lift the brownies right out with the greatest of ease.

Blondies

When I was looking for the perfect blondie, I went to the source on all things chocolate chipified: my good friend and fellow baker Dede Wilson, author of *A Baker's Field Guide to Chocolate Chip Cookies*. I knew she'd come through with a killer recipe, and boy, did she ever.

$^1/_2$ cup (115 g) unsalted butter

1 cup (140 g) flour

$^1/_2$ teaspoon baking powder

$^1/_8$ teaspoon baking soda

$^1/_8$ teaspoon salt

1 cup (215 g) packed light brown sugar

1 teaspoon vanilla extract

1 large egg

$^2/_3$ cup (115 g) chocolate chips

$^2/_3$ cup (75 g) pecans or walnuts, toasted (see page 13) and coarsely chopped

Preheat the oven to 350°F (175°C).

Butter an 8-inch (20-cm) square pan and cut a square of parchment or wax paper to fit the bottom.

Melt the butter in a medium saucepan, then let it cool to room temperature.

In a large mixing bowl, whisk together the flour, baking powder, baking soda, and salt. Stir the brown sugar and vanilla into the melted butter, then stir in the egg.

Stir the melted butter mixture into the dry ingredients, then fold in the chocolate chips and nuts.

Scrape the batter into the prepared pan. Smooth the top and bake for 30 minutes, until slightly puffed in the center. Remove from the oven and let cool completely.

Serve topped with ice cream and sauce.

STORAGE: Wrap the pan with foil and store at room temperature. They will keep for up to 3 days.

Chocolate Ice Cream Sandwich Cookies

These resemble the classic ice cream sandwich cookies but taste much better, and are far fudgier, than those soggy dark rectangles you'll soon forget about.

$^1/_2$ cup (115 g) unsalted butter, at room temperature

1 cup (200 g) sugar

1 large egg, at room temperature

1 teaspoon vanilla extract

6 tablespoons (50 g) unsweetened Dutch-process cocoa powder

$1^1/_2$ cups (210 g) flour

1 teaspoon baking powder

$^1/_8$ teaspoon salt

Preheat the oven to 350°F (175°C). Line 2 baking sheets with parchment paper or silicone baking mats.

Beat together the butter and sugar in the bowl of an electric stand mixer, or by hand, until smooth. Beat in the egg and vanilla.

In a separate bowl, whisk together the cocoa, flour, baking powder, and salt. Stir the dry ingredients gradually into the creamed butter mixture until completely incorporated and there are no streaks of butter.

Form the dough into sixteen $1^1/_2$-inch (4-cm) rounds. On the baking sheets, flatten the rounds so they're 3 inches (8 cm) across, spacing them evenly. You can get 8 on a normal 11 by 17-inch (28 by 43-cm) baking sheet, with 3 going lengthwise down the sides and 2 in the center in between.

Bake for 20 minutes, rotating the baking sheets midway during baking, then remove from the oven.

Once cool, sandwich ice cream between 2 cookies, then wrap each ice cream sandwich in plastic wrap and store in the freezer.

Chocolate Chip
Ice Cream Sandwich Cookies

These oversized cookies are packed with nuts and chocolate chips, perfect for making the best ice cream sandwiches you've ever had. Feel free to use as much ice cream as you like inside.

$^1/_2$ cup (115 g) unsalted butter, at room temperature

$^1/_4$ cup (50 g) granulated sugar

$^1/_3$ cup (70 g) packed light brown sugar

1 large egg, at room temperature

1 teaspoon vanilla extract

1 cup (140 g) flour

Slightly rounded $^1/_4$ teaspoon baking soda

$^1/_4$ teaspoon salt

$^3/_4$ cup (120 g) semisweet or bittersweet chocolate chips

$^1/_2$ cup (50 g) walnuts or pecans, toasted (see page 13) and chopped

Beat the butter with the granulated and brown sugar in the bowl of an electric stand mixer, or by hand, until smooth. Beat in the egg and vanilla.

In a separate bowl, whisk together the flour, baking soda, and salt, making sure there are no lumps of baking soda. Stir the dry ingredients into the creamed butter mixture, then mix in the chocolate chips and nuts. Wrap the dough in plastic wrap, flatten it into a disk, and chill for at least 1 hour.

Preheat the oven to 350°F (175°C). Line several baking sheets with parchment paper or silicone baking mats.

Form the dough into sixteen 1$^1/_2$-inch (4-cm) rounds. Flatten the rounds of dough into 3-inch (8-cm) disks, spaced evenly apart on the baking sheets. You should get 6 on a normal 11 by 17-inch (28 by 43-cm) baking sheet. Since they don't spread much, you can leave 1 inch (3 cm) of space between them.

Bake the cookies for 15 minutes, rotating the baking sheets midway during baking, then remove from the oven.

Once cool, sandwich ice cream between 2 cookies, then wrap each ice cream sandwich in plastic wrap and store in the freezer.

Oatmeal
Ice Cream Sandwich Cookies

MAKES 16 COOKIES, FOR 8 ICE CREAM SANDWICHES

This recipe makes jumbo-sized, chewy oatmeal cookies, ideal for sandwiching ice cream. They stay nice and moist after they're frozen and are especially good (in my humble opinion) filled with Plum Ice Cream (page 77). Let them cool completely before trying to lift them off the baking sheet. They'll be somewhat soft, since they're designed to be retain their tenderness even after they're frozen.

Since these cookies are larger than normal, I find that I can get 6 onto a standard baking sheet (11 by 17 inches, or 28 by 43 cm), so that even when they spread, they don't touch. If you have several baking sheets, this is a great time to put them into service. If not, let your baking sheet cool completely before baking the next batch of cookies.

$^2/_3$ cup (90 g) flour

$^1/_4$ cup (50 g) granulated sugar

6 tablespoons (90 g) packed light brown sugar

$^1/_2$ teaspoon baking soda

$^3/_4$ teaspoon ground cinnamon

$^1/_4$ teaspoon salt

$1^1/_2$ cups (150 g) rolled oats (not instant)

$^1/_2$ cup (80 g) raisins

$^1/_2$ cup (125 ml) unflavored vegetable oil

3 tablespoons (45 ml) whole milk

1 large egg

Preheat the oven to 350°F (175°C). Line several baking sheets with parchment paper or silicone baking mats.

Whisk together the flour, granulated and brown sugars, baking soda, cinnamon, and salt in a large mixing bowl, being sure to break up any lumps of brown sugar. Stir in the oats and raisins.

Make a well in the center, then pour in the oil and milk. Add the egg and stir until the batter is smooth.

Drop 6 heaping tablespoons at a time, evenly spaced, on each baking sheet. Spread the batter with the back of the spoon, making each circle 3 inches (8 cm) wide.

Bake the cookies for 20 minutes, rotating the baking sheets midway during baking, then remove from the oven.

Once completely cool, sandwich ice cream between 2 cookies, then wrap each ice cream sandwich in plastic wrap and store in the freezer.

Almond Butterscotch Cookie Cups

These edible cups are easiest to bake on baking sheets lined with parchment paper, rather than thick silicone baking mats, since they're whisper thin and somewhat fragile. Overturned teacups make the perfect molds, although you can use anything that's relatively wide with a flat bottom, such as a custard cup.

After baking, if any cookies cool before you've had a chance to mold them into cookie cups, simply pop the baking sheet back in the oven for about 30 seconds to make them supple and try again.

4 tablespoons (60 g) butter, salted or unsalted

$1/4$ cup (60 ml) light corn syrup

$1/4$ cup (60 g) packed light brown sugar

$1/8$ teaspoon almond extract

$1/2$ cup (40 g) sliced almonds

6 tablespoons (60 g) flour

Preheat the oven to 350°F (175°C). Line a baking sheet with parchment paper. Have ready 4 overturned teacups or custard cups.

Melt the butter in a small saucepan with the corn syrup and brown sugar. Stir in the almond extract, almonds, and flour.

Drop 4 slightly rounded tablespoons of batter, evenly spaced, on the baking sheet and use the back of the spoon to spread them into circles 2 inches (5 cm) across. Bake the cookies for 12 minutes, until they're deep golden brown. Let rest for 30 to 45 seconds, then lift each cookie off the baking sheet with a flexible metal spatula and flip it over onto an upended teacup. (If the cookies get too firm to shape, return them to the oven for 30 seconds to soften them.)

Let the baking sheet cool, then repeat with the remaining batter.

STORAGE: Store these cookie cups in an airtight container. They are best served the day they're made. The batter can be made and refrigerated up to 1 week in advance. Let it come to room temperature before baking.

Lemon-Poppy Seed Cookie Cups

The unexpected crunch of poppy seeds in these very pretty, delicate cookie cups is the perfect foil for any homemade ice cream or a fruity sorbet.

3 tablespoons (45 g) butter, salted or unsalted

2 tablespoons freshly squeezed lemon juice

7 tablespoons (85 g) sugar

3 tablespoons (25 g) flour

1/2 cup (40 g) sliced almonds

2 tablespoons poppy seeds

In a small saucepan, melt the butter. Remove from the heat and stir in the lemon juice, sugar, and flour. Mix in the almonds and poppy seeds and let the mixture rest for 1 hour.

Preheat the oven to 350°F (175°C). Line a baking sheet with parchment paper. Have ready 4 overturned teacups or custard cups.

Put 4 level tablespoons of batter, evenly spaced, on the baking sheet and use the back of the spoon to spread them into circles 2 inches (5 cm) across. Bake the cookies for 10 minutes, until they're deep golden brown. Let rest for 30 to 45 seconds, then lift each cookie off the baking sheet with a flexible metal spatula and flip it over onto an upended teacup. (If the cookies get too firm to shape, return them to the oven for 30 seconds to soften them.)

Let the baking sheet cool, then repeat with the remaining batter.

STORAGE: Store these cookie cups in an airtight container. They are best served the day they're made. The batter can be made and refrigerated up to 1 week in advance. Let it come to room temperature before baking.

Ice Cream Cones

Making ice cream cones at home is very easy. It's quite fun if you have an electric waffle-cone maker (see Resources, page 237), although you can bake them in the oven with great success as well.

The batter is simplicity itself: just a few ingredients mixed together, baked, and rolled up into cones...which is the fun part! You will need a conical cone-rolling form made of wood or plastic (see Resources, page 237), or you can simply shape them around overturned teacups to make a cone-bowl hybrid.

A few tips for baking cones by hand: The batter recipe can easily be doubled, allowing for a few practice cones, which may come in handy your first time making them. When baking them in the oven, I prefer to use parchment paper to line the baking sheet, rather than a silicone baking mat. Also, I let the baking sheet cool between batches or have another baking sheet handy, as the batter is much easier to handle when the baking sheets are at room temperature. To roll the cones, you may wish to wear clean rubber gloves or use a tea towel, since the just-baked cookies may be too warm for you to handle with bare hands.

If using an electric ice cream cone maker, most models require 3 tablespoons of batter for each cone, so you may get 4 cones from this recipe. Follow the instructions that come with your unit.

> $1/4$ cup (60 ml) egg whites (about 2 large egg whites)
>
> 7 tablespoons (85 g) sugar
>
> $1/2$ teaspoon vanilla extract
>
> $1/8$ teaspoon salt
>
> $2/3$ cup (90 g) flour
>
> 2 tablespoons (30 g) unsalted butter, melted

Preheat the oven to 350°F (175°C).

In a small mixing bowl, stir together the egg whites, sugar, and vanilla. Stir in the salt and half of the flour, then mix in the melted butter. Beat in the rest of the flour until smooth.

Line a baking sheet with parchment paper and use a small offset spatula or the back of a spoon to spread 2 level tablespoons of the batter into a circle 6 inches (15 cm) across. Try to get the circles as even and smooth as possible (you're likely to get 2 rounds on one standard baking sheet).

Put the baking sheet in the over and begin checking the cones after about 10 minutes. Depending on your oven, they'll take between 10 and 15 minutes to bake. The circles should be a deep golden brown throughout (some lighter and darker spots are inevitable, so don't worry). Remove the baking sheet from the oven. Use a thin metal spatula to loosen the edge of one disk. Slide the spatula under the disk, quickly flip it over, and immediately roll it around the cone-rolling form, pressing the seam firmly on the counter to close the cone and pinching the point at the bottom securely closed. Let the cone cool slightly on the mold until it feels firm, then slide it off and stand it upright in a tall glass to cool. Roll the other cone the same way. (If it's too firm, return the baking sheet to the oven for a minute or so until it's pliable again.)

Repeat, using the remaining batter. You'll find it easier to spread the batter if you slide the reusable parchment paper off the baking sheet; any heat from the baking sheet will make the batter fussy to spread.

STORAGE: The batter can be made up to 4 days in advance and stored in the refrigerator. Let the batter come to room temperature before using. Once baked and cooled, store the cones in an airtight container until ready to serve. They're best eaten the same day they're baked.

(continued)

VARIATIONS: For Sesame or Poppy Seed Ice Cream Cones, stir 3 tablespoons (35 g) toasted sesame or poppy seeds and a bit of grated lemon zest into the batter.

To make Chocolate Ice Cream Cones, increase the sugar to $^1/_2$ cup (100 g), and use 6 tablespoons (60 g) flour and 3 tablespoons (21 g) unsweetened Dutch-process cocoa powder in place of the $^2/_3$ cup (90 g) flour.

For Gingersnap Ice Cream Cones, add 1 tablespoon mild molasses and $^1/_4$ teaspoon each ground cinnamon, ginger, and nutmeg to the batter. Increase the sugar to $^1/_2$ cup (100 g).

For Honey-Cornmeal Ice Cream Cones, substitute 1 large egg and 1 egg white for the $^1/_4$ cup (60 ml) egg whites. Melt 2 teaspoons of strongly flavored honey with the butter, and substitute $^1/_2$ cup (70 g) of flour and $^1/_4$ cup (35 g) of stone-ground cornmeal for the $^2/_3$ cup (90 g) flour.

For Rosemary Ice Cream Cones, add 2 teaspoons finely chopped fresh rosemary to the Honey-Cornmeal Ice Cream Cone batter.

Tartufi

MAKES 8 TARTUFI

Tartufo means "truffle" in Italian and refers to how these ice cream mounds look when dipped in pure chocolate, which forms a neat, crispy coating for a favorite ice cream. You can make them any size you wish, but I usually make mine about golf ball size (about 2 ounces, 60 g, each) and serve two per person.

The trick to making Tartufi is to work rather quickly and neatly. Keep the ice cream mounds in the freezer until the absolute last moment prior to dipping.

> 2 cups (500 ml) ice cream
>
> 6 ounces (170 g) bittersweet or semisweet chocolate, chopped
>
> 6 tablespoons (85 g) unsalted butter, cut into pieces
>
> $1^1/_2$ tablespoons light corn syrup

Line two large dinner plates with plastic wrap or parchment paper and put them in the freezer. Once the plates are chilled, use an ice cream scoop to make balls of your favorite ice cream, setting them on one of the plates. Take care that the scoops are solid and well formed, with no dangling bits of ice cream; use your hands if necessary. Freeze the ice cream scoops thoroughly.

To dip the Tartufi, melt the chocolate, butter, and corn syrup in a medium bowl set over a pan of simmering water. Once the chocolate is melted and the mixture is smooth, remove the bowl of chocolate from the improvised double boiler. Remove the ice cream balls from the freezer, and the second plate as well.

Here the trick is to going to be to try to get as thin a shell as possible around the ice cream. Using two soup spoons, drop a frozen scoop of ice cream into the melted chocolate mixture and toss it quickly until it's coated. Transfer it onto the unused dinner plate. Repeat with the remaining scoops of ice cream, then return the scoops to the freezer until ready to serve.

Profiteroles

Many people come to Paris with dreams of falling in love, and I know more than one person who's returned home starry-eyed after a steamy love affair—with profiteroles. Who can resist eggy, buttery pastry filled with vanilla ice cream, heaped on plates, served with a gleaming silver pitcher of warm chocolate sauce? It's a tableside ritual that takes place nightly in romatic restaurants and cozy cafés across the city as dashing waiters douse profiteroles with warm sauce and the molten chocolate gushes over the golden puffs, filling every little nook and crevice possible. The profiteroles are served forth with a sly grin (and perhaps a bit of a wink), leaving you free to indulge.

Profiteroles are seductively simple to make at home, and you can't go wrong with any ice cream and sauce combination that sounds good to you. My personal favorite is profiteroles filled with Chartreuse Ice Cream (page 57), drizzled with Classic Hot Fudge (page 164), and scattered with lots and lots of crispy French Almonds (page 189). *J'adore!*

> 1 cup (250 ml) water
>
> 2 teaspoons sugar
>
> $^1/_2$ teaspoon salt
>
> 6 tablespoons (85 g) unsalted butter, cut into small chunks
>
> 1 cup (140 g) flour
>
> 4 large eggs, at room temperature
>
> 1 egg yolk
>
> 1 teaspoon milk

Preheat the oven to 425°F (220°C). Line a baking sheet with parchment paper or a silicone baking mat.

Heat the water, sugar, salt, and butter in a small saucepan, stirring, until the butter is melted. Remove from the heat and dump in the flour all at once. Stir briskly until the mixture is smooth and pulls away from the sides of the pan.

Allow the dough to cool for 2 minutes, then briskly beat in the eggs, one at a time, until smooth and shiny.

Using two spoons, scoop up a mound of dough roughly the size of an unshelled walnut with one spoon and scrape it off with the other spoon onto the baking sheet (or you can use a pastry bag or spring-loaded ice cream scoop). Place the mounds, evenly spaced, on the baking sheet. Lightly beat the egg yolk and milk together and brush the top of each mound with some of the egg yolk glaze.

Bake the cream puffs for 30 minutes, or until puffed and well browned. Turn off the oven and leave them in for another 5 minutes.

STORAGE: The cream puffs are best eaten the same day they're made. Once cooled, they can be frozen in a zip-top freezer bag for up to 1 month. Defrost at room temperature, then warm briefly on a baking sheet in a moderate oven until crisp again.

Crêpes

MAKES 8 CRÊPES

If you've never made crêpes before, you'll find that it's one of life's most satisfying accomplishments. You spend a few minutes dipping, swirling, and flipping and end up with a neat stack of delicious crêpes. As with traditional pancakes, the first one is usually a dud, so don't be discouraged. Once you've slid a few out of the frying pan, you'll feel like a pro. This recipe can easily be doubled and they freeze beautifully, so there's no reason not to keep an extra stack in the freezer for a last-minute crêpe fix.

> ¾ cup (180 ml) whole milk
>
> 2 tablespoons (30 g) butter, melted
>
> 3 large eggs
>
> 1 teaspoon sugar
>
> ¼ teaspoon coarse salt
>
> ¾ cup (110 g) flour

Pour the milk and melted butter into a blender. Add the eggs, sugar, and salt. Blend briefly. Add the flour and blend until smooth. Transfer to a bowl and refrigerate for at least 1 hour. (The batter can be made in advance and refrigerated overnight.)

To fry the crêpes, let the batter come to room temperature, then whisk it to thin it out a bit.

Heat a 12-inch (30-cm) nonstick skillet over medium to high heat. When a few drops of water sprinkled on the pan sizzle, pour in ¼ cup (60 ml) of batter and quickly tilt the pan so the batter covers the bottom. Cook the crêpe for about 45 seconds, until the edges begin to darken. Use a flexible spatula to flip it over, then cook for another 45 seconds on the reverse side.

Slide the crêpe onto a dinner plate, then repeat with the remaining batter.

To serve, fold the crêpes in half and arrange them, overlapping slightly, in a buttered baking dish. Cover with foil and heat in a 300°F (150°C) oven for 10 to 15 minutes, until hot. Serve the hot crêpes topped with a scoop of ice cream and a drizzle of sauce.

STORAGE: Crêpes can be made in advance and, once cool, wrapped in plastic wrap. Store in the refrigerator for up to 2 days. To freeze crêpes, wrap them in plastic wrap and then in aluminum foil. Crêpes can be frozen for up to 2 months.

Meringue Nests

MAKES 8 MERINGUE NESTS

Crispy nests of meringue—also known as *vacherins*—add a certain *savoir faire* and offer a very dramatic presentation for any ice cream or sorbet, especially when you add a ladleful of sauce as well. The combination of crackly meringue, luscious ice cream, and a complimentary sauce is justifiably known as one of the great French dessert classics. It is certain to become a well-loved part of your repertoire as well.

Use a deft hand when folding in the confectioners' sugar. Aggressive overmixing can cause the meringue to start deflating.

> 4 large egg whites (about $1/2$ cup, 125 ml), at room temperature
>
> Pinch of salt
>
> $1/2$ cup (100 g) granulated sugar
>
> $1/4$ teaspoon vanilla extract
>
> $1/4$ cup (35 g) confectioners' sugar

Preheat the oven to 200°F (100°C).

Line a baking sheet with parchment paper or a silicone baking mat.

In the bowl of an electric stand mixer, begin whipping the egg whites with the salt at medium speed until frothy.

Increase the speed of the mixer to medium-high and whip until the egg whites thicken and begin to hold their shape. Continue whipping the whites while adding the granulated sugar, 1 tablespoon at a time. Once the sugar's been added, add the vanilla and continue to whip for 2 minutes, until stiff and glossy.

Remove the mixer bowl from the stand and sift the confectioners' sugar over the meringue while simultaneously folding it in.

Divide the meringue into 8 portions, evenly spaced, on the baking sheet. (They'll all fit if you arrange 3 down each side lengthwise and 2 in the center.)

Take a spoon, dip it in water, tap off the excess, and make a hollow in the center of each meringue, like mashed potatoes in preparation for gravy.

Bake the meringues for 1 hour. Turn the oven off and continue to let the meringues dry out in the oven for 1 hour more.

The meringues are done when they feel dry and lift easily off the parchment paper or silicone baking mat.

STORAGE: Once cool, store the meringues in an absolutely airtight container until ready to serve. They can be made 1 week in advance.

VARIATIONS: Meringue nests lend themselves to many variations. Here are some of my favorites. Simply fold the additional ingredients into the meringue after adding in the confectioners' sugar.

Cinnamon: 1 tablespoon ground cinnamon

Coconut: $1/2$ cup (40 g) dried shredded coconut, toasted

Cocoa Nib: 6 tablespoons (60 g) cocoa nibs

234   The Perfect Scoop

Coffee: 1 tablespoon best-quality instant coffee (crush the crystals into a fine powder with the back of a spoon first) or espresso powder

Chocolate: 3 tablespoons (21 g) unsweetened Dutch-process cocoa powder

Chocolate Chip: $^1/_2$ cup (80 g) semisweet or bittersweet chocolate chips (regular or mini)

Chocolate–Chocolate Chip: 3 tablespoons (21 g) unsweetened Dutch-process cocoa powder and $^1/_3$ cup (60 g) semisweet or bittersweet chocolate chips (regular or mini)

Green Tea and Black Sesame: $1^1/_2$ teaspoons *matcha* (green tea powder) and 2 tablespoons black sesame seeds

For Almond Meringue Nests: Replace the vanilla with $^1/_4$ teaspoon almond extract, and press 2 tablespoons sliced almonds into the top of each meringue before baking.

ACKNOWLEDGMENTS

Who hasn't dreamed of spending months and months churning out ice cream all day long and creating all the mix-ins, sauces, and everything else that's served along-side? While I tinkered all day in my kitchen, and all night on my laptop, I was always encouraged by the many people who gave me support, tested recipes, provided valuable information...and ate lots and lots of ice cream in the process.

Thanks to my perfect editor, Clancy Drake, who embraced the idea of this book right off the bat and was always on the same page as I was every step of the way. To copyeditor Rebecca Pepper, for making sure everything was in the right place. Thanks to the rest of the staff at Ten Speed: Nancy Austin who came up with the super design for this book; Kristin Casemore and Lisa Regul in publicity; and Aaron Wehner, for his guidance from day one. Big thanks to Lara Hata, who beautifully photographed the recipes, and to stylist George Dolese for doing such a fabulous job coaxing the ice creams into perfect scoops.

Appreciation also to friends who contributed recipes and information: Carrie Bachman, Frank Browning, Mary Canales, Elizabeth Falkner, Maureen Fant, Susan Loomis, Nikki Nealeigh, Adam Roberts, Heidi Swanson, Mary Jo Thoresen, Dede Wilson, Judy Witts, and Lee Wooding.

I'm very grateful to my diligent team of testers, Cliff Colvin, Joanna Miller, Cindy Meyers (who I'm outing as an "over-swirler"), Jeanette Hermann Rosenblum, and Janet Taddeo, for churning away in their kitchens, near and far. And *merci* to Colette Rivaton, for her palate extraordinaire.

To my cyber-dude Ben McCullough, for keeping my web site and food blog humming and up-to-date.

As always, I am grateful to Lindsey Shere for teaching me much of what I know about making ice cream and pursuing pure flavors during the time I was lucky enough to work with her. And to Alice Waters, for providing fertile (and organic) grounds for all of us to grow from.

Thanks to Frederic Arbaud at Cuisinart in the United Kingdom, who let me test his company's latest equipment. Appreciation to the lovely Lisa Callaghan of All-Clad, as well as Valerie Gleason at Chef's Choice; Muriel Bellaïche, Brian Maynard, Paul McCauley, Kris Van Den Bossche, and the rest of the gang at KitchenAid; and Gretchen Holt at Oxo, for making sure I was always fully equipped and in the know about the latest and greatest ice cream making equipment.

To my agent, Fred Hill, for continuing to remind me who's the boss in our relationship. And to Romain Pellas, who ate his first egg white omelet. *Oh! la vache!...et merci beaucoup pour tout.*

RESOURCES

Baker's Catalogue
www.bakerscatalogue.com

Candied citrus peel, chocolate and cocoa powder in bulk, malted milk powder, and thermometers.

Bialetti
www.bialetti.com

The best-quality stovetop espresso makers.

Boyajian
www.boyajianinc.com

Peppermint flavoring, as well as natural orange and other citrus oils.

Chef's Choice
www.edgecraft.com

Ice cream cone making machines, cone-rolling forms, and cone stands.

Chocosphere
www.chocosphere.com

Online chocolate source with high-quality brands from around the world. Cocoa powder and cocoa nibs available as well.

Cuisinart
www.cuisinart.com

Comprehensive line of ice cream making machines, as well as blenders and food processors.

Dagoba
www.dagobachocolate.com

Organic chocolate, chocolate chips, cocoa nibs, and cocoa powder.

Donvier
www.donvier.com

Nonelectric ice cream makers.

E. Guittard
www.eguittard.com

Fine chocolate and chocolate chips.

Frontier
www.frontiercoop.com

Organic mint oils and extracts.

Green & Black's Organic
www.greenandblacks.com

Organic chocolate and cocoa powder.

KitchenAid
www.kitchenaid.com

Ice cream making machines and ice cream freezing attachments for their stand mixers. Powerful blenders and food processors as well.

Krups
www.krups.com

Ice cream making machines.

Oxo
www.oxo.com

Makers of heatproof spatulas, as well as sturdy measuring cups and spoons, ice cream scoops, and strainers.

Pacojet
www.pacojet.com

Revolutionary ice cream maker, intended mostly for professionals.

The Perfect Purée
www.perfectpuree.com

Frozen passion fruit purée, as well as other fruit and berry purées.

Rival
www.rivalproducts.com

Ice cream makers, including classic White Mountain machines.

Saltworks
www.saltworks.us

Large selection of sea salts, including French fleur de sel and Maldon salts from Great Britain.

ScharffenBerger
www.scharffenberger.com

Fine chocolate and cocoa nibs.

Star Kay White
www.starkaywhite.com

Almond and mint extracts.

Sur la Table
www.surlatable.com

Cookware, espresso makers, ice cream making machines, ice cream cone forms, and thermometers.

Trader Joe's
www.traderjoes.com

Nationwide grocery chain with a wide selection of dried fruits, nuts, sour cherries in light syrup, and unsweetened coconut. Also chocolate sold in bulk and baking ingredients.

Williams-Sonoma
www.williams-sonoma.com

Ice cream freezers, espresso makers, scoops and a variety of equipment for making ice cream.

Vanilla.com
www.vanilla.com

Outstanding pure Bourbon, Mexican, and Tahitian vanilla extracts, whole vanilla beans as well as dried, ground beans.

Vanns Spices
www.vannsspices.com.

Flavored citrus and mint oils as well as spices and extracts.

Zeroll
www.zeroll.com

High-quality professional ice cream scoops.

INDEX